MORE POEM PORTRAITS

BOOKS BY JAMES J. METCALFE

More Poem Portraits

Poem Portraits

Garden In My Heart

James J. Metcalfe Poems for Children

More Poem Portraits

A FURTHER COLLECTION OF VERSE

by

JAMES J. METCALFE

Garden City Books

GARDEN CITY, NEW YORK

1951

GARDEN CITY BOOKS

DEDICATION

I contemplate the passing world . . . And with my pen in hand
. . . I dedicate these lines to all . . . The humble of the land . . .
To all who look upon their deeds . . . With modesty and grace
. . . And do not feel entitled to . . . A more important place . . .
It matters not how rich they are . . . Or whether they are poor
. . . No more than if they happen to . . . Be famous or obscure
. . . As long as they appreciate . . . The blessings that are theirs
. . . And give their gratitude to God . . . In unpretentious
prayers . . . I dedicate my efforts to . . . The ones who do their
part . . . Sincerely and completely with . . . Humility of heart.

Foreword

Author of the popular books, *Poem Portraits, Garden In My Heart*, and *Poems For Children*, James J. Metcalfe now offers his readers this new collection of verse from his daily newspaper column, syndicated throughout the United States, and in Canada, Mexico, and Ireland.

His philosophical lines stem from the rich and wide experiences of his forty-five years, including the dangerous days of his gang-busting for the Federal Bureau of Investigation, his exciting exposé of the German and German-American Bunds for the Chicago *Times*, and other phases of his colorful career as a journalist.

The rhymes about his family and their typical American home life are inspired by his wife, Lillian, and their children—Jimmie, eighteen, Don, fifteen, and Kristina Maria, eight. Jimmie, incidentally, left college at seventeen to enlist in the Navy.

Jim Metcalfe, who was born in Berlin, Germany, and Lillian, a native of Stavanger, Norway, met at a high school dance in Chicago. For some years now the Metcalfes have been making their home in Dallas, Texas.

Other thoughts that flow from Jim's pen are those about friendship, patriotism, business, and various occupations, but as his fan mail testifies, it is love that makes the world go around, and with each Poem Portrait on the subject of love, hearts flutter and the letters come pouring into his mail box.

Humble in the midst of his international acclaim, James Metcalfe is profoundly grateful to God for having blessed him with his ability to express the thoughts of others as they would like to be able to put them into words. His beautiful prayer-poems are his way of saying, "Thank You, God."

The Publishers

Contents by Subject

x

Your Seventh Birthday . 229

LIFE

xii

xiii

xiv

xv

xvii

MORE POEM PORTRAITS

BY THE GRACE OF GOD

All things are by the grace of God . . . Including life and death
. . . Maturity and wisdom and . . . A newborn baby's breath
. . . The sun and moon, the mountain peaks . . . The weather
and the sea . . . And everything upon this earth . . . Of time and
memory . . . Yet some forget this vital fact . . . While in their
selfish way . . . They try to take the credit for . . . The glory of
the day . . . They praise themselves for what they do . . .
And hold themselves apart . . . As being so much better than . . .
The ones of humble heart . . . But they must know they cannot
live . . . Forever on this sod . . . And therefore even they
themselves . . . Are by the grace of God.

LANDSCAPE ARTIST

The landscape artist is the one . . . Who spends his working
hours . . . Designing pretty patterns for . . . The bushes and the
flowers . . . Who knows the type of tree and grass . . . To build
the best attraction . . . And if the rose or zinnia . . . Will give
more satisfaction . . . He is the garden architect . . . Who figures
out the measure . . . Of every shrub and every bed . . . For horti-
cultural pleasure . . . He has to make his living and . . . Fulfill
his business duty . . . But all his pride and happiness . . . Are
in creating beauty . . . And every lawn and every yard . . . That
visitors admire . . . Is one more rung of praise on which . . . He
climbs his ladder higher.

MY FRIENDSHIPS

My friendships are the homing ships . . . That touch the evening shore . . . And they are all the flowers fair . . . That blossom
at my door . . . They are the stars that twinkle when . . . The
sun has slipped away . . . They are my windows and my roof
. . . Against a rainy day . . . My friendships warm the winter snow
. . . And cool the summer breeze . . . And bring to life the pages
of . . . My book of memories . . . They are the jewels in my
box . . . The hopes that fill my chest . . . The courage of my
effort and . . . My comfort when I rest . . . And I shall keep
and cherish them . . . As long as I may last . . . To live for some
tomorrow and . . . To dream about the past.

TICKET CLERK

The ticket clerk is one who tells . . . The routing and the rate . . . And schedules trips according to . . . The hour and the date . . . He has to read the table and . . . To figure out the run . . . And in its complicated style . . . It is not any fun . . . He must be quite familiar with . . . The pages in his book . . . And equal to some nasty words . . . Or just a dirty look . . . His helping hand is bound by strings . . . That tie him in a knot . . . And many are the tickets that . . . He simply hasn't got . . . But always he is willing and . . . Prepared to do his best . . . To get your transportation and . . . Your comfort and your rest.

WITH YOU FOREVER

I want each moment of my life . . . And everything I do . . . To be the happy memories . . . That I may share with you . . . Each golden hour of the day . . . Each silver star at night . . . And every breath that leaves my lips . . . By dawn or candlelight . . . I want to walk with you beyond . . . The clouds that gather rain . . . Unto the land where dreams come true . . . And nothing is in vain . . . Where spring is filled with flowers and . . . The autumn is a song . . . And beauty paints a masterpiece . . . Of faith and courage strong . . . I want to share your summer and . . . Your winter white with snow . . . I want to hold you close to me . . . And never let you go.

HARDWARE STORE

The hardware store is where we buy . . . The items large and small . . . That fix the premises at home . . . From living room to hall . . . The doorknobs and the nails and screws . . . The kitchenware and mop . . . And what it takes to keep a door . . . From slamming to a stop . . . And then there are the garden tools . . . The spade and fork and hoe . . . That do their part to keep away . . . The weeds that want to grow . . . The hose and sprinkler that convey . . . The water to the lawn . . . And showers for the children when . . . The heat is really on . . . The hardware store is valuable . . . And practical and good . . . Because it fills so many needs . . . For every neighborhood.

THE PERFECT HOME

When faith abides within the house . . . Then truly there is love . . . As constant and eternal as . . . The silver stars above . . . And when affection fills the house . . . Then surely there is peace . . . And happy are the gentle hearts . . . In joys that never cease . . . For faith and love and peace are one . . . And as they blend together . . . They form the perfect rainbow bright . . . Beyond the darkest weather . . . And always God is present there . . . To comfort and to bless . . . The ones who join in prayer to Him . . . For health and happiness . . . And so as faith and love and peace . . . And God surround each deed . . . There is no endless shadow and . . . There is no desperate need.

JOB

A job is something we must have . . . To buy our daily bread . . . To get some clothes to wear and find . . . A place to rest our head . . . But more than that it is the chance . . . To take our place in life . . . And to support as best we can . . . Our children and the wife . . . To have respectability . . . And hold our head up high . . . And prove we have the courage and . . . The willingness to try . . . It may be quite a prominent . . . Or just a humble task . . . But doing it and doing well . . . Are all the world can ask . . . It may not pay a fortune and . . . It may not be a song . . . But when we have and hold a job . . . It shows that we belong.

ROAD TO HAPPINESS

The road to happiness begins . . . In front of every door . . . If we are certain that we know . . . What we are looking for . . . If we are just prepared to face . . . The problems that arise . . . And do not fear the gloomy clouds . . . That gather in the skies . . . For we must have the strength and will . . . To see our efforts through . . . And we must do our part in life . . . To make our dreams come true . . . No victory is easy and . . . No goal is quickly gained . . . And prizes are not given to . . . The one who has complained . . . Our road may be a winding path . . . And it may twist and bend . . . But everlasting happiness . . . Is waiting at the end.

WHEN YOU BECAME MY FRIEND

Along a path of flowers fair . . . I saw the rainbow's end . . .
And all the world was wonderful . . . When you became my
friend . . . My heart was young, my step was light . . . As I
went on my way . . . And everywhere my soul embraced . . .
The beauty of the day . . . Because your friendship seemed to
melt . . . My troubles and my cares . . . As though it were a
miracle . . . In answer to my prayers . . . It gave me hope and
courage new . . . And faith that I had lost . . . And taught me
that a sacrifice . . . Is worth whatever cost . . . And whether I
succeed or fail . . . I know that in the end . . . I shall be grateful
for the day . . . When you became my friend.

THE SKY IS GOD'S

Sometimes the sky is filled with joy . . . And sometimes it is
sad . . . In rain that seems to shower tears . . . Or sunshine
that is glad . . . Sometimes it shakes with thunder and . . . It
glares with lightning bright . . . Or softly smiles in silence through
. . . The silver stars of night . . . It hurls the hail and says
farewell . . . To flakes of falling snow . . . And forms a backdrop
for the moon . . . Wherever lovers go . . . But whether black or
beautiful . . . The sky belongs to God . . . And always it is
subject to . . . His beckon and His nod . . . And as it blends a
rainbow, so . . . It seems to blend the years . . . According to
His holy will . . . In all our smiles and tears.

WE BOW OUR HEADS

We bow our heads before the graves . . . Of our unselfish sons
. . . Who gave their all to quell the foe . . . And still his blazing
guns . . . Who donned the blue or khaki and . . . Went bravely
into war . . . That we might live in liberty . . . And peace for
evermore . . . Their names are written in our hearts . . . And on
Old Glory too . . . In everlasting memory . . . Of red and white
and blue . . . We honor them for courage and . . . For loyalty
sincere . . . With silent praise in each salute . . . And love in
every tear . . . And while our gratitude exceeds . . . Our power
to express . . . We hope and pray that they have found . . .
Eternal happiness.

TILE-SETTER

It takes a truly expert hand . . . To set a piece of tile . . .
And one that is familiar with . . . Design and modern style . . .
Each piece must have its special place . . . With mortar in between . . . To bring about a masterpiece . . . For some domestic
scene . . . The setter uses float strips and . . . A level here and
there . . . To build a bath and kitchen and . . . To give them
greater wear . . . With pink and gray or gold and blue . . .
Or simply black and white . . . He decorates the walls and floors
. . . To everyone's delight . . . And if it is a large estate . . .
Where thrift is not the rule . . . He also lays the patio . . . and
lines the swimming pool.

WHO ELSE ON EARTH?

There will be songs to comfort you . . . And hands to hold your
hand . . . And there will be enchanting lips . . . That say they
understand . . . But who will keep you company . . . When
months and years go by . . . And who will smooth your silver
hair . . . And listen to your sigh? . . . And who will kiss your
tears away . . . And be forever true . . . As lovingly and happily
. . . As I would promise you? . . . I may not offer you the world
. . . Or half its wealth and fame . . . And I may give you nothing
more . . . Than just my common name . . . But I will hunger
every night . . . And suffer every day . . . To bless your heart
and fill your dreams . . . With joy in every way.

OUR BUSY MIRROR

It used to be that Jimmie spent . . . An hour every day . . .
Before the bathroom mirror when . . . He went to school or play
. . . And he is not allergic now . . . To looking at his face . . .
Whenever he is sprucing up . . . To go some special place . . . But
when it comes to primping, he . . . No longer is alone . . . Be-
cause his brother Donnie is . . . Prepared to do his own . . .
And so the mirror constantly . . . Reflects a studied stare . . .
As both our boys apply the comb . . . And neatly part their hair
. . . We wonder what will happen and . . . Whatever we will do
. . . When our Kristina will begin . . . To want the mirror too.

RUMOR

However well it may describe . . . The dark or brighter side . . .
A rumor is a message that . . . Is never justified . . . It is an
idle tale that has . . . No factual support . . . And would not
be admissible . . . As evidence in court . . . And yet it is a
common thing . . . That flies from door to door . . . And causes
deep dissension and . . . Eventually a war . . . A rumor is the
wishful thought . . . Of women and of men . . . Who want to rush
to new renown . . . Or guide a poison pen . . . It thrives upon
suspicion and . . . Creates a certain doubt . . . And gives the
gossips everything . . . They want to talk about.

HATS OFF TO LABOR

We give our tribute and our thanks . . . To all who sweat and
toil . . . The ones who fill the factories . . . And those who till
the soil . . . The carpenters and plumbers and . . . The men who
mine our coal . . . The ones who man the ships at sea . . . Or
merely dig a hole . . . We honor labor on this day . . . For all that
it has done . . . To multiply production in . . . The battles we
have won . . . For building up America . . . Through home and
foreign trade . . . And for the faith and courage and . . . The
strength it has displayed . . . May labor always lead the way . . .
Through struggle and through strife . . . To victory and glory and
. . . The more abundant life.

FIREMAN'S PRAYER

When I am called to duty, God . . . Wherever flames may rage
. . . Give me the strength to save some life . . . Whatever be its
age . . . Help me embrace a little child . . . Before it is too late
. . . Or save an older person from . . . The horror of that fate
. . . Enable me to be alert . . . And hear the weakest shout . . .
And quickly and efficiently . . . To put the fire out . . . I want
to fill my calling and . . . To give the best in me . . . To guard
my every neighbor and . . . Protect his property . . . And if
according to Your will . . . I have to lose my life . . . Please bless
with Your protecting hand . . . My children and my wife.

FRIENDS IN MY HEART

I know that I am lazy and . . . I do not even try . . . To
recognize an old hello . . . Or hold a new good-by . . . I make
no effort to recall . . . The faces or the names . . . That fill my
working hours or . . . The time I have for games . . . And every
now and then it is . . . Embarrassing to meet . . . Some old
acquaintance whom I should . . . Be very prompt to greet . . .
Who ought to be familiar and . . . Remembered every day . . .
No matter what occasion or . . . However far away . . . But
whether I recall the name . . . Or I am not so smart . . . The
friendly eyes that look in mine . . . Are always in my heart.

CAR CONDUCT

The courtesies of driving are . . . So simple and so few . . .
That everyone should follow them . . . Without the least ado . . .
The signal for a sudden stop . . . Or turning left or right . . .
The cutting down of lamps that glare . . . When passing cars at
night . . . The patience to remain behind . . . Upon a hill or
curve . . . And holding back the epithets . . . That others may
deserve . . . They are the courtesies that keep . . . Unpleasant-
ness away . . . And usually they also are . . . The laws we should
obey . . . But more importantly they are . . . The courtesies we
give . . . That all of us who drive may have . . . A longer life to
live.

RUNNING AWAY

The nightly dream that I endure . . . Is not my only one
. . . For I have many others while . . . I walk beneath the sun
. . . Indeed sometimes they interfere . . . With what I ought to
do . . . And very likely that is why . . . So few of them come true
. . . But I am constantly intent . . . On reaching for a star . . .
And running from the things of life . . . The way they really are
. . . I do not like a morbid mood . . . Or any sign of wrath . . .
And I am always miserable . . . When shadows cross my path
. . . And so I go on dreaming and . . . Pretending I have fun
. . . Although of course I know that I . . . Am getting nothing
done.

TOASTMASTER

He is the banquet boss whose job . . . Is not an easy one . . .
Because he has to guide the course . . . Of business and of fun
. . . He introduces speakers in . . . A pleasant sort of way
. . . And gives a hint or two of what . . . They are about to say
. . . He calls attention to the guests . . . And tells a joke or
two . . . And he must have a parting word . . . When all the rest
are through . . . Sometimes this kind of creature knows . . . Pre-
cisely when to pause . . . And how to hold the audience . . .
And draw the most applause . . . But sometimes he is not so hot
. . . Or does not know the score . . . And by his smart or clumsy
style . . . Turns out to be a bore.

HAVE YOU GOT A PENNY?

Santa Clauses everywhere . . . Are ringing bells today . . . Do
you have a quarter or . . . A dime to give away? . . . Have you got
a nickel or . . . A penny for the poor? . . . Every little bit will
help . . . To make their Christmas sure . . . You can make it
possible . . . For them to have a tree . . . Bright with lights and
presents for . . . A smiling family . . . You can gain their gratitude . . . And fill their lives with joy . . . Blessing them with food
and clothes . . . Or just a little toy . . . Be a friend to Santa Claus
. . . And help him fill his pack . . . Give as much as you can spare
. . . And God will pay you back.

YOUR DAY, DEAR DON

Your birthday, Don, is very much . . . A day in history . . .
Because you bring so many joys . . . To all our family . . .
Your mother and your brother and . . . Your little sister dear . . .
And I are grateful unto God . . . And glad that you are here
. . . We all are deeply fond of you . . . And proud of your success
. . . And wish on every candle bright . . . Your lifelong happiness . . . We hope you have the best of luck . . . In everything
you do . . . And every day in every way . . . Your dreams will all
come true . . . Congratulations to you, Don . . . A barrel full of
cheers . . . And may God bless you on this day . . . When you are
fourteen years.

GETTING MAIL

I used to wonder why my mail . . . Was never very much . . .
And why I had so few good friends . . . Who cared to keep in
touch . . . It seemed the postman never stopped . . . To ring my
bell or knock . . . Although he always had some news . . . For
others in the block . . . And then one ordinary day . . . With
nothing else to do . . . I wrote a lot of letters to . . . The
different folks I knew . . . Well, much to my amazement I . . .
Received a message back . . . And magically my daily mail . . .
Amounted to a stack . . . And so it was not very long . . . Before
I saw the light . . . And learned that letters come to those . . .
Who take the time to write.

TRAIN CONDUCTOR

He punches tickets on the train . . . And settles each dispute
. . . Of where and how the passenger . . . Is presently en route
. . . Perhaps the train is not the one . . . The person meant to
get . . . Or someone overlooked the fare . . . And has to pay the
debt . . . And then there are the youngsters who . . . Contribute
only half . . . But when he sees how big they are . . . He tries
to hide a laugh . . . He answers every question as . . . Politely
as can be . . . And does his best to make the trip . . . A pleasant
memory . . . The train conductor has a job . . . That is not any
fun . . . And he deserves much credit for . . . The way he gets it
done.

WILL YOU WAIT?

How many days and nights are you . . . Prepared to wait for
me? . . . How many hours will your heart . . . Be warm with
sympathy? . . . And if the seasons turn to years . . . And moments
never end . . . Will you remember me, my sweet . . . As more
than just a friend? . . . Will you be faithful when the wind . . .
Is whirling in the dust . . . And when you cannot help but feel
. . . The urge to wanderlust? . . . I know I do not have the right
. . . To ask so much of you . . . And yet I love you so, my sweet
. . . What else am I to do? . . . Because when some tomorrow
comes . . . And time is ours to share . . . The world will be an
empty place . . . Unless I know you care.

KRISTINA'S DOLLS

Kristina has so many dolls . . . She can not count them all . . .
Indeed there are enough of them . . . To reach from wall to
wall . . . They are so very pretty in . . . Their dresses bright and
gay . . . And they are always smiling when . . . They help
Kristina play . . . She hugs them and she kisses them . . . And
sees that they are fed . . . And when the stars come out at night
. . . She puts them all to bed . . . Of course she has her favor-
ites . . . But each one gets a share . . . Of motherly attention
and . . . The very best of care . . . And though she has so many
dolls . . . She always shouts with glee . . . Each time another one
arrives . . . To keep her company.

LIGHT OF THE WORLD

God made the heaven and the earth . . . And He commanded
light . . . The glory of the sun by day . . . The moon and stars
at night . . . The light of all the universe . . . That we might
walk and see . . . Not just the path of progress but . . . To His
eternity . . . He formed the flame of fervor and . . . The glow
of wisdom great . . . That we might find the way to peace . . .
And freedom from all hate . . . The blaze of true benevolence
. . . The gleam of every hope . . . To reach the sparkle of success
. . . And never have to grope . . . He is The Light of all the
world . . . And only in His name . . . Can we destroy the darkness of . . . Our sinfulness and shame.

COUNTY FAIR

The greatest fun I have each year . . . Is at the county fair
. . . When farmers take a holiday . . . And all the folks are
there . . . When horses, hogs, and cows receive . . . The ribbons
they deserve . . . And women are rewarded for . . . The pies and
cakes they serve . . . I like that carnival for kids . . . With candy
and balloons . . . Where barkers shout and lovers see . . . A dozen
different moons . . . Where there are wheels and bingo games
. . . On which to take a chance . . . And music for the big parade
. . . Or those who want to dance . . . And whether I take home
a prize . . . Or both my hands are bare . . . The greatest fun I
have each year . . . Is at the county fair.

WONDERFUL YOU

My darling, you are wonderful . . . And perfect as can be . . .
And every day I thank my God . . . That you belong to me . . .
Your loving faith inspires me . . . To reach a nobler height . . .
And in so many other ways . . . You are my guiding light . . . You
are my morning sunshine and . . . The peaceful sky of blue . . .
And you are all the silver stars . . . That make my dreams come
true . . . I speak your name as softly as . . . My lips would say a
prayer . . . Though I could not begin to tell . . . How much I
really care . . . I love you, darling, more than life . . . Could ever
mean to me . . . Because you are my every hope . . . And happy
memory.

HE GAVE HIS ALL

He was a man who fought his way . . . Against whatever odds
. . . And found reflected in this life . . . The glory that is God's
. . . He was the soul of character . . . And great religious strength
. . . Who measured not the path he trod . . . By any selfish
length . . . His every breath was like a song . . . That echoed in
the sky . . . And like a smile that could not fade . . . Or ever say
good-by . . . And thus the world remembers him . . . Who gave
his all each day . . . That other men might learn to walk . . . The
more courageous way . . . Who never flinched when duty called
. . . Or asked to be relieved . . . But truly earned the high reward
. . . He surely has received.

ALWAYS A RAINBOW

When all the sunlight disappears . . . And there is only rain
. . . I may be somewhat lonely but . . . The time is not in vain
. . . Because my thoughts are with me and . . . I contemplate the
past . . . And I remember that no rain . . . Was ever known to
last . . . And I remember that no wound . . . Has ever failed to
heal . . . However deep the agony . . . That I have had to feel
. . . There is no storm or hurricane . . . That does not spend its
force . . . There are no tears of bitterness . . . That do not run
their course . . . And always somewhere in the midst . . . Of
moments passing by . . . The lamp of faith is lighted by . . . A
rainbow in the sky.

REPORTER'S PRAYER

I want to be impartial, God . . . In everything I do . . . And
know that all the news I write . . . Is accurate and true . . .
I want to phone in time to meet . . . Each deadline every day
. . . And please the reading public with . . . A scoop or exposé
. . . Not just to get a by-line and . . . Its personal success . . .
But more to build a better world . . . Through freedom of the
press . . . To be informative and fair . . . For everyone to know
. . . The things that happen daily and . . . The lessons they be-
stow . . . And so I pray that I may be . . . Proficient and sincere
. . . To serve the least subscriber and . . . To further my career.

EXCESS ECONOMY

We save our money for the day . . . When we may take a rest
. . And when at last we can afford . . . To buy the very best . . .
And in a way this plan is good . . . For people to pursue . . . With
perseverance great enough . . . To see the project through . . .
Provided we protect ourselves . . . From cold, financial facts . . .
And do not fail to take some time . . . To play and to relax
. . . But all too often we are so . . . Intent upon our goal . . .
That we neglect the comforts of . . . The body and the soul
. . . And when our hoard has reached the height . . . Of all we
want to buy . . . Our feebleness informs us it . . . Is almost time
to die.

GOD BLESS YOU, FRIEND

God bless you, friend, for all the things . . . That you have done
for me . . . With faith and understanding and . . . With love and
sympathy . . . God bless you for your thoughtfulness . . . And for
the way you say . . . Good morning and good evening or . . .
Whatever time of day . . . Your confidence inspires me . . . To
reach a greater height . . . In every brave ambition and . . . In
doing what is right . . . I can not thank you half enough . . .
For all the deeds you do . . . But all my heartfelt gratitude . . .
Belongs at last to you . . . And so this special message is . . .
The fondest I could send . . . To tell my deepest feeling when
. . . I say "God bless you, friend!"

WISH FOR TOMORROW

October leaves my calendar . . . And now it is November . . .
And now I tell myself again . . . The dreams that I remember
. . . The dreams of all the days and nights . . . We used to spend
together . . . With never any thought of time . . . Or what might
be the weather . . . Our promise to be true as long . . . As
both of us were living . . . To be considerate and kind . . .
Devoted and forgiving . . . We wanted just to be alone . . .
For hours and forever . . . With nothing to disturb our hearts
. . . And no remorse whatever . . . And now I wish that I could
take . . . Each little joy and sorrow . . . And make today the
yesterday . . . Of our complete tomorrow.

OUR DEAR BOYS

Our boys are not extragavant . . . And yet somehow we find
. . . They constantly are keeping us . . . Financially behind . . .
Their shirts and sox and trousers too . . . Are always wearing out
. . . And we are buying shoes for them . . . Each time we turn
about . . . At breakfast, lunch, and dinner time . . . They never
get their fill . . . Until it seems impossible . . . To pay our grocery
bill . . . And then at school they need supplies . . . And tickets
to a show . . . And trolley fare to carry them . . . Wherever they
would go . . . No, they are not extravagant . . . But surely it
appears . . . Our youngsters do the best they can . . . To keep
us in arrears.

GETTING A DAY OFF

Among the toughest things in life . . . Is how to find a way
. . . To get the boss to let you have . . . Your freedom for a day
. . . There was a time when Grandma died . . . And funerals
took place . . . Precisely when the ball clubs fought . . . To win
the pennant race . . . And once upon a time a guy . . . Could
take a harmless pill . . . That gave him all the facial signs . . .
Of being somewhat ill . . . But nowadays the bosses are . . . Alert
to each excuse . . . And thinking up an alibi . . . Is hardly any
use . . . Though now and then if you are fair . . . And truthfully
implore . . . The boss may smile and let you have . . . An afternoon or more.

COURT HOUSE

The court house is a gloomy place . . . Where criminals are tried . . . And every lawyer tries to get . . . The jury on his side . . . Where judges rule with dignity . . . And bailiffs keep the peace . . . While clerks record the cost of each . . . Conviction or release . . . The court house is a picture show . . . Of fascinating sights . . . Where people stare at others who . . . Demand their common rights . . . Where damages are figured up . . . And contracts are enforced . . . And married couples separate . . . Or get themselves divorced . . . It is the hall of justice in . . . A land where all are free . . . And every law is one that strives . . . For full equality.

SAYING HELLO

There is a kind of quick hello . . . That does not offer much . . . And then there is another one . . . That has a friendly touch . . . A fond hello that warms the heart . . . And seems to linger on . . . Although the hurried handshake and . . . The passer-by are gone . . . It means a great deal more than just . . . The greeting it conveys . . . Because it is so comforting . . . In many different ways . . . It brightens up the darkest sky . . . It penetrates the rain . . . And somehow when a wound appears . . . It takes away the pain . . . So why be brusk and cold as ice . . . Or unconcerned and slow . . . When so much good may flourish from . . . The way we say hello?

TREASURER

His title marks him as the one . . . Who keeps the cash on hand . . . Or in the bank where it may be . . . Obtained upon demand . . . Provided each withdrawal is . . . An authorized request . . . And all the signatures are there . . . To stand the final test . . . He has to keep a record of . . . The money he receives . . . And what the proper balance is . . . When any of it leaves . . . Invariably the funds by far . . . Exceed his salary . . . And so he furnishes a bond . . . To bind his honesty . . . But while the matter of that bond . . . Is usually a "must" . . . He would not have his job unless . . . He merited the trust.

THE WAY WE PRAY

Our lips may memorize and speak . . . A dozen prayers a day
. . . And yet they may not mean a word . . . Of anything we
say . . . We may repeat mechanically . . . The phrases we were
taught . . . Without regard to anything . . . Of real religious
thought . . . And that is wrong because a prayer . . . Should be a
message clear . . . And as we say it we should be . . . Devoted and
sincere . . . No words can reach the throne of God . . . Or set
our sins apart . . . Unless we love Him and we have . . . Contrition of the heart . . . Unless we mean the prayers we say . . .
And place our faith in Him . . . That hope may never falter and
. . . The light may never dim.

DAWN IN THE FOREST

If I could be an artist now . . . With all my memories . . . I
think that I would paint the sun . . . That penetrates the trees
. . . The sun that fills the forest at . . . The starting of the day
. . . When all the stars have vanished and . . . The shadows slip
away . . . The sun that seeks the flowers out . . . To make their
beauty bright . . . And sweeps the darkest corner with . . . A ray
of golden light . . . Because it is the symbol true . . . Of courage
in the dawn . . . And of the hope that faces life . . . With fears
and fancy gone . . . It is the hand that heals the wound . . . And
turns the clock of time . . . To draw us ever closer toward . . . The
mountain we would climb.

WHY I LOVE YOU

You ask me why I love you, dear . . . And I can only say . . .
It is because you are sincere . . . In every little way . . . Because
the brightness of your eyes . . . Is like a shining light . . . That
reaches through the darkest skies . . . And beautifies the night
. . . I love you for the words you speak . . . When you and I are
glad . . . And for the tears upon your cheek . . . Whenever life is
sad . . . Your kiss is like a thousand charms . . . Your sigh is like a
song . . . And in the comfort of your arms . . . My heart is young
and strong . . . I love you, dear, because you are . . . So wonderful
and sweet . . . And like an everlasting star . . . That makes my
life complete.

DEPARTMENT STORES

Department stores are places where . . . A person goes to buy
. . . A thousand different items, from . . . A carpet to a tie . . .
Refrigerators, radios . . . A table or a chair . . . A spool of thread,
a safety pin . . . Or shiny kitchen ware . . . They are the special
meeting spots . . . For wives who like to munch . . . On spicy bits
of gossip while . . . They wait to order lunch . . . Department
stores have charge accounts . . . And they have few restraints . . .
On those who want to cash their checks . . . Or register complaints
. . . And whether you are wealthy or . . . You work for every
dime . . . They welcome every purchase and . . . Deliver it on
time.

OUR RIGHT TO LIVE

The colonists insisted on . . . Their right to work and play
. . . And that is all we ask the world . . . To let us have today
. . . The right to live in freedom and . . . To worship as we
choose . . . And to express whatever thoughts . . . May honor or
accuse . . . It is our independence and . . . The heritage we give
. . . To all our sons and daughters for . . . As long as they may live
. . . The liberty of home and hearth . . . And courts where we
may go . . . To settle in equality . . . The problems that we know
. . . So let us always carry on . . . And be prepared to fight . . .
For our pursuit of happiness . . . And every human right.

YOUR BIRTHDAY

Your birthday, dear, means more to me . . . Than all the other
days . . . Because you are so charming in . . . So many different
ways . . . Because you are my partner and . . . My understanding wife . . . My constant inspiration and . . . The essence of
my life . . . You take away my loneliness . . . And fill my heart
with bliss . . . By every word you whisper and . . . With every
loving kiss . . . And so it is no wonder that . . . I love you more
and more . . . Each time another birthday cake . . . Is coming to
your door . . . Or why I hope that all your skies . . . Will be
forever blue . . . And why, my sweet, I wish a world . . . Of
happiness for you.

URCHIN

He is the poor, neglected boy . . . Who runs around the street
. . . Without sufficient cover for . . . His body or his feet . . . Who
steals from stores and tries to pick . . The pockets in a throng
. . . Because he has not had the chance . . . To learn the right
from wrong . . . He sleeps in doorways and he digs . . . In every
garbage pail . . . To satisfy his hunger when . . . The stuff is not
too stale . . . For him there is no future while . . . The world goes
on its way . . . Ignoring and abhoring him . . . And leaving him
to stray . . . They pass him by and never try . . . To see or understand . . . That all he needs is sympathy . . . And just a helping
hand.

DRUGSTORE

The drugstore used to be a shop . . . Where medicine was sold
. . . To heal an ulcer or to cure . . . A headache or a cold . . .
But now it is a meeting-place . . . For youngsters in their 'teens
. . . To browse around or stand and read . . . The comic magazines . . . Where sandwiches and malts are made . . . And sodas
taste so good . . . When flavored with the gossip of . . . The
school or neighborhood . . . Of course prescriptions still are filled
. . . And cough drops may be had . . . And there is lots of castor
oil . . . For every little lad . . . But nowadays the drugstore is
. . . The place where people go . . . To buy a lampshade or to
see . . . The television show.

AS THERE IS LIFE

No eyes can ever be more blind . . . Than those that do not
see . . . The light of faith in one true God . . . And His eternity
. . . No mind is so unconscious and . . . So shallow and alone
. . . As that which thinks there is no God . . . Or any great unknown . . . For as the sun is set in space . . . And drops of water
fall . . . And as we live, there has to be . . . A power over all
. . . There has to be a reason for . . . The human heart and hand
. . . The sense of feeling and the gift . . . To speak and understand . . . No earthly science can explain . . . The secret of a
breath . . . But only by the will of God . . . Can there be life
and death.

17

TIRED KRISTINA

One day Kristina disappeared . . . And we looked everywhere
. . . But our young daughter obviously . . . Had vanished into
air . . . We searched the whole wide neighborhood . . . And went
through every store . . . And in our house we checked each room
. . . And every closet door . . . Her mother wept and worried
and . . . My hair began to creep . . . Until at last we found her
in . . . The bathtub—sound asleep! . . . Another time, quite
late at night . . . I heard a thumping sound . . . So I put down
my pencil and . . . Began to look around . . . Well, our beloved
little girl . . . Had fallen out of bed . . . And on the floor she slept
right on . . . Just like a sleepy head!

YOU ARE SO DEAR

I love you every hour, dear . . . I love you every day . . . I love
you for your gentle smile . . . And every word you say . . . I love
you every second and . . . Each moment I am here . . . Because
you are so darling and . . . So wonderful and dear . . . And that
is why I call you "dear" . . . Because to me you are . . . As
brilliant and as perfect as . . . The brightest silver star . . . You
are the only one I love . . . The only one I will . . . The only
dream I ever pray . . . That heaven will fulfill . . . Oh, let me be
a part of you . . . And share your life with me . . . And bless me
with the happiness . . . Of your dear company.

VALEDICTORIAN

He is the chosen orator . . . Who represents the class . . . Of
those who had the diligence . . . And competence to pass . . . His
speech will tell the story true . . . Of what the school has meant
. . . And why their youthful spirits are . . . Imbued with sentiment
. . . Perhaps he will elaborate . . . On what the future holds . . .
And how the character of man . . . Has many different molds
. . . But whether he is wonderful . . . Or merely up to par . . .
He is the chosen scholar and . . . The graduation star . . . And
many students envy him . . . And wish that they could be . . .
The lucky ones who linger in . . . Scholastic history.

SELF-RELIANT

The most important traits in life . . . Are those that one applies
. . . To conquer every trouble when . . . Emergencies arise . . .
The knack of knowing what to do . . . When anything goes wrong
. . . And how to work a problem out . . . With faith and courage
strong . . . For only as we help ourselves . . . Can we avoid defeat
. . . And carry on the fight to make . . . Our victory complete . . .
We have to be equipped to face . . . Whatever odds there are
. . . Without the aid of miracles . . . Or any magic star . . . And
so we ought to exercise . . . A little common sense . . . And build
up our abilities . . . Through wide experience.

FARM

A farm is where the chickens roost . . . And horses eat their hay
. . . While hogs are herded in a pen . . . And little children play
. . . It is the place where seeds take root . . . In cultivated rows
. . . According to the kind of crop . . . The busy farmer grows . . .
Where windmills furnish power and . . . The friendly cows pro-
vide . . . The butter and the milk and cream . . . That keep the
world supplied . . . A farm requires sunshine and . . . A certain
share of rain . . . To be successful and to show . . . A real financial
gain . . . But in the weary winter it . . . Becomes a cozy nest . . .
Where nature seems to slumber and . . . The farmer takes a rest.

MY REAL FRIENDS

The friends who mean the most to me . . . Are not the rich and
great . . . Who offer me their money and . . . Who help me
celebrate . . . And not the ones who tag along . . . Because they
want to be . . . A part of any wealth or fame . . . That may
belong to me . . . But they are those who cheer me up . . . Whenever I am blue . . . And who are really interested . . . In everything I do . . . The ones who are concerned about . . . My
children and my wife . . . And whether we need anything . . . To
live a better life . . . The friends who mean the most to me . . .
Are those who do their part . . . To show me how to serve the
world . . . With all my grateful heart.

GIFT GADGETS

I like the little gadgets that . . . I gather here and there . . .
From salesmen and commercial firms . . . Or at the county fair
. . . The calendars and paper weights . . . The pencils bright and
new . . . The memo books and blotters and . . . The letter
openers too . . . I know they clutter up my desk . . . And make
my coat expand . . . And advertising constantly . . . Appears on
every hand . . . But most of them are practical . . . And useful as
can be . . . And after all each one of them . . . Is absolutely free
. . . Although sometimes the gift is so . . . Attractive to the eye
. . . That simply out of gratitude . . . I am inclined to buy.

BE GOOD TO US

O God, be good to all the world . . . In which we live today
. . . Forgive us for our foolishness . . . And help us find the way
. . . Let not the fury of Your wrath . . . Envelop us with fear . . .
However selfish we may be . . . Or false and insincere . . . But
please consider this our plight . . . Whatever time or place . . .
That we are always weak and frail . . . Without Your guiding grace
. . . We may grow lax and we may seem . . . To be indifferent too
. . . But deep within the heart, O God . . . We do remember
You . . . We do believe in You with all . . . The fervor of the soul
. . . And with Your help we hope to reach . . . Our everlasting
goal.

YOU IN MY ARMS

I held you in my arms one night . . . And whispered love to you
. . . And in that hour I believed . . . That all my dreams came
true . . . And I was not mistaken, dear . . . For now you are my
own . . . And every moment of this life . . . Is ours to share alone
. . . You are the depth of all my thoughts . . . The soul of every
song . . . My happiness and sorrow and . . . My faith and courage
strong . . . You are the magic of the stars . . . The glory of the
dawn . . . And all the gentle helpfulness . . . I need to carry on
. . . And while I know I can not say . . . Sufficient thanks to you
. . . I promise you that I will try . . . To make your dreams come
true.

HIDE OUR HATE

Sometimes we cannot help our thoughts . . . Of bitterness and hate . . . Or those of wishing someone else . . . A most unpleasant fate . . . And maybe we have reason to . . . Be angry and complain . . . And let our spirits wander in . . . The darkness and the rain . . . But we are never justified . . . In being vain and proud . . . And there is no excuse for words . . . That say our wrath out loud . . . And there is nothing to be gained . . . From deeds designed to hurt . . . Or by ignoring tragedy . . . That we could help avert . . . So let us hide our spiteful thoughts . . . And do our best to be . . . A paragon in word and deed . . . Of Christian charity.

ONLY OUTLOOK

I do not like the loneliness . . . That fills my room at night . . . When day is done and when I know . . . My friends are out of sight . . . I have to live in solitude . . . With foolish fantasies . . . Or gather my companionship . . . From books and memories . . . And that is difficult to do . . . Because my joy depends . . . Upon the opportunity . . . Of being with my friends . . . I have to hunt for happiness . . . When I am all alone . . . And usually I cannot find . . . The kind to call my own . . . My room is filled with loneliness . . . Until the night is gone . . . And I may have my best of friends . . . To share another dawn.

TONSILS OUT

Kristina had her tonsils out . . . And all her adenoids too . . . And now she is herself again . . . And just as good as new . . . She did not mind the pain too much . . . And when the job was done . . . It was not long till she returned . . . To all her play and fun . . . She was so brave and willing and . . . Obedient and sweet . . . That everything we did for her . . . Was really quite a treat . . . And now she eats and drinks real well . . . And it is plain to see . . . That she has made a perfect and . . . A quick recovery . . . And though she may not fully know . . . What it is all about . . . Kristina is a happy girl . . . To have her tonsils out.

LORD, LET ME HELP

Lord, let me live a friendly life . . . Of willingness sincere . . .
To help the world defeat despair . . . And overcome its fear . . .
I want to speak of comfort to . . . The lonely soul and sad . . .
And lead the way to loving You . . . And being always glad . . . I
want to touch the humble heart . . . And take away its pain . . .
That it may never find itself . . . Forgotten in the rain . . . Give
me the grace to give myself . . . To someone else today . . . So
I may be of service in . . . A special sort of way . . . Inspire me to
carry on . . . In everything I do . . . Until I gain as many souls
. . . As I can bring to You.

TOO MUCH IS BETTER

I have so many things to do . . . I never get them done . . .
But keeping always busy is . . . The way I have my fun . . . Because if I were idle I . . . Would feel depressed and blue . . . For
want of mental exercise . . . And something more to do . . . I
would not be content if all . . . My work were put away . . . And
every morning merely meant . . . Another lazy day . . . And that
is why I truly like . . . The tasks in front of me . . . Regardless of
how difficult . . . Or many they may be . . . And I would rather
have too much . . . Than not enough to do . . . Because each
project peps me up . . . When I have seen it through.

VICE-PRESIDENT

Of all the many titles that . . . A business may present . . . I
think the most fictitious is . . . The poor vice-president . . . Of
course there are occasions when . . . He gets a decent pay . . .
And when directors listen to . . . The words he wants to say . . .
But frequently it designates . . . A person who is there . . . To
lend importance and respect . . . To some routine affair . . .
To authorize his signature . . . On check or document . . . And
save the time of higher-ups . . . At least to that extent . . . And
in that situation he . . . Is more or less a clerk . . . Whose title far
exceeds the pay . . . They give him for his work.

PARTNERS IN LIFE

We think about our parents and . . . Our sisters and our brothers . . . But do we ever take the time . . . To care for any others? . . . Do we remember all our friends . . . Our neighbors on the street . . . And do we ever think about . . . The strangers whom we meet? . . . Do we consider life at large . . . In sorrow and in pleasure . . . Where everyone must make his way . . . According to his measure? . . . The world was never meant to be . . . A small one of our own . . . Where we may hold our happiness . . . And live our life alone . . . For we are all in partnership . . . And there is no partition . . . Except as each of us may sin . . . And owe a true contrition.

OUR IDLE HOME

We have a cozy little home . . . That we are proud to own . . . Where we may share our happiness . . . And live our life alone . . . We got it for our children and . . . We struggled to begin it . . . But when the summer days are here . . . We never find them in it . . . They leave it in the early dawn . . . And they are out of sight . . . Until the sun is slipping down . . . And it is nearly night . . . Of course we know that in their hearts . . . It is a priceless treasure . . . And in the winter it becomes . . . Their special place for pleasure . . . And so we do not really mind . . . Their absence in the sun . . . Because we know the summer is . . . The time for outdoor fun.

EXPENSE ACCOUNT

I figure my expenses and . . . Submit them to the boss . . . In order that my own accounts . . . Will not reflect a loss . . . But every time I turn them in . . . The boss begins to shout . . . And every item he reviews . . . He is inclined to doubt . . . He tells me it appears that I . . . Am in a spending mood . . . And that I could not possibly . . . Have eaten so much food . . . He questions my hotel bill and . . . My travel cost and such . . . And has a fit because he thinks . . . I entertain too much . . . Regardless of how carefully . . . I try to live and eat . . . The boss insists that my account . . . Is just a swindle sheet.

MIRACLE

A miracle is not a dream . . . Or any fantasy . . . But it is just
as real and true . . . As our humanity . . . And it is not a thing
that is . . . Unusual or rare . . . Because it happens every day
. . . To people everywhere . . . Although indeed it is beyond
. . . The powers of the earth . . . And it is fairly sure to have . . .
Some everlasting worth . . . A miracle, however great . . . Is nothing more or less . . . Than just the answer to our prayer . . . When
we are in distress . . . It is the way of God when we . . . Have
asked His timely aid . . . And He bestows the gift for which . . .
Our humble hearts have prayed.

EDGAR GUEST

These many years his pen has moved . . . In rhythm and in
rhyme . . . To give us beauty, faith and love . . . And courage
in our time . . . A truly Christian gentleman . . . Devout in all
his ways . . . He does not look for glory and . . . He does not ask
for praise . . . But always he is echoing . . . The nobler way to
live . . . With every inspiration his . . . Ability can give . . . His
words instill the human heart . . . And stir the sleeping soul . . .
To honor God and country and . . . To reach a higher goal . . .
We thank him for his gentle thoughts . . . So gracefully expressed
. . . The Poet of the People—our . . . Beloved Edgar Guest.

HOW OFTEN, LOVE!

How often I have wanted you . . . To cherish and to keep! . . .
How often I have thought of you . . . And cried myself to sleep!
. . . I see the city street and park . . . The country road and lane
. . . I walk beside you in the snow . . . And hug you in the
rain . . . I hear your laughter in the wind . . . The same as yesterday . . . And then I turn your face to mine . . . And kiss your tears
away . . . But now my arms are empty, love . . . And when I
dream of you . . . Your lips are hushed forever and . . . The wind
is silent too . . . And in the park, along the street . . . The highway or the lane . . . I only feel the melting snow . . . Or touch the
tired rain.

BEGGAR'S PRAYER

I am a lowly beggar, God . . . Who has to ask for meals . . .
And who must worry daily how . . . The population feels . . .
I have to beg the passer-by . . . For nickels and for dimes . . . And
I am fed or I am starved . . . According to the times . . . I wish
that I could make my way . . . And never seek a cent . . . That
comes from pity, charity . . . Or other sentiment . . . Indeed I
know how many frauds . . . Are on the street today . . . And how
they grab the money that . . . The people toss their way . . . But
I am truly crippled and . . . I need what folks may give . . . And
all I ask this day, O God . . . Is just enough to live.

AIRLINE PILOT

Each time I fly I think about . . . The pilot of the plane . . .
And how no doubt he must endure . . . A certain nervous strain
. . . His eyes and hands are busy but . . . The minutes seem so
long . . . That there must be monotony . . . In every motor's song
. . . And as the clouds go drifting by . . . Or raindrops fill the air
. . . I know he must have many thoughts . . . That he would
like to share . . . Perhaps his heart is lonely for . . . The one he
loves the most . . . Or he has private problems that . . . Extend
from coast to coast . . . In any case I really think . . . His credit
ought to climb . . . For his devotion to the task . . . That saves
me so much time.

OUR NEW YEAR'S EVE

Each time another year must end . . . My darling wife and I
. . . Discuss the fortunes of the months . . . That now have drifted
by . . . We do not go to parties and . . . We do not have our
own . . . But we enjoy the New Year's Eve . . . Together and
alone . . . We count the many blessings that . . . Have multiplied
our wealth . . . Especially our children and . . . Their happiness
and health . . . We figure out the future on . . . The basis of today
. . . And plan to do the best we can . . . For progress and for play
. . . We give our gratitude to God . . . And as the New Year
starts . . . We kiss each other and renew . . . The promise in
our hearts.

HIS OWN OPINION

Each person has or ought to have . . . Opinions of his own
. . . And if he tells them he will learn . . . That he is not alone
. . . For many folks will sympathize . . . And many will agree
. . . And anyway the common right . . . To think and speak is
free . . . There are some governments that tell . . . Their subjects
what to say . . . But that is not the way it is . . . Inside the U.S.A.
. . . Indeed there is no subject on . . . The population rolls . . .
Except the government itself . . . According to the polls . . . And
so each citizen may smile . . . Or he may weep and moan . . . For
he has every right to have . . . Opinions of his own.

GARDEN

A garden is the special place . . . To plant the flowers fair . . .
That bloom in gay profusion if . . . They get our loving care . . .
It is a corner of the earth . . . Where bright carnations grow
. . . And lilacs and forget-me-nots . . . Invite the winds that blow
. . . But also every garden is . . . A glorious retreat . . . Where
life is filled with silver stars . . . And happy lovers meet . . .
Where loving words are whispered and . . . Where promises are
made . . . And youthful hearts are fondly joined . . . In dreams
that never fade . . . A garden is a fairyland . . . Of love and
flowers fair . . . For those who cherish beauty and . . . Who try to
find it there.

HOW LONG THE DAY

The shortest day of all the year . . . Is not that certain one
. . . When there is more of moonlight and . . . So little of the sun
. . . But it is every day, my dear . . . When I may be with you
. . . To share your thoughts and hold your hand . . . The way all
lovers do . . . Each second sweet is all too brief . . . The day is
swiftly gone . . . And I must meditate and wait . . . Until another
dawn . . . The moon is like a silent thief . . . Who steals the
world from me . . . And draws another golden date . . . Into
eternity . . . So too the sun's enduring pace . . . Is not the longest
day . . . But on the clock there is no face . . . When you are far
away.

PALACE OF DREAMS

At last we have the home we want . . . With all the space we need . . . And it is wonderful to see . . . Our name upon the deed . . . The boys have ample quarters now . . . In which to sleep and groom . . . While sister has the privacy . . . And pleasure of her room . . . My wife and I are comfortable . . . Throughout the day and night . . . And in my cozy study here . . . I read my mail and write . . . In all the world there could not be . . . A more delightful place . . . For any family to live . . . In fullness and with grace . . . It is the culmination of . . . Our happy plans and schemes . . . And in a thousand ways it is . . . The palace of our dreams.

OUR BROTHERHOOD

There is no greater aim in life . . . Or one that does more good . . . Than striving for perfection in . . . The bond of brotherhood . . . To work and play, to rest and pray . . . And do the best we can . . . For God and country, for our home . . . And every fellowman . . . To live in faith and friendship and . . . In peace from day to day . . . To greet the stranger on the street . . . And help him on his way . . . For only as we build the world . . . Can we expect to earn . . . The happiness and favors that . . . Are given in return . . . And only as we persevere . . . In doing what is good . . . May there be confidence that God . . . Will bless our brotherhood.

GIFT SHOP

The gift shop is a treasure house . . . Of presents bright and gay . . . And greeting cards for everyone . . . At home and far away . . . The store of glass and chinaware . . . A book or picture frame . . . And stationery printed with . . . Initials or your name . . . A lamp to light your living room . . . An ash tray quaint and new . . . And vases for the flowers fair . . . Your dear ones send to you . . . The gift shop is the place to browse . . . When you have time to spend . . . In search of something pretty for . . . A relative or friend . . . Or just to pass the time of day . . . And maybe treat yourself . . . With just a bit of bric-a-brac . . . To decorate your shelf.

I AM YOUR OWN

If I have loved you in the past . . . I love you more today . . .
Because you are so gentle and . . . So sweet in every way . . .
Because you understand me, dear . . . As no one else can do
. . . And in your sympathy and love . . . My heart belongs to you
. . . I cherish you in every dawn . . . Of sunshine or of rain . . .
And when the frost of snow or sleet . . . Is on my window pane
. . . When stars are in the heavens and . . . The moon is in the
sky . . . And when my lips are touching yours . . . To say a soft
good-by . . . I love you more than all the world . . . Could ever
mean to me . . . And I will be your very own . . . And yours
eternally.

MY HUMBLE PLEA

O God, Who rules the universe . . . And all the things there
are . . . Who sets the sun and moon in space . . . And every
shining star . . . Consider now my common clay . . . And hear
my humble plea . . . And bless me with Your guiding grace . . .
And generosity . . . Let not my heart be hardened to . . . The
heartaches of today . . . Let not my soul be strange or cold . . .
To those who go astray . . . But help me to be helpful to . . .
The smallest and the least . . . That Your eternal glory will . . .
Be evermore increased . . . That all the world will keep Your word
. . . And everyone will do . . . The kindly deeds for other souls
. . . That praise and honor You.

TRAVEL

They say that travel broadens one . . . And that indeed is true
. . . No matter what your age may be . . . Or what you strive to do
. . . By plane or train, upon a bus . . . Or in your private car . . .
You learn the most according to . . . How wide your travels are
. . . You need not go around the world . . . Or sail the seven seas
. . . But just to visit different states . . . And their communities
. . . To know how other people live . . . And what they do and
say . . . And whether it is warm or cold . . . And skies are blue or
gray . . . And then you grow in wisdom and . . . In common
interest too . . . With traveled friends from near and far . . . Who
come to visit you.

TRUE GLORY

Some people wonder if their lives . . . Are fruitful as can be . . .
And if their work and income have . . . Sufficient dignity . . .
They fear that their appearance may . . . Be just a bit below . . .
The level of their neighbor's or . . . Some other folks they know
. . . When all the while they ought to see . . . That glory does
not stem . . . From wealth or fame or anything . . . That has to
do with them . . . It is sincerity that counts . . . And whether
people try . . . To do some good for others and . . . To help the
passer-by . . . And if they are contributing . . . The best that they
can do . . . To bring about a better world . . . Where common
dreams come true.

GLAD JANUARY

The month of January seems . . . The longest of the year . . .
Perhaps because the air is cold . . . And skies are seldom clear
. . . Perhaps because in snow and sleet . . . We long to see the
spring . . . And dream of green surroundings when . . . The birds
begin to sing . . . But January always holds . . . A warm and
gentle place . . . With friendly fire in the hearth . . . And some
familiar face . . . The carnivals, toboggan slides . . . The children
on their sleds . . . The steaming supper on the stove . . . And
babies in their beds . . . Yes, January means a lot . . . To those
who try to see . . . How happy and how wonderful . . . This
month can really be.

VOLUNTEER FIREMAN

The fireman who volunteers . . . Is he who works all day . . .
And wants to serve his neighborhood . . . Without reward or pay
. . . Who always is available . . . To jump right up and go . . .
Whenever warning bells ring out . . . Or fire whistles blow . . .
He braves the blaze and fights the smoke . . . With all his energy
. . . To save as much as possible . . . Of life and property . . .
And whether flames are quickly quenched . . . Or only ruins stand
. . . The volunteer will linger there . . . To lend a helping hand
. . . He does not look for credit or . . . A medal on his chest . . .
But he would be a neighbor true . . . Who tries to do his best.

29

MY SOUL IS GOD'S

I know my soul belongs to God . . . Wherever I may be . . . Because He rules the universe . . . And He created me . . . And well I know that when I die . . . And when at last we meet . . . I shall be called upon to stand . . . Before His judgment seat . . . But also I belong to Him . . . Because of how I feel . . . And just because He always is . . . So friendly and so real . . . He comforts me when I am sad . . . He tells me what is right . . . And when the shadows shroud my path . . . He guides me through the night . . . And though I know I have a will . . . That is my own and free . . . I want to serve my God because . . . He is so good to me.

OUR STREET IS PAVED

Today the city paved our street . . . And now it looks real good . . . And now we speak with special pride . . . About our neighborhood . . . The dust and dirt are there no more . . . The holes have disappeared . . . And less will be the accidents . . . That we have always feared . . . It is a great improvement and . . . Is beautiful to see . . . And naturally it benefits . . . The whole community . . . Of course it cost some money and . . . We have to foot the bill . . . And some of us may swallow it . . . As quite a bitter pill . . . But it provides a picture that . . . Is practical and new . . . And every piece of property . . . Is raised in value too.

TO MEET AGAIN

No, I have not forgotten you . . . Your laughter and your tears . . . Not even after all the months . . . Of all these many years . . . Perhaps your brow is wrinkled now . . . Perhaps your hair is gray . . . And some may think your charm is gone . . . As much as yesterday . . . But in the memories I hold . . . You are the very same . . . And I am still inspired by . . . The blessing of your name . . . The blessing of your gentleness . . . The goodness of your soul . . . And everything about you, dear . . . So happy, sweet, and whole . . . And even if you smile no more . . . At least I knew you then . . . And I can always hope and pray . . . That we shall meet again.

REALLY FRIENDS

I like the steady person who . . . Is always there to serve . . .
No matter how much happiness . . . Or sorrow I deserve . . . The
one I can depend upon . . . To do the greatest task . . . Or who
will even undertake . . . The smallest thing I ask . . . For that is
really friendship in . . . The finest sense on earth . . . And that
is what will always prove . . . A person's final worth . . . It matters
not how strong we are . . . Or powerful our name . . . Because
when friendship deals the hand . . . The cards are all the same
. . . We live together in this world . . . And we should try to be
. . . An equal and unselfish part . . . Of all humanity.

WAGGING TONGUE

Beware the wicked, wagging tongue . . . That blabbers through
the town . . . To criticize the government . . . Or tear the neighbors down . . . The tongue that laps up gossip and . . . Proceeds
to spread it out . . . Until a whisper in the night . . . Becomes a
mighty shout . . . There is sufficient poison in . . . The passing
world today . . . Without the vicious venom of . . . The words
some people say . . . For gossip takes the truth apart . . . And
turns it into lies . . . Until no single fact remains . . . That one
may recognize . . . And so beware the wagging tongue . . . That
wants to slur and scoff . . . And when you hear it, do your best
. . . To break and cut it off.

GOD BLESS THE IRISH

God bless the Irish everywhere . . . On this St. Patrick's Day
. . . For all their sunny smiles and for . . . Their friendly, cheerful way . . . They are among the bravest and . . . The finest folks
on earth . . . Whose progress and traditions are . . . Of everlasting
worth . . . The shamrock and shillalah and . . . The wearin' o'
the green . . . The pipe of clay, the blarney, and . . . The beautiful colleen . . . The songs of ancient Ireland and . . . The dances
old and new . . . The fairy and the banshee and . . . The buckle
on a shoe . . . God bless the Irish for their faith . . . Their hope
and charity . . . And may the world rejoice and grow . . . In their
philosophy.

31

TO MY JUNE BRIDE

I love you more than any sun . . . Or any star or moon . . .
Because, my dear, you have agreed . . . To be my bride in June
. . . Because there is no other girl . . . Who is as good as you . . .
Or one whose smile could do as much . . . To make my dreams
come true . . . You are the beauty of my love . . . The music of
each song . . . And when I look at you I feel . . . Forever young
and strong . . . You lift my soul above the clouds . . . And you
are sweet to me . . . In every way that life becomes . . . A treas-
ured memory . . . I love you, darling of my heart . . . Each morning, night, and noon . . . But most of all because you are . . . My
loving bride in June.

PHANTOM PALS

Our daughter has some playmates whom . . . We do not see or
hear . . . But who are constant company . . . For our Kristina
dear . . . Including little Rusty and . . . Delightful Marianne . . .
Red Riding Hood and Goldilocks . . . And sprightly Peter Pan
. . . She talks to them continually . . . When it is light or dark
. . . And now and then she scolds them and . . . She makes them
toe the mark . . . But she is always quite prepared . . . To plead
in their behalf . . . If ever we get in their way . . . Or have the
nerve to laugh . . . And being just a little girl . . . She really has
the right . . . To all the playmates far beyond . . . Our hearing
and our sight.

FORGETFUL BOSS

They talk about professors and . . . Their absent-minded way
. . . But you should know the boss we have . . . And what goes
on each day! . . . He has a memorandum pad . . . A calendar
and clock . . A file for every letter and . . . A key to every lock
. . . He has a secretary who . . . Informs him constantly . . . Of
what he should be getting done . . . And where he ought to be
. . . And yet there is not anything . . . That he can ever find . . .
Or any date or business deal . . . That lingers in his mind . . .
And more than any other time . . . He wanders in a daze . . .
Whenever someone mentions that . . . He promised us a raise.

WEB OF LIFE

I watched a spider spin its web . . . With patience and with
care . . . To build its slight and slender bridge . . . Across the
silent air . . . It never wandered from its course . . . Or strayed
beyond its task . . . While every strand was perfect and . . . With-
out the smallest mask . . . And as I watched I thought of life . . .
And how we strive to spin . . . The web that is the golden goal
. . . Of what we want to win . . . How easily we tire and . . .
How often we relax . . . Whenever we must work our brains . . .
Or bend our brittle backs . . . How frequently we look around . . .
For comfort and for cheer . . . To give us greater courage and
. . . To help us persevere.

CLERGYMAN'S PRAYER

Help me, O Lord, to lead in prayer . . . The members of our
church . . . And guide them ever faithfully . . . In their eternal
search . . . Help me to say my sermon well . . . And wisely counsel all . . . Who come to worship in Your house . . . And heed
Your loving call . . . Let me forget myself for them . . . With all
the best in me . . . And minister to every need . . . In our community . . . That I may comfort those who weep . . . And heal
the sick of mind . . . To help the proud be humble and . . . The
selfish to be kind . . . That I may live my every day . . . To tell
Your gospel true . . . And with the power of Your grace . . . To
bring more souls to You.

GOOD MOVIES

I do not like the movies that . . . Are full of tears and crime
. . . Or those that are so silly that . . . They are a waste of time
. . . Or those where horror holds the screen . . . Until I get the
chills . . . As savages and demons try . . . To manufacture thrills
. . . I do not like hysteria . . . Or violence or shame . . . Or pic-
tures where the hero is . . . The one who takes the blame . . .
But I prefer the common scenes . . . At home and on the street
. . . Where life is real and human and . . . The music soft and
sweet . . . Because it seems to me that my . . . Admission and the
tax . . . Entitle me to rest my eyes . . . And help my mind relax.

TO TOUCH YOUR LIPS

You tell me that you love me and . . . I say I love you, dear . . .
And nothing more is needed now . . . To make our meaning clear
. . . And yet there is a loneliness . . . That lingers in my heart . . .
And every day is gray because . . . We have to be apart . . . I read
your words and hear your voice . . . And know that you are true
. . . But, oh, I want you, darling, and . . . I long to be with you
. . . I cannot hold your hand by mail . . . Or kiss you on the
phone . . . And in a thousand other ways . . . I have to be alone
. . . I want to see your smile again . . . And take you in my arms
. . . To touch your lips and feel the warmth . . . Of all your lov-
ing charms.

RECORD OF FRIENDS

I wish I had a record of . . . The friends that I have known . . .
Who gave me so much comfort when . . . I would have been
alone . . . The ones who still are somewhere and . . . The ones
who passed away . . . That they would be in all my thoughts . . .
And every time I pray . . . My heart is deeply grateful for . . . The
blessings they bestowed . . . And for the seeds of faith and hope
. . . And charity they sowed . . . I do remember most of them
. . . But some I cannot name . . . However much they helped
me or . . . Regardless of their fame . . . I wish I had a record now
. . . Of every faithful friend . . . That they might share the gratitude . . . That I would like to send.

MY SPECIAL PRAYER

Eternal God, I offer You . . . This special prayer today . . .
That You will keep me in Your care . . . And never let me stray
. . . Encourage me to give my best . . . In everything I do . . .
That every deed and word may bring . . . Some happiness to You
. . . And if the way seems difficult . . . Let not my lips complain
. . . But help my heart be reconciled . . . To loneliness and
rain . . . Bestow on me Your loving grace . . . That I may persevere . . . Beyond the night of darkness and . . . The sorrow of
a tear . . . And when the shadows lengthen and . . . At last You
summon me . . . I pray that I may be with You . . . For all eternity.

BUTTONS

Among the useful items we . . . Are fortunate to share . . . Are those important buttons on . . . The garments that we wear . . . The gold and silver, bone and brass . . . The pewter and the shell . . . The ivory, plastic, horn, and cloth . . . And wooden ones as well . . . They decorate the uniform . . . And grace the gown of lace . . . And keep the coats and pants and shirt . . . And underwear in place . . . And then there is the kind that tells . . . The party of our choice . . . Or that society or club . . . In which we have a voice . . . Indeed the button ought to get . . . A special word of praise . . . For holding us together in . . . So many helpful ways.

WE MAKE MISTAKES

As time goes on there will be words . . . And actions to regret . . . And there will be some other things . . . We wish we could forget . . . But it is only natural . . . To know the pains and aches . . . Of being somewhat foolish and . . . Of making more mistakes . . . We seem to think the hands of time . . . Are all we ever need . . . To help us harvest wisdom for . . . Our every word and deed . . . We feel that our experience . . . Will sort of pave the way . . . To all the golden glory of . . . A more successful day . . . And now and then we may receive . . . Some unexpected breaks . . . But usually our goal is gained . . . By learning from mistakes.

PARENTAL HOMEWORK

The Sunday church or Sunday school . . . Can only do so much . . . And all the rest depends upon . . . The parents' final touch . . . A child needs counsel in the home . . . And guidance every day . . . To understand the word of God . . . And how to love and pray . . . To be considerate and kind . . . Obedient and good . . . And strive to gain a worthy place . . . In town and neighborhood . . . But there are parents who neglect . . . Their duties and their cares . . . And who depend upon the church . . . To teach their children prayers . . . When it is really up to them . . . To do the greater part . . . To bring their little ones to God . . . For happiness of heart.

35

COUNTRY WINTER

The air is cold, the ground is hard . . . The fields are white with snow . . . The trees are bare, and everywhere . . . The wind begins to blow . . . The river bed is covered with . . . A sheet of solid ice . . . And all the countryside is caught . . . And held in winter's vise . . . But here and there along the road . . . A chimney seems to sigh . . . As now and then a wisp of smoke . . . Is wafted to the sky . . . A school bell rings and painted sleds . . . Go laughing down a hill . . . While stocking caps and mittens gay . . . Are hoping for a spill . . . And when the shadows yawn and stretch . . . The windowpanes grow bright . . . With blazing logs that light the hearth . . . And stars that watch the night.

SO MANY FRIENDS

I have so many faithful friends . . . Wherever I may go . . . It seems that everyone on earth . . . Is somebody I know . . . Dear Berta, Joe, and Anna Mae . . . And Jan and Ginger too . . . Young Mary, Trudy, Gayle, and Clare . . . To name a very few . . . And, oh, there are so many more . . . By telephone and mail . . . That I could never feel alone . . . And I could never fail . . . Because they all encourage me . . . To do my very best . . . And just in knowing them I am . . . Their everlasting guest . . . I have so many friends today . . . I cannot count them all . . . For they are legion as the stars . . . That shape a silver shawl.

BANK TELLER

The teller in a bank appears . . . To have an easy task . . . But actually his quiet eyes . . . Are peering through a mask . . . For he is held accountable . . . For every dime he takes . . . And when he cashes people's checks . . . He must avoid mistakes . . . He has to know your signature . . . Or judge you by your looks . . . And he must be alert against . . . The counterfeits and crooks . . . He must be quick, efficient, and . . . Congenial and discreet . . . And always ready to prepare . . . A perfect balance sheet . . . But if he has the aptitude . . . His ultimate reward . . . May be the post of president . . . Or chairman of the board.

OUR CHURCH ATTIRE

If we put on some fancy clothes . . . To go to church today . . .
Then let it be for God and not . . . For neighborhood display
. . . And let us be unmindful of . . . The manner of our dress . . .
As we implore forgiveness and . . . Petition Him to bless . . . For
God is not persuaded by . . . The garments that we wear . . . But
only by the color and . . . Appearance of our prayer . . . And
only by the texture and . . . The quality of soul . . . And how the
humble heart may weave . . . The fabric of its goal . . . It matters
not how new the suit . . . Or bright the hat and gown . . . But
only how sincere we are . . . When we are kneeling down.

PITCHER DON

When baseball season comes around . . . Our Don has got the
itch . . . And when his team is on the field . . . He is prepared to
pitch . . . He hurls the horsehide high and low . . . His aim is
true and straight . . . And usually his curves will cut . . . A corner
of the plate . . . He seldom walks a player, and . . . A circuit clout
is rare . . . And when the ball is slammed his way . . . He grabs
it from the air . . . His batting average well deserves . . . A word
or two of praise . . . And he can run and slide in time . . . To ruin
double plays . . . He's only fourteen years of age . . . But he is
going great . . . And some big club should sign him up . . . Before
they are too late.

BY TRAIN AT NIGHT

I like to ride the train at night . . . Whatever style or class . . .
And look outside and see the towns . . . And cities that I pass . . .
And watch the lights that blink and nod . . . As though to say
hello . . . And wish me all the best of luck . . . Wherever I may go
. . . A ride upon the train at night . . . Is happy as can be . . .
With food for every appetite . . . And pleasant company . . . And
when at last I go to sleep . . . My slumber is secure . . . And there
is no discomfort or . . . Misgiving to endure . . . I may be late or
early in . . . The morning dark or fair . . . But when the porter
calls my stop . . . I know that I am there.

UNTIL THAT TIME

The golden sun has disappeared . . . The sky is dull and
gray . . . And I am lonely in my heart . . . Because you went
away . . . Not just around the corner or . . . A measurement of
miles . . . But to the vast eternity . . . Beyond our tears and
smiles . . . I miss you more each moment, love . . . And, oh, I
long for you . . . The while my life goes on and there . . . Is
nothing I can do . . . Tomorrow is an empty word . . . And if I
say good night . . . It seems to have a hollow sound . . . That
switches off the light . . . And I can only wait and pray . . . Until
the time when we . . . May look upon each other in . . . That vast
eternity.

WHATEVER WEATHER

I wish that I could always smile . . . When there are clouds of
gray . . . And when the gushing rain appears . . . To wash the
world away . . . And sometimes when the sun comes out . . . I am
inclined to sigh . . . Because I cannot shed a tear . . . No matter
how I try . . . The weather seems to rule my life . . . From morning until night . . . And there must be a perfect sky . . . To keep
my spirits bright . . . I am a prisoner of rain . . . A servant to the
snow . . . And I am buffeted about . . . By all the winds that
blow . . . I live in fear when thunder roars . . . And lightning
stabs the ground . . . And I am lost in dreams of love . . . When
stars are all around.

THANKS FOR WRITING

I thank you for your letter, friend . . . And for the words you
said . . . To urge me and inspire me . . . And help me forge
ahead . . . You have encouraged me to live . . . A better life on
earth . . . And in that humble way to do . . . Some deed of
greater worth . . . I may not ever see you and . . . I may not
answer you . . . But you will be in all my thoughts . . . And
every dream come true . . . Because your letter gave me strength
. . . And confidence and pride . . . And it revealed you as a friend
. . . Forever at my side . . . And so I say "God bless you" and . . .
I thank you evermore . . . For having sent that message to . . .
The mailbox at my door.

OUR CONSOLATION

We have our friends to comfort us . . . In sorrow and distress
. . . And always there are worldly goods . . . To give us happiness . . . But consolation deep and real . . . Can come from God
alone . . . And only if we ask Him with . . . A fervor all our
own . . . There is no other way for us . . . To overcome our fears
. . . And find the path to perfect peace . . . In trouble or in
tears . . . There is no sympathy on earth . . . That ever can compare . . . With all the everlasting joy . . . And solace of a prayer
. . . Because we know that God gives ear . . . To every word we
say . . . And when we feel that we are lost . . . He helps us find
the way.

CHRISTMAS CARDS

My Christmas cards are signed and sealed . . . And ready to be
mailed . . . And in remembering my friends . . . I hope I have
not failed . . . Because I want to say hello . . . To each and every
one . . . And wish them Merry Christmas and . . . A New Year
full of fun . . . But just in case I did forget . . . To file their names
away . . . I have some extra greeting cards . . . To make their
spirits gay . . . And so if I should hear from one . . . Who did not
hear from me . . . I shall be fairly ready to . . . Defend my
memory . . . Except of course I would not take . . . The time to
fret and fuss . . . If my delay in mailing cards . . . Would be too
obvious.

POP-UP TOASTER

We have a pop-up toaster now . . . That makes the bread get
brown . . . Each time we put a slice in there . . . And push the
lever down . . . It is a simple gadget that . . . We plug into the
wall . . . And that in hardly any time . . . Produces toast for all
. . . Of course it is no miracle . . . And nothing really new . . .
But we maintain a budget book . . . For everything we do . . .
And that is why we are so proud . . . To have a toast-machine
. . . The very best and costliest . . . That we have ever seen . . .
And that is why we always smile . . . And why we like to boast
. . . That every day at breakfast we . . . Enjoy the finest toast.

IF EVER YOU LEFT

I would remember you, my love . . . If Heaven closed your eyes . . . And angels came to carry you . . . Beyond tomorrow's skies . . . I would remember every song . . . We sang together, love . . . When there was moonlight on the sea . . . And there were stars above . . . The sweetness of your wistful smile . . . The softness of your touch . . . And all the beauty of this life . . . That we enjoyed so much . . . And when the flowers bloomed in spring . . . And rain came falling down . . . I would recall each country lane . . . And every street in town . . . I would remember every dream . . . You ever shared with me . . . And pray that we would meet again . . . In God's eternity.

CLEAN CLOTHES

When I send any garment out . . . To get it cleaned and pressed . . . Invariably I find myself . . . Considerably distressed . . . For if I want it right away . . . It usually is late . . . And I must dread some business call . . . Or fear my social fate . . . But if there is no hurry and . . . There is no special need . . . The item of apparel is . . . Returned with extra speed . . . And then I never seem to have . . . Sufficient cash on hand . . . To take the package and to pay . . . The sum that they demand . . . I wish my clothes would keep their crease . . . And never soil or tear . . . So I would always be equipped . . . For functions everywhere.

WHEN WE COMPLAIN

Whenever we are somewhat sad . . . Or we complain and fuss . . . We ought to stop and think about . . . What God expects of us . . . Because He does not ask us all . . . To qualify as saints . . . And He is not unreasonable . . . In seeking some restraints . . . He merely asks of each of us . . . The best that we can do . . . And that we help our neighbors in . . . The struggles they go through . . . He wants us to be gentle and . . . Avoid the way of sin . . . That we may be deserving of . . . The goal we hope to win . . . He only longs to look upon . . . The willingness in us . . . And find that we are not ourselves . . . When we complain or fuss.

PICNIC PRAYER

O Lord, protect our picnic on . . . This special summer day
. . . And keep all fear and trouble and . . . All tragedy away . . .
Let not the rain come pouring down . . . To drown our happy
mood . . . Or ants or spiders interfere . . . To spoil our tasty food
. . . Let not the slightest harm occur . . . To anyone out here . . .
Especially our little ones . . . So precious and so dear . . . But give
us all Your blessing and . . . The inspiration true . . . To rest and
play together and . . . To try to be like You . . . Let us enjoy our
picnic, Lord . . . And keep us safe and well . . . And we will sing
Your praise on earth . . . For everyone to tell.

CLOCK

A clock is something that we use . . . To tell the time of day
. . . And many are the reasons that . . . We put it on display . . .
Like keeping dates and knowing when . . . We ought to eat a bite
. . . And how much time is left until . . . We have to say good
night . . . It warns us not to linger if . . . We want to catch a train
. . . And when to swallow one more pill . . . To kill that certain
pain . . . But many times it seems to me . . . That all it has to do
. . . Is order me around each day . . . To see my struggles through
. . . It wakes me up to go to work . . . It sends me off to lunch
. . . And constantly reminds me of . . . The card I have to punch.

YOUR FRIENDLY COP

You may not like his uniform . . . His manner or his talk . .
And when he stops your auto you . . . May be inclined to squawk
. . . But he is there to help you and . . . He really is your friend
. . . And warm and willing is the hand . . . That he is glad to
lend . . . Your friendly officer in blue . . . Is at your beck and call
. . . To guard your home and family . . . However large or small
. . . To give first aid and watch your child . . . En route to school
or play . . . Recover stolen property . . . And guide you on your
way . . . He is the genial member of . . . The governmental ranks
. . . Who gives his all, while all he wants . . . Is just to get your
thanks.

THANK YOU, FRIEND

When things go wrong and life takes on . . . A disappointing trend . . . I do not sigh or weep but I . . . Remember you, my friend . . . I keep my courage and my faith . . . Because I know that you . . . Have shown me how the grayest sky . . . Can turn to one of blue . . . Your smile has illustrated that . . . This world is not in vain . . . And confidence is all I need . . . To keep away the rain . . . I contemplate the kindly words . . . That you have said to me . . . And measure every moment small . . . Against eternity . . . And then I feel as though my heart . . . Has reached the rainbow's end . . . And all the gratitude in me . . . Belongs to you, my friend.

READ TO ME, DADDY

Kristina likes to have me read . . . The storybooks to her . . . Especially the fairy tales . . . That little girls prefer . . . And so I turn the pages and . . . Explain the pictures there . . . To make my daughter happy and . . . To show how much I care . . . Sometimes it gets monotonous . . . As ancient stories do . . . And then I try to hurry on . . . And skip a line of two . . . But instantly Kristina dear . . . Is set to yell and cry . . . And says I have no right to let . . . The smallest word slip by . . . She seems to know each tale by heart . . . And yet I get no rest . . . Until at last I satisfy . . . Her every book request.

WHO EAT TOO MUCH

Not many people pass away . . . From eating not enough . . . But quite the opposite is true . . . Of those who gorge and stuff . . . The connoisseurs, the gourmets or . . . Whatever name they bear . . . Who order nearly everything . . . Upon the bill of fare . . . The human stomach would not fit . . . An elephant or bull . . . And surely it was not designed . . . To hold a barrel-full . . . But there are people who will eat . . . And satisfy their thirst . . . Until it is a miracle . . . Their bodies do not burst . . . And while they never think that they . . . Are doing any wrong . . . They wonder why the doctor says . . . They may not live so long.

COLUMBUS DAY

Columbus gained a golden place . . . In modern history . . .
Because he had the courage to . . . Explore beyond the sea . . .
He braved the water and the wind . . . To prove the world was
round . . . And when he landed on these shores . . . He knelt and
kissed the ground . . . And thus America became . . . A country
known to all . . . That thrives today on fertile farms . . . And
teems with cities tall . . . Columbus well deserves our praise . . .
And our most grateful prayer . . . And every plaque and monu-
ment . . . In public park or square . . . He found a new and
brighter world . . . In which to work and play . . . And that is
why we honor him . . . And celebrate today.

IF LOVE WERE NOT

What would the world be like without . . . The element of love
. . . And what would be the meaning of . . . The moon and stars
above? . . . The fragrance of the flowers fair . . . That blossom in
the spring . . . And all the magic melodies . . . That birds and
lovers sing? . . . How could the grass be green again . . . Or children laugh and play . . . Without affection of the heart . . . To
take the tears away? . . . Without a friendly smile or word . . . To
show we understand . . . And now and then the comfort of . . . A
kind and helping hand? . . . And how could life be worth the
while . . . Or any dream come true . . . Unless I knew the ecstasy
. . . And joy of loving you?

GETTING A RAISE

Sometimes we slave and never get . . . The smallest word of
praise . . . And only as we ask for it . . . Do we obtain a raise . . .
It seems the boss is cruel and . . . The world is hard and cold . . .
And we are never recognized . . . Until we are too old . . . But
actually the average boss . . . Is really fair and square . . . And
figures out each salary . . . According to our share . . . He knows
his profit and his loss . . . And what we do each day . . . And
whether we are wasting time . . . Or we are worth our pay . . .
And always he is glad to give . . . A suitable reward . . . In keeping with our efforts and . . . The cash he can afford.

LET US ADORE HIM

Let us adore The Lord, our God . . . On this His Christmas
Day . . . And with the shepherds let us kneel . . . And fold our
hands and pray . . . With all the angels let us sing . . . And let us
join with them . . . In praise and benediction to . . . The Babe of
Bethlehem . . . For on this day He blessed the earth . . . With
faith and courage great . . . That we might live in lasting peace
. . . And overcome all hate . . . Let us be like the Magi good . . .
Who traveled from afar . . . To worship Him and offer gifts . . .
Beneath His brilliant star . . . And let us try to follow Him . . .
As once He lived and died . . . And in the comfort of His love
. . . For evermore abide.

WHY ARGUE?

Why do we have to disagree . . . And glare with angry eyes . . .
When it is such an easy thing . . . To think and compromise? . . .
Why do we merely argue points . . . Instead of reasoning . . .
When perfect peace and joy are all . . . That harmony can bring?
. . . We cannot conquer all the world . . . And always have our
way . . . And no one can be right each time . . . In what he wants
to say . . . Each person is entitled to . . . Opinions of his own . . .
And it is our prerogative . . . To let our thoughts be known . . .
So let us be forebearing in . . . Our queries and replies . . . And
let us try to understand . . . And somehow compromise.

WHITE CANE

Be courteous and careful when . . . You see a cane of white
. . . Because it means the carrier . . . Has been deprived of sight
. . . He uses it to feel his way . . . By tapping on the street . . .
And trying not to brush against . . . The people he may meet
. . . It is the only way he has . . . To let you know that he . . . Is
handicapped at every turn . . . Because he cannot see . . . So let
him pass or give him room . . . Wherever he would stand . . . And
be not ever hesitant . . . To lend a helping hand . . . Be grateful
unto God that He . . . Has given you your sight . . . And be
respectful of the one . . . Who holds a cane of white.

WHY I WRITE

If there is one who reads my lines . . . And one whose heart will
say . . . That my mundane philosophy . . . Has helped him on
his way . . . If there is anyone whose sky . . . Is brighter than before . . . And who by virtue of my words . . . May make a higher
score . . . Then I shall know my life is not . . . Entirely in
vain . . . Because I have contributed . . . Some comfort in the
rain . . . And that is all I ever ask . . . That I may do my bit . . .
To help the world consider life . . . And make the best of it . . .
I only want to share my thoughts . . . With everyone on earth
. . . In soft and simple phrases for . . . Whatever they are worth.

WHY FEAR OR FRET?

When we allow ourselves to fret . . . And we indulge our fears
. . . We are inviting tragedy . . . And turning on our tears . . .
There is no need to worry and . . . No cause to be afraid . . . If
we just keep our confidence . . . And try to make the grade . . .
Sometimes the road looks mighty rough . . . And things get in our
hair . . . And now and then our burdens seem . . . Much more
than we can bear . . . But if we go on fighting and . . . Our flag is
flying high . . . The chances are our fears will fade . . . And all
our troubles die . . . And if we go on living and . . . Contributing
our best . . . At least our conscience will be clear . . . And God
will do the rest.

MY TAILORING WIFE

My wife is back in school again . . . Despite her many years
. . . Because she wants to learn the way . . . To use a pair of
shears . . . She wants to be a tailor and . . . To make herself a
suit . . . So she can wear it here and there . . . And look divine
and cute . . . She is an expert when it comes . . . To dresses, coats,
and such . . . And in so many sewing ways . . . She has that perfect touch . . . And I must say she looks divine . . . And cute as
she can be . . . On any street, in church or home . . . Or in society
. . . But she would be a tailor now . . . And that is quite okay
. . . If only she will cut and sew . . . A suit for me some day.

45

FORGIVE ME, GOD

Forgive me, God, for having sinned . . . Forgive the fool in me
. . . And help my heart to make amends . . . For my iniquity . . .
I did not mean to hurt You, God . . . Or ever disobey . . . Your
great and good commandments for . . . The way to live each day
. . . I know that I am guilty and . . . Unworthy in Your sight . . .
And I have not the least excuse . . . To offer for my plight . . . I
should have been courageous when . . . Temptation came along
. . . And prayed to You for special grace . . . To keep my spirit
strong . . . But please forgive my fickleness . . . And save me,
God, from sin . . . That I may serve You faithfully . . . And every
struggle win.

WHY IS IT?

Why is it when you struggle hard . . . And when you reach your
goal . . . Some people seem to think that you . . . Are just a lucky
soul? . . . They do not give you credit for . . . The work that
you have done . . . But they would grab your fortune and . . .
The laurels you have won . . . They do not save their money and
. . . They never want to toil . . . But when you get ahead of them
. . . It makes them fairly boil . . . And then they want to take
from you . . . The goods that you have gained . . . Or otherwise
impose upon . . . The height you have attained . . . Why is your
golden harvest time . . . The only time they care . . . And only
for the wealth and fame . . . They hope somehow to share?

IF YOU WILL HAVE ME

I promise you a sky of blue . . . The moonlight on the sea . . .
And all the dreams that lovers dream . . . If you will marry me
. . . The sunshine in the morning and . . . The silver stars at night
. . . And everything that life can bring . . . To make your hours
bright . . . A cottage with a garden where . . . The flowers never
fade . . . And you will never be alone . . . Or ever be afraid . . . I
promise you a world of fun . . . And everlasting friends . . . And
more than just a pot of gold . . . Where every rainbow ends . . .
I promise you I will be true . . . And every day will be . . . A
paradise of love and joy . . . If you will marry me.

THE FRIEND I WANT

I do not want the kind of friend . . . Who sneaks me out of
trouble . . . Or one who makes a promise that . . . Is just another
bubble . . . I do not like the one whose mouth . . . Is always full
of praise . . . According to my salary . . . Or when I get a raise
. . . Whose smile and generosity . . . Depend upon the weather
. . . And how much influence I have . . . Each time we get together . . . I want the friend who understands . . . And who believes in me . . . And never gives me any cause . . . To doubt his
loyalty . . . Who does not hesitate to ask . . . For what he wants
to borrow . . . But who, without my asking it . . . Will bring it
back tomorrow.

WINDOW ENVELOPES

I like to open envelopes . . . That come addressed to me . . .
For they may hold some friendly words . . . To keep me company
. . . And they may carry messages . . . Of happiness and cheer
. . . As sweet as any whisper soft . . . That ever touched the ear
. . . But when I get those envelopes . . . With windows on the
front . . . I knit my brow and heave a sigh . . . Or else I groan
and grunt . . . Because I know that they contain . . . The bills I
have to pay . . . And nothing more effectively . . . Can darken
any day . . . The sight of window envelopes . . . Is painful to my
neck . . . Except on rare occasions when . . . They bring a welcome check.

LIBRARIAN

The good librarian is one . . . Who knows not only books . . .
But how to handle people and . . . To judge them by their looks
. . . Who also knows a thousand facts . . . Or finds them in a
hurry . . . To satisfy the doubtful minds . . . That cogitate and
worry . . . From ancient words to current news . . . And how to
spell a name . . . The wars that shaped geography . . . And who
was most to blame . . . The best there is in juveniles . . . In poetry
and fiction . . . The latest thing in science and . . . The key to
better diction . . . The good librarian is kind . . . And yet politely stern . . . Whose knowledge is abounding but . . . Who
does not cease to learn.

MY HOUSE IS YOURS

My house is always yours to share . . . Whatever day or night
. . . With all the shelter of its walls . . . And all its warmth and
light . . . With food and drink, an easy chair . . . A choice of
books to read . . . And everything of what I have . . . That you
may like or need . . . My garden walk is yours to trod . . . My
flowers yours to pluck . . . And when you touch my wishing well
. . . I hope it brings good luck . . . Because you are my friend and
so . . . You are a welcome guest . . . And I am happy when you
come . . . And take the time to rest . . . Just make yourself at
home and do . . . Whatever you may care . . . My heart is here to
please you and . . . My house is yours to share.

FOR THEM, O GOD

Be with me in that hour, God . . . When I am old and gray . . .
And help me to appreciate . . . My every yesterday . . . Let me
be sorry for my sins . . . And grateful for each gain . . . And let
me not complain about . . . A single drop of rain . . . Endow me
with the wisdom to . . . Inspire other souls . . . To take the path
of virtue to . . . Their everlasting goals . . . Give me the grace
and strength I need . . . To turn whatever tide . . . That all my
friends may follow You . . . And have no fear to hide . . . Enable
me, O God, to be . . . Sincere and kind and true . . . And teach
Your children everywhere . . . To live their lives for You.

WEDDING WISHES

I hope your wedding day will be . . . A beautiful success . . .
And love will always light the way . . . To lasting happiness . . .
I hope the sun will shine on you . . . Much brighter than before
. . . And stars will keep you comforted . . . When night is at your
door . . . May all your phrases harmonize . . . And all your feelings blend . . . Like colors in a rainbow, from . . . Beginning to
the end . . . I wish you many blissful years . . . As husband and as
wife . . . And pray that God will bless you with . . . The richest
fruits of life . . . And when the shadows lengthen in . . . The
hour of your ease . . . I hope your hearts will hold the joy . . . Of
golden memories.

LIVESTOCK BUYER

He buys the hogs and cattle for . . . The packing house he
serves . . . And strives to give the one who sells . . . As much as he
deserves . . . He wants to pay the proper price . . . To get the best
of meat . . . And satisfy his customers . . . Wherever they may
eat . . . And so he checks the animals . . . As they go marching by
. . . And cautiously appraises them . . . With his discerning eye
. . . He has to be an expert in . . . The field of pork and steak . . .
To carry out his duty well . . . For everybody's sake . . . For
farmer and for rancher and . . . The butcher in his store . . . And
every struggling housewife with . . . Her daily dinner chore.

WHY NOT FORGET?

Why do we always call to mind . . . Some old and hidden hurt
. . . Or worry over little words . . . That sounded somewhat curt?
. . . Why do we make an issue now . . . Of what is gone at last
. . . Instead of overlooking it . . . And burying the past? . . .
Instead of spreading happiness . . . By turning wrath aside . . .
And thereby helping other souls . . . To overcome their pride?
. . . There is no good in jealousy . . . Or any vengeful gain . . .
And every ounce of selfishness . . . Is finally in vain . . . They
only lead to sorrow and . . . The deepest of regret . . . When it is
so much better to . . . Forgive and to forget.

GUESS WHO?

My memory may not be keen . . . For faces or for names . . .
But I have no desire to . . . Indulge in guessing games . . . And
nothing more effectively . . . Can make me mad or blue . . .
Than having someone say hello . . . And then exclaim, "Guess
who?" . . . It may be at a party or . . . When we are quite alone
. . . Along a crowded thoroughfare . . . Or on the telephone . . .
No matter where or how we meet . . . I do not like the one . . .
Who banks on my embarassment . . . To manufacture fun . . .
And usually it's somebody . . . I never really knew . . . So why
should I be wasting time . . . By guessing who is who?

49

KRISTINA WRITES

Kristina wants to write some verse . . . And that is very well . . .
But I must help her get ideas . . . And teach her how to spell . . .
She comes into my study when . . . I labor at my task . . . And
countless are the questions that . . . My little girl will ask . . . She
rhymes a couple lines and then . . . She smiles and looks at me
. . . And hopes that I will help her to . . . Complete her poetry
. . . It slows the work I have to do . . . And interrupts my thought
. . . And correspondence does not get . . . The promptness that it
ought . . . But she is such a darling that . . . I never can resist . . .
And somehow all the time I lose . . . Is not too greatly missed.

WE WALKED TOGETHER

We went to church together and . . . We tried to understand
. . . And on the way to work and school . . . I used to hold your
hand . . . I held it hidden in your coat . . . And squeezed it now
and then . . . And always there were promises . . . That we
would walk again . . . That we would walk and we would talk . . .
About the happy schemes . . . That filled our hearts and touched
the sky . . . With all our youthful dreams . . . I went to work, you
went to school . . . And time went rolling by . . . And then one
night I walked with you . . . And you began to cry . . . I did not
know the answer then . . . But I deserved the blame . . . And now
I wish your lips were mine . . . And I could call your name.

RADIO COMEDIAN

He is the jester of the waves . . . Who makes us laugh out loud
. . . And takes away the troubled thoughts . . . That linger like a
cloud . . . He is the genie who responds . . . When happy dials
spin . . . To serve with mirth and merriment . . . The ones who
tune him in . . . It may be just a joke or two . . . A jingle or a play
. . . Or just the way his voice appeals . . . And brightens up the
day . . . Of course he can be corny to . . . A wearisome degree
. . . And thereby lose his rating and . . . Perhaps his salary . . .
The radio comedian . . . Is generally a whiz . . . Unless it is
apparent that . . . He merely thinks he is.

FOR YOU, DEAR GOD

Dear God, I wish with all my heart . . . And every deed I do
. . . That I could show my loyalty . . . And prove my love for
You . . . That I sincerely mean each prayer . . . And every vow I
say . . . And I would serve You faithfully . . . Each moment of
the day . . . You are The Guardian of my life . . . The Shepherd
of my soul . . . And Your eternal paradise . . . Will always be my
goal . . . I know my sins are many and . . . My flesh is weak indeed . . . As I implore Your mercy in . . . This hour of my need
. . . But I adore and praise You and . . . I promise You anew
. . . That I will keep Your word, dear God . . . And try to be like
You.

HANDS

There is a hand that tills the soil . . . And gathers in the grain
. . . And one that serves the factory . . . Or operates a train . . .
A hand that plays piano keys . . . Or moves the pen to write . . .
And one that clasps in fond hello . . . Or doubles up to fight
. . . There is a hand that leads a child . . . Or stiffens in salute
. . . That sweeps and scrubs and cooks the meals . . . Or polishes
a boot . . . Yes, there are many human hands . . . According to
their kind . . . And what they strive to say or do . . . And what
they hope to find . . . The hands that steal and plunder or . . .
That beg for food each day . . . And those that close in love's
embrace . . . Or gently fold and pray.

BUZZING THE BOSS

So many times an office is . . . A hive of busy bees . . . That
thrive on selfish motives and . . . On petty jealousies . . . The
busy bees that flit about . . . To catch the boss's eye . . . And
always seem so hard at work . . . When he is passing by . . . They
mark their progress and they count . . . Their blessings and their
breaks . . . By criticizing others and . . . Exposing their mistakes
. . . They try to stab and undermine . . . And bring about distrust
. . . And point to those ahead of them . . . As old and worn with
rust . . . And some may keep their honeycomb . . . And flap a
flippant wing . . . But often they themselves become . . . The
victim of their sting.

51

SPRING IS HERE

I know that spring has come because . . . I hear the old complaint . . . That our abode needs cleaning and . . . Another coat of paint . . . The floors should have their share of wax . . . The walls should be more gay . . . And all the trash of winter should . . . Be swept or hauled away . . . The flower beds require care . . . The yard is filled with weeds . . . And it is up to me to do . . . These huge domestic deeds . . . And yet when I have time to spare . . . And look around the lawn . . . I dream about vacation time . . . And I begin to yawn . . . It may be just my lazy way . . . Of handling everything . . . Or it may be the fever that . . . Is common to the spring.

ADVICE

Advice is something most of us . . . Are always glad to give . . . Especially in telling folks . . . The way they ought to live . . . We know what foods are best for them . . . And what they ought to wear . . . The kind of medicine they need . . . And how to comb their hair . . . The proper time to quit a job . . . And look for something new . . . Where they can make a million bucks . . . Instead of just a few . . . We like to give advice to those . . . Who want a home or car . . . Who fall in love or turn to golf . . . And try to better par . . . Indeed it is the perfect thing . . . For someone else's sake . . . But when advice is offered us . . . We find it hard to take.

DOCTOR'S PRAYER

O God, I say this prayer to You . . . That You will help me be . . . A faithful doctor to the folks . . . Of my community . . . Let me attend to every want . . . And lessen every plight . . . Whatever be the illness or . . . The time of day or night . . . Enable me, O God, to make . . . A diagnosis true . . . And always do my level best . . . To pull the patient through . . . To overcome each dread disease . . . Dissolve a sudden spell . . . And tell the healthy human how . . . To keep his body well . . . Give me the strength to practice and . . . Pursue the ethics clear . . . That guide and guard the doctor in . . . Fulfilling his career.

GAYLE

There never was a kinder man . . . Or any finer friend . . . Or
one who lived more usefully . . . The time he had to spend . . .
He was not famous in the sense . . . Of wealth or great renown
. . . But he was loved and praised by all . . . The neighbors in
his town . . . Devoted husband to his Clare . . . Obedient to God
. . . Forever faithful to the flag . . . Above his native sod . . . He
was among the dearest friends . . . I ever had on earth . . . A
truly Christian gentleman . . . Of real and solid worth . . . God
bless him for the many ways . . . His life inspired me . . . And
keep him in His loving care . . . For all eternity.

ALL IN THE HEART

The value of this life on earth . . . Depends upon the scales . . .
Of whether one succeeds at last . . . Or ultimately fails . . . Not
by the weight of money or . . . A single ounce of fame . . . Or
such seclusion as would seem . . . A freedom from all blame . . .
But by the comfort of a word . . . The kindness of a deed . . .
And by the boundless charity . . . To somebody in need . . . The
sacrifice of time and toil . . . To help the world survive . . . And
keep ambition, faith, and hope . . . And fortitude alive . . . And
so as there is victory . . . Or every effort fails . . . The answer is
the human heart . . . And how it tips the scales.

I TREASURE YOU

I treasure every word you say . . . And every line you write . . .
And after you have filled my day . . . I think of you at night . . .
I follow every step you take . . . Wherever you may go . . . I live
for your beloved sake . . . Because I love you so . . . You are the
everlasting dawn . . . That makes my life worth while . . . And I
could never carry on . . . Without your loving smile . . . In every
dream I kiss your hand . . . And gaze into your eyes . . . And ask
your heart to understand . . . And try to sympathize . . . I treasure
you beyond the sun . . . And all the stars above . . . Because you
are the only one . . . With whom I am in love.

JIMMIE WILL WIN

Our Jimmie likes the comics and . . . The movies full of fun
. . . And always he is asking for . . . A motorbike or gun . . . He
never volunteers for work . . . And seldom seems to care . . . For
any interference with . . . The time he has to spare . . . And yet
he gets good marks in school . . . And takes a certain pride . . . In
every undertaking where . . . His efforts are applied . . . And
when we call on him to do . . . Some job around the place . . . He
usually dispatches it . . . With willingness and grace . . . And so
although he likes to loaf . . . Our hearts are not afraid . . . Because he shows sufficient signs . . . That he will make the grade.

GIVE ME PATIENCE

Dear God, there are so many things . . . That I would like to
get . . . And often I complain because . . . I do not have them
yet . . . I know that I should be resigned . . . To Your most holy
will . . . And give You my desires to . . . Deny or to fulfill . . .
But I am somewhat restless and . . . I find it hard to wait . . .
Especially if certain gains . . . May seem a little late . . . And that
is why I ask You for . . . The patience that I need . . . To gather
all the benefit . . . Of every word and deed . . . The patience to
keep fighting and . . . To conquer every strife . . . And constantly
improve myself . . . To win my goal in life.

AFRAID?

If you are superstitious now . . . Then keep yourself in bed . . .
And challenge not the ladder long . . . That looms above your
head . . . Beware the wobbly mirror and . . . The sidewalk with a
crack . . . And do not cross the pathway of . . . A kitty that is
black . . . Because today is Friday and . . . It is the 13th day . . .
And all the very worst of luck . . . May come along your way
. . . But if you have the sense to keep . . . Your feet upon the
ground . . . You will not mind the silly things . . . That simple
folks expound . . . Each day is like another day . . . Regardless of
the date . . . And in the freedom of your will . . . There is no
magic fate.

HOME

The home is that establishment . . . The parents have to keep
. . . So boys and girls will have a place . . . Where they may eat
and sleep . . . Where children learn to walk and talk . . . To
putter and to pound . . . To mark the walls and bring in mud . . .
And throw their clothes around . . . The house where high school
youngsters stop . . . To call and make a date . . . Or daughter
primps and powders while . . . The boy friend has to wait . . .
But all too soon the home becomes . . . A big and empty place
. . . Where little lines of loneliness . . . Adorn a loving face . . .
Where tidiness is tiresome . . . And fingers gently feel . . . The
stains and scars on furniture . . . That once were very real.

WHEN WE ARE OLD

When you and I are old, I hope . . . That we shall be together
. . . To share the wonders of this world . . . In every kind of
weather . . . I pray that we shall sit before . . . The same inviting
fire . . . With all the golden memories . . . That lovers could
desire . . . And if my hair is gray and yours . . . Reflects a silver
beauty . . . May both of them be evidence . . . That we fulfilled
our duty . . . May there be nothing tragic or . . . In any way
distressing . . . But may we both belong to God . . . And gain
His every blessing . . . I hope our partnership will bear . . . The
fruit of each endeavor . . . And you will be with me, my love . . .
Forever and forever.

APPLE

The apple is a piece of fruit . . . That grows upon a tree . . .
And that is generally enjoyed . . . By all the family . . . Some say
it is so healthful that . . . If eaten every day . . . Its vitamins will
surely keep . . . The doctor far away . . . Of course when it is
still too green . . . It should be used to bake . . . For otherwise it
may produce . . . An awful tummy ache . . . The apple is a target
for . . . The would-be William Tell . . . And it will make the
cider that . . . Some people like so well . . . It is the tasty filling
for . . . A strudle or a pie . . . And sometimes it is someone who
. . . Attracts another's eye.

GIVE ME YOUR LIGHT

O Lord, I need Your guiding light . . . To help me on my way
. . . Not only in the dark of night . . . But all throughout the
day . . . Because the sun can do no more . . . Than keep my
body warm . . . And lift my spirits up before . . . And after every
storm . . . It does not show me how to walk . . . Along the
proper path . . . Or try to teach my tongue to talk . . . Without
contempt or wrath . . . It has no power to reveal . . . My selfishness to me . . . Or make me understand and feel . . . My human
frailty . . . And that is why, O Lord, I ask . . . Your guiding light
today . . . That I may do my every task . . . According to Your
way.

ATHLETE'S PRAYER

Be with me, God, and help me win . . . The contest of today
. . . But let me hear with humble heart . . . The praises people
say . . . Let me be perfect in my form . . . And let each aim
be true . . . And let me take a certain pride . . . In everything I
do . . . But fill my soul with honesty . . . And listen to my prayer
. . . That every time I play the game . . . I play it fair and
square . . . Because the glory of this world . . . Can only last
so long . . . And there is bound to be an end . . . To every
magic song . . . And every victory I gain . . . Belongs at last to
You . . . Because You give me all the strength . . . To see each
struggle through.

QUITE THE SAME

I like to walk along the street . . . And watch the people pass
. . . The women and the children and . . . The men of every
class . . . I study their appearance and . . . The friendly smiles
they wear . . . As well as every little frown . . . Of weariness and
care . . . I wonder what ambitions and . . . What hopes are in
their hearts . . . And whether they are happy here . . . Or long
for other parts . . . And as I try to analyze . . . The faces that I see
. . I tell myself that they are not . . . So far apart from me . . .
That now and then I smile or frown . . . To show the way I feel
. . . And every day my life is just . . . As fanciful or real.

56

BRIGHTER SIDE

Each night I hope tomorrow will . . . Be brighter than today
. . . And there will not be many clouds . . . I have to chase
away . . . Because there are a thousand tears . . . I long to leave
behind . . . That I may live in happiness . . . And have my
peace of mind . . . I want each moment to improve . . . Beyond
the one before . . . With golden opportunities . . . And greater
things in store . . . For what is life to me unless . . . I have eternal
hope . . . And there are no dark corners where . . . I have to
hunt and grope? . . . And so whatever miseries . . . I have to
take in stride . . . I always do the best I can . . . To see the
brighter side.

APRIL FOOL

If you get a commendation . . . Or a sudden raise in pay . . .
Or they tell you that the office . . . Has proclaimed a holiday . . .
If you see a bulging billfold . . . On the sidewalk or the street
. . . Or a silk hat seems to tempt you . . . To propel your football feet . . . Or if somebody informs you . . . That your shoe-
string is untied . . . Or your underwear is showing . . . And you
better run and hide . . . Just remember it is April . . . And that
first, mischievous day . . . When all folks forget their troubles . . .
And they want to laugh and play . . . When the tricksters get
together . . . At the office, home, or school . . . With their eagerness to crown you . . . As another April fool.

WITH EVERY LETTER

I like to send you letters, dear . . . Wherever I may be . . . And
try to tell your gentle heart . . . How much you mean to me . . .
To whisper words of love to you . . . With paper, pen, and ink
. . . And say again the sweetest thoughts . . . That I could ever
think . . . I like to call you darling and . . . To thank you for
your smiles . . . And paint the dreams I dream of us . . . Across
the many miles . . . Each morning, noon, or evening when . . . I
take my pen in hand . . . I cherish you and trust that you . . .
Will always understand . . . With every letter that I write . . . I
send my faith and hope . . . And with a thousand kisses, dear
. . . I seal the envelope.

HOSPITAL

It is the house of suffering . . . Where human life is weighed
. . . According to the strength of heart . . . It takes to make the
grade . . . Where doctors try and nurses help . . . To make the
body well . . . And where sometimes they have to wait . . . While
only time will tell . . . It is a place for flowers and . . . A greeting
card or two . . . And books and magazines to read . . . With
nothing else to do . . . Where trays convey the simple fare . . .
Of food and drink each day . . . And medicine is plentiful
. . . For taking pain away . . . And where the welcome visitor . . .
May linger for a while . . . And cheer the lonely patient with
. . . A sympathetic smile.

KRISTINA'S MEASLES

Kristina has the measles and . . . She has to stay in bed . . .
And she must take her medicine . . . And rest her pretty head
. . . She cannot go outside to play . . . Or see a picture show . . .
Or feel the breath of early spring . . . When gentle breezes blow
. . . But she is not the one to cry . . . Or ever to complain . . . Be-
cause she knows that every rose . . . Must have a little rain . . .
And also she is quite aware . . . That it is just a spell . . . And
everybody loves our girl . . . And wants her to get well . . . While
both her brothers wait on her . . . And Mommy dear and Dad
. . . Are spoiling her with toys and things . . . To keep Kristina
glad.

A CHILD SHOULD PRAY

Whatever else a child may learn . . . It should be taught to
pray . . . In loving gratitude to God . . . For every night and day
. . . For sunlight and for beauty and . . . For every breath of air
. . . A happy home and parents good . . . Who give the
best of care . . . It is the rightful heritage . . . Of every child to
know . . . There is a life beyond this world . . . To which we all
must go . . . To understand the right from wrong . . . And which
provides the path . . . To happiness in Heaven or . . . To God's
eternal wrath . . . Throughout each wakeful moment in . . . The
home, at school, or play . . . A child should learn the word of
God . . . And what it means to pray.

TO SAY MY THANKS

My eyes are weary and I wish . . . That I could sleep tonight
. . . But if I did not say these words . . . I would not feel all right
. . . I want to speak my gratitude . . . For all your kindly praise
. . . And thank you for your aid to me . . . In many other ways
. . . You have been more than generous . . . And more than just a
friend . . . And that is why I tie my heart . . . To every thought I
send . . . I want you to believe me when . . . I say I am sincere
. . . And I will always be with you . . . Whatever day or year . . .
Because you are so friendly and . . . Because you are so true . . .
That I would like with all my heart . . . To be of help to you.

CALENDAR OF LIFE

Some calendars begin their span . . . When it is New Year's
Day . . . And some have fiscal attributes . . . That start in June or
May . . . Our government commences on . . . The first of each
July . . . While schools select September for . . . The students
low and high . . . It does not matter overmuch . . . Where they
may start or end . . . As long as there are just twelve months . . .
To figure on and spend . . . A year of life is still a year . . . Wherever it begins . . . For everyone who struggles and . . . Who loses
or who wins . . . And only God himself can choose . . . The day
that we arrive . . . And mark the few or many dates . . . That we
may be alive.

MY SHOPPING GUIDE

When I decide to get some clothes . . . I take my wife along . . .
Because she knows the latest styles . . . And what is right and
wrong . . . Oh, I may buy some sox myself . . . Or just a shirt or
two . . . But as for other articles . . . My choice would never do
. . . For she must stamp approval on . . . The suits and ties I
wear . . . Despite the fact that frequently . . . She drives me to
despair . . . She argues with the salesman and . . . She laughs at
what I choose . . . And spends an hour to select . . . A hat or pair
of shoes . . . But when we leave the store and when . . . The
project is complete . . . I must confess my person looks . . . Re-
spectable and neat.

59

GIVE THANKS TODAY

The river of our gratitude . . . Would overflow its banks . . . If all the blessings we possess . . . Received our heartfelt thanks . . . But always there are things that we . . . Are prone to overlook . . . Including all the joys we fail . . . To enter in our book . . . Although the soul is warm inside . . . The countenance is cold . . . Because we do not think about . . . The happiness we hold . . . And yet we ought to recognize . . . The freedom of our shore . . . And all the opportunities . . . That knock upon our door . . . So let our hearts appreciate . . . The chance to work and play . . . And give our gratitude to God . . . On this Thanksgiving Day.

LOAN-SHARK

The money-lender has the cash . . . To liquidate a debt . . . And keep the one who borrows it . . . From worry and from fret . . . Until the hour is at hand . . . To pay the borrowed sum . . . And he who got it wonders where . . . It will be coming from . . . And then the courtesy grows cold . . . And kindness seems to pale . . . Between the choice of paying up . . . Or going straight to jail . . . I do not mean the banker or . . . The understanding friend . . . The government or relative . . . Who has enough to lend . . . But I refer to him who keeps . . . His dealings in the dark . . . And who is commonly described . . . As being quite a shark.

I KNOW I LOVE YOU

Although I know it is a fact . . . That we have merely met . . . Your friendly smile is something sweet . . . That I cannot forget . . . I gazed into your eyes and saw . . . The answer to my prayer . . . That somebody would come along . . . Who really seemed to care . . . I know you only gave a glance . . . And spoke a word or two . . . And yet that was enough for me . . . To fall in love with you . . . I may have been mistaken when . . . I looked at you tonight . . . But I have never seen the world . . . So beautiful and bright . . . And I just hope we never will . . . Be very far apart . . . Because the moment that we met . . . You won my loving heart.

I LONG TO CALL YOU

When I am in this empty room . . . I feel so all alone . . . And
as I linger here I long . . . To lift the telephone . . . I want
to call your number and . . . To hear your voice again . . . Your
sweet hello and soft good-by . . . That seems to say "Amen" . . .
Just like an angel's whisper at . . . The closing of a prayer . . . To
take me in your loving arms . . . And keep me in your care . . .
But all I ever do is dream . . . And wish that you were here . . .
And try to find the fitting words . . . To make my meaning clear
. . . I walk around my empty room . . . In silence and alone . . .
Without the courage in my heart . . . To lift the telephone.

GOD, HELP ME SOME

O gracious God, I know that I . . . Should always turn to You
. . . Whenever I need any help . . . For what I want to do . . .
But now I want so many things . . . That it would not be fair . . .
To ask consideration for . . . My every fervent prayer . . . And
furthermore I know that I . . . Should strive with all my might
. . . To grow in grace and make myself . . . More worthy in Your
sight . . . I weigh the hours that I could . . . Have put to better
use . . . And every reason I may give . . . Is just a poor excuse . . .
And so I do not ask for all . . . The gifts for which I sigh . . . But
just the blessings that will be . . . Enough to get me by.

BE GENEROUS

If we complain about our lot . . . Just let us think today . . .
About the crippled boys and girls . . . Who cannot run and play
. . . The ones who sit in wheelchairs or . . . Who have to lie in
bed . . . And wonder by what method they . . . May earn their
daily bread . . . Who cannot live the fullest life . . . With bodies
strong and well . . . Including all the sports where they . . .
Might otherwise excel . . . Then let us all be generous . . . And
buy the sunshine stamps . . . For hospital facilities . . . And
medicine and camps . . . The Easter Seals that mean so much
. . . For children everywhere . . . Whose little limbs are crippled
and . . . Who need our special care.

TOO LITTLE TIME

I have so many genial friends . . . And yet it seems that we . . .
Too seldom find the time to share . . . Each other's company . . .
We do not get together for . . . Those visits of the heart . . . Because our work or weariness . . . Is keeping us apart . . . Or else
there is an illness or . . . Some travel out of town . . . Or problems that envelop us . . . And sort of get us down . . . And so the
days and weeks go by . . . Without a social call . . . And even
months will disappear . . . With no hello at all . . . And that is
why each time I see . . . A fond, familiar face . . . I wish this
world were not so fast . . . And such a busy place.

RADIO ENGINEER

He is the man behind the scene . . . Who keeps your voice in
tune . . . When you declaim or yodel or . . . You undertake to
croon . . . He holds the pulse and temperature . . . Of all that
you emit . . . At just the proper volume for . . . The air to carry
it . . . He magnifies your whisper so . . . That every sound is
heard . . . And if your tone becomes too loud . . . He levels every
word . . . He cannot change your diction nor . . . Improve upon
your pace . . . Nor alter any emphasis . . . That echoes into space
. . . But he conveys your vocal cords . . . Along that even keel
. . . That makes them sound inviting and . . . More natural and
real.

IN EVERY WIND

When you are lonely and the wind . . . Is blowing through your
hair . . . It is the gentle breeze I send . . . To tell you that I care
. . . However warm and soft the day . . . However cold and bleak
. . . Each surge of air is from my lips . . . To kiss your lovely
cheek . . . Because my every breath is yours . . . Wherever you
may be . . . And every song I sing is one . . . Of love and sympathy . . . I walk with you where skies are blue . . . And in the
rain that pours . . . And all throughout the darkest night . . . A
waiting world endures . . . So let it be for evermore . . . In sunshine and in snow . . . For I would keep you close to me . . .
Wherever winds may blow.

KRISTINA'S PRAYER

Kristina says this little prayer . . . To keep her in God's loving care . . . "Dear Lord, before I go to bed . . . I fold my hands and bow my head . . . Please take good care of me tonight . . . And wake me up with sunshine bright" . . . I wrote the words for her to say . . . When she is tired from her play . . . And while she knows it all by heart . . . And does not skip the smallest part . . . She has a notion to complain . . . When she wakes up and sees the rain . . . Until I tell her God intends . . . Both rain and sunshine for His friends . . . And as His gentle waters flow . . . All little girls and flowers grow.

GOD IS FAIR

God does not favor anyone . . . According to his name . . . His worldly goods or poverty . . . Or his immortal fame . . . He does not offer prizes for . . . Material success . . . Or praise the lonely one who lives . . . A life of emptiness . . . But He rewards the faithful soul . . . That struggles day and night . . . To win a worthy place on earth . . . By doing what is right . . . God blesses him who guards himself . . . Against the slightest sin . . . And who unselfishly would serve . . . His neighbor and his kin . . . Who does not argue or complain . . . However steep the hill . . . But who accepts the way of life . . . As God's eternal will.

IN MEMORY OF YOU

I hold you in my dreams at night . . . I call you in the dawn . . . And yet I have to tell myself . . . That you are really gone . . . That you are gone beyond recall . . . Forever and a day . . . And there is nothing I can do . . . And nothing I can say . . . You were so wonderful to me . . . So gentle, sweet, and kind . . . It seemed that I was always in . . . Your heart and in your mind . . . No, there is nothing I can say . . . Except a loving prayer . . . That God will bless you, dearest one . . . And keep you in His care . . . And in my silent sorrow there . . . Is nothing I can do . . . Except to live a better life . . . In memory of you.

SUMMER COLD

A cold is bad enough to have . . . In winter, spring, or fall . . .
But when it comes in summertime . . . It is the worst of all . . .
Because it seems to take a hold . . . And never go away . . . And
all it does is make us sick . . . And interrupt our play . . . It ruins
our vacation and . . . Our disposition too . . . And it is just as fatal
to . . . The work we have to do . . . A summer cold is something
that . . . We do not like to own . . . Because our neighbors are
inclined . . . To let us be alone . . . And we are isolated from . . .
The flowers and the trees . . . While we remain at home and try
. . . All sorts of remedies.

RECEPTIONIST

Sometimes with haughty attitude . . . And sometimes soft and
low . . . She greets the people who come in . . . And shows them
where to go . . . Or tells them they must wait awhile . . . Until
their turn to see . . . The doctor, lawyer, or the one . . . Who
heads a company . . . Her job is simply to receive . . . And get
the person's name . . . Together with his history . . . And why he
ever came . . . And keep the fellow waiting there . . . Until the
moment when . . . He is permitted to go in . . . Or asked to come
again . . . Her title is receptionist . . . But it would not be wrong
. . . To call her interceptionist . . . To all who come along.

WISHING YOU JOY

May Christmas bring you happiness . . . And fill your heart
with love . . . And may you richly share in all . . . The blessings
from above . . . May there be many presents bright . . . Around
your Christmas tree . . . And greeting cards from near and far . . .
For all the family . . . It is the hour to rejoice . . . It is the time
of year . . . When everyone should dwell in peace . . . And in
good will and cheer . . . And when December disappears . . . May
there be even more . . . Of pleasure and fulfillment and . . . Of
happiness in store . . . May every season, day, and month . . .
Throughout the new year bring . . . Prosperity and progress and
. . . The best of everything.

IN MY LONELINESS

I fold my hands behind my back . . . And slowly pace the floor
. . . I stop at every window and . . . I listen at the door . . . I gaze
into the fireplace . . . And stir the ashes gray . . . But all that I
can find is just . . . A dream of yesterday . . . I cannot hear your
friendly voice . . . That used to fill the room . . . Or any fleeting
echo that . . . Might penetrate the gloom . . . I cannot seem to
reach your hand . . . Or see your wistful face . . . Not even in the
magic flames . . . That light the fireplace . . . And yet somehow
within myself . . . I feel your presence near . . . And in my loneliness I wish . . . That you were really here.

CATALOGUE OF DREAMS

I keep a catalogue of dreams . . . To which I always turn . . .
When I have time to think about . . . The things for which I yearn
. . . The hopes that fill the days to come . . . With brighter atmos-
pheres . . . And all the songs that seem to stir . . . The ghosts of
yesteryears . . . I thumb the pages and I see . . . The sundry pictures there . . . Of every disappointment and . . . Each answer to
a prayer . . . Of every longing and regret . . . And every tear and
smile . . . The promise of tomorrow and . . . The memory worth
while . . . My catalogue can never fade . . . Or ever fall apart . . .
Because its pages hold the dreams . . . That linger in my heart.

KRISTINA'S PURSES

Kristina has a little purse . . . She takes to school each day . . .
To ride the bus and get the lunch . . . For which she has to pay
. . . But if I may correct myself . . . I ought to make it clear . . . A
single purse is not enough . . . For our Kristina dear . . . It seems
that every other day . . . Another one is gone . . . Because she left
it somewhere or . . . She dropped it on the lawn . . . And so to
what her lunches and . . . Her transportation cost . . . We have
to add the prices of . . . The purses that are lost . . . Her school
expense is bad enough . . . But what is really worse . . . Is that of
always purchasing . . . Another little purse.

FROM NINE TO FIVE

I go to work from nine to five . . . To earn my daily bread . . .
And gather facts and figures that . . . I crowd into my head . . .
I hurry to get down on time . . . And when I walk in late . . . I
try to make my boss believe . . . The trolley wouldn't wait . . . At
noon I put my pencil down . . . And grab a bite to eat . . . And
when the final whistle blows . . . I dash into the street . . . It
seems a sort of useless way . . . For hours to be spent . . . But then
I have to have some cash . . . For groceries and rent . . . Indeed
it is the only means . . . To keep myself alive . . . And so I guess
I'll go right on . . . And slave from nine to five.

I PROMISE YOU

Whatever moon may meet the dawn . . . Or stars look down
on me . . . I promise you my deepest love . . . For all eternity . .
I promise you that I will spend . . . The hours and the years . . .
To bring you every happiness . . . And keep away your tears . . .
To cherish and to honor you . . . With loyalty and pride . . . And
never doubt your loving lips . . . Or ever leave your side . . .
Whatever sun may light the sky . . . Or fortune come along . . . I
promise you that every day . . . Will be a brighter song . . . I
promise you with all my heart . . . That I will live for you . . .
And I will never rest until . . . Your dreams have all come true.

SUMMER RAIN

The rain is good for flowers and . . . The crops the farmers sow
. . . And when the summer heat is here . . . It cools the winds that
blow . . . It washes off the dusty street . . . And leaves its puddles
there . . . To entertain the children when . . . Their little feet are
bare . . . It always helps the merchant sell . . . Umbrellas, coats,
and such . . . And gives the town and countryside . . . A fascinating touch . . . Indeed it is a blessing in . . . A thousand ways and
one . . . But from another point of view . . . It is not any fun . . .
Because it gets the grass to grow . . . And makes it doubly hard
. . . To trim the lawn and fight the weeds . . . That permeate the
yard.

TO GOD ALONE

I dedicate myself to God . . . In all my work and play . . . And
more profoundly in the prayers . . . I move my lips to say . . . I
kneel before the altar of . . . His majesty and might . . . To ask
His blessing for my soul . . . Each morning and each night . . . I
ask His pardon for the sins . . . For which I am to blame . . .
And grace to live a better life . . . In honor of His name . . . With
humble heart I thank my God . . . For all His gifts to me . . . And
for the hope that I will share . . . In His eternity . . . In everything I do and with . . . Whatever I may own . . . I dedicate and
give myself . . . To God, and God alone.

I WAIT AND PRAY

The streets are crowded every day . . . And yet they seem so
bare . . . And I am lonely in my heart . . . Because you are not
there . . . And when the mailman comes along . . . I merely
dream and sigh . . . Because I know so well, my love . . . That he
will pass me by . . . No matter where I search for it . . . There is
no joy for me . . . In town or valley or beyond . . . The reaches of
the sea . . . From winter into springtime and . . . From summer
into fall . . . The sky is dark and dreary and . . . The shadows
form a wall . . . I cannot see the sun that shines . . . Or hear the
birds that sing . . . But I can only wait and pray . . . And keep
remembering.

COWARD

The coward is a person who . . . Is always sure to fail . . . Because his heart and soul and mind . . . Are timorous and frail . . .
And usually the fault is his . . . For if his will would try . . . He
could be brave and virtuous . . . And hold his head up high . . .
He need not prove his prowess in . . . A pugilistic fight . . . But
just to sign the nasty notes . . . He takes the time to write . . .
To have the courage to confess . . . His dark duplicity . . . Instead of putting on the cloak . . . Of black hypocrisy . . . To toss
away his cheating stilts . . . Admit his midget size . . . And be
prepared to tell the truth . . . And to apologize.

THE FRIENDLY TOUCH

There is no feeling in this life . . . That I enjoy so much . . . As
just to shake the hand of one . . . Who has that friendly touch . . .
The one who smiles and says hello . . . Wherever we may meet
. . . In happiness or sorrow and . . . In glory or defeat . . . Who is
not ever jealous of . . . Another person's gain . . . And does not
try to run and hide . . . Each time it looks like rain . . . There is
no greater comfort and . . . No more enduring theme . . . Than
just to know that someone else . . . Rejoices in my dream . . .
That someone wishes me the best . . . Of health and wealth and
such . . . And in so many other ways . . . Displays that friendly
touch.

WIGGLY KRISTINA

Kristina has a way with me . . . I never can resist . . . And that
is why from day to day . . . Her schemes have never missed . . .
She merely tells me what she wants . . . And then she sort of sighs
. . . And wistfully she looks at me . . . With those enchanting
eyes . . . From gorgeous dolls and Teddy bears . . . To candy,
gum, and such . . . My beautiful Kristina knows . . . I am an easy
touch . . . I call her "Wiggly" just because . . . Wherever we may
be . . . There are so many toys and things . . . She wiggles out of
me . . . But she is such a lovely girl . . . And always good as gold
. . . That I would buy up all the world . . . To please my 5-year-
old.

JOYOUS WEDDING

Beloved bride and bridegroom, may . . . Your wedding day be
bright . . . And may the light of silver stars . . . Adorn your
wedding night . . . May God bestow His gentle grace . . . And
keep you ever true . . . And may the best there is in life . . .
Belong to both of you . . . There will be disappointments and
. . . There will be little tears . . . But they will serve to strengthen
you . . . Throughout the married years . . . And they will magnify your love . . . And multiply your smiles . . . As long as you
go arm in arm . . . Along the passing miles . . . And so the best
of luck to you . . . And may your children be . . . As beautiful and
happy as . . . Your sweetest memory.

SUNSHINE STAMP

Let each of us who loves a child . . . Extend a helping hand . . .
To all the crippled children who . . . Are living in our land . . .
The little boy who lost a leg . . . Or wears an empty sleeve . . .
The little girl who lies upon . . . A bed she cannot leave . . . Let
us be good enough to buy . . . Some Easter Seals today . . . To
stamp the sunshine on their hearts . . . And blot their tears away
. . . To bring them comfort in their plight . . . And ease their
every pain . . . And teach their souls to understand . . . That life
is not in vain . . . Let us be generous for those . . . Who are so
young and frail . . . By helping out to buy up all . . . The Easter
Seals on sale.

JUST MEETING YOU

I never really knew how much . . . This life could mean to me
. . . Until I had the happiness . . . To share your company . . .
Until we met the other night . . . And we exchanged hellos . . .
And after while we whispered words . . . Of poetry and prose
. . . I know it is too early now . . . To offer you my heart . . . But
I cannot conceal the hope . . . That we will never part . . . And I
am confident that time . . . Will prove this much is true . . . That
you were always meant for me . . . And I belong to you . . . I
dream of you each moment and . . . I treasure all your charms
. . . And oh, I long to hold you, dear . . . Forever in my arms.

DAY WORTH WHILE

I count that day as wisely spent . . . In which I do some good
. . . For someone who is far away . . . Or shares my neighborhood
. . . A day devoted to the deed . . . That lends a friendly hand
. . . And demonstrates a willingness . . . To care and under-
stand . . . I long to be of usefulness . . . In little ways and large
. . . Without a selfish motive and . . . Without the slightest charge
. . . Because in my philosophy . . . There never is a doubt . . .
That all of us are here on earth . . . To help each other out . . . I
feel that day is fruitful and . . . The time is worth my while . . .
When I promote the happiness . . . Of one enduring smile.

TABLE

The table is an article . . . On which to work and eat . . . A place where people play with cards . . . And board directors meet . . . Where junior does his homework and . . . His mother sews a dress . . . And diplomats and generals . . . Their attitudes express . . . It holds the happy picnic and . . . The spot of social tea . . . The telephone, the billiard ball . . . Research and surgery . . . It may be quaint and valuable . . . Or just a common thing . . . On which to stand the flowers and . . . The presents people bring . . . But every table has its use . . . In office, home, and hall . . . However huge and handsome or . . . However plain and small.

THEY ARE SO FEW

I seem to have so many friends . . . And yet I have so few . . . Because so many do not have . . . The warmth there is in you . . . The feeling of affection and . . . The willingness to serve . . . No matter what the task I ask . . . Or what I may deserve . . . No matter what the problem or . . . The sorrow to be faced . . . Or what may be the injury . . . That ought to be erased . . . So many friends appear at dawn . . . And disappear at night . . . So many set their torch ablaze . . . And then put out the light . . . There are so few who are like you . . . Forever true and warm . . . Forever faithful in their hearts . . . Against whatever storm.

PAPER HANGER

He puts the paper on the wall . . . With patience and with paste . . . And yet his brush is speedy and . . . It has no time to waste . . . The color scheme may be the kind . . . His customers select . . . Or it may be the masterpiece . . . That critics would expect . . . The pattern may be beautiful . . . Or dismal as the rain . . . And it may show the largest spot . . . Or hide the smallest stain . . . But whether poor or perfect, it . . . Is still a special art . . . And he who hangs the paper, plays . . . A most important part . . . For he must climb the ladder and . . . Adorn the humblest wall . . . With beauty and with harmony . . . Wherever life may call.

FARMER'S AMBITION

The farmer strives for progress and . . . He wants some luxuries . . . But he is not intent on wealth . . . Or huge monopolies
. . . His dream is not a palace with . . . A chauffeured limousine
. . . Expensive clothes and jewels and . . . A brilliant social scene
. . . But just the fullness of his farm . . . With freedom from all
debt . . . And certain comforts and delights . . . He always hopes
to get . . . A modern stove and washer and . . . Refrigerator new
. . . A recent model auto and . . . A radio or two . . . He does
not want the whole wide world . . . Or some extensive part . . .
But just his measured acres and . . . The friendships of his heart.

DIRTY LOOK

Some people always are prepared . . . To give a dirty look . . .
And try to make a fellow feel . . . As though he were a crook . . .
They seem to be chagrined because . . . Of something that oc-
curred . . . Or having been reminded of . . . The way in which
they erred . . . And so they hope their gaze will have . . . A wither-
ing effect . . . Regardless of the damage to . . . Their meager self-
respect . . . They never seem to realize that . . . They give themselves away . . . As plainly as the anger that . . . They show but do
not say . . . That anyone with common sense . . . Can read them
like a book . . . And see the lines of cowardice . . . Behind their
dirty look.

YOUR HOLY DAY

However bright or dark, O God . . . This day belongs to You
. . . With all the thoughts we ever think . . . And every deed we
do . . . Of course we know that You create . . . And You design
each day . . . But this is one we set aside . . . To honor You and
pray . . . Because it is the special one . . . That You Yourself have
blest . . . And dedicated as the day . . . For all the world to rest
. . . And so it is the time for us . . . To sort of take our stock . . .
And contemplate the sins that we . . . Commit around the clock
. . . And ask for all the grace we need . . . To live a better
way . . . Because today is Sunday and . . . It is Your holy day.

THEY NEED OUR HELP

We have our work and other things . . . To keep us occupied
. . . But in this life from day to day . . . There is another side . . .
There are the ones who need our help . . . To keep their courage
strong . . . To teach them how to say hello . . . And how to get
along . . . The ones who hunger and who thirst . . . For just a
word or two . . . To fill them with the confidence . . . For what
they want to do . . . They do not look for miracles . . . They do
not ask for much . . . Indeed they only hope to find . . . A kind
and friendly touch . . . So let us give a little of . . . The time that
we can spare . . . To help the ones who need us and . . . To show
we really care.

KIND OF A KISS

In this peculiar world in which . . . We are compelled to live
. . . There are all kinds of kisses that . . . We human beings
give . . . There is the after-breakfast kiss . . . That never comes
too soon . . . And one that seems to make a dream . . . Dissolve
into the moon . . . The special kind for Mom and Dad . . . Or
Junior in his crib . . . Or which the latter lavishes . . . With never
any bib . . . The kiss of one is just for fun . . . Or seals a vow for
life . . . And there is he who gives it to . . . The mother of his
wife . . . In this peculiar world we have . . . A kiss of every kind
. . . Because each one depends upon . . . The current state of
mind.

OUR YOUNG FISHERS

Our boys are able fishermen . . . And like the sport real well
. . . And it could just about be said . . . They equally excel . . . It
seems that Jimmie always gets . . . The biggest fish of all . . . But
Donnie holds his own when he . . . Has counted up his haul . . .
They try the lake, the pond, the creek . . . And every kind of
stream . . . In search of perch and bass and trout . . . To satisfy
their dream . . . Their spending money goes for hooks . . . And
fancy plugs and flies . . . And special rods and reels and lines . . .
That every expert tries . . . And while their gaudy tackle boosts
. . . Their pride and happiness . . . It is the lowly worm with
which . . . They have the most success.

LETTER OF LOVE

Tonight I write this letter, dear . . . And hope it will convey
. . . The sentiment of love sincere . . . That I would like to say
. . . The fact that I admire you . . . And you mean more to
me . . . Than any other dream come true . . . Of hope or memory
. . . I love you for yourself alone . . . The good that you have
done . . . And for the joy that I have known . . . With you, my
only one . . . I long for your enchanting smile . . . And for your
fond embrace . . . To make each moment more worth while . . .
With nothing to erase . . . And so I take my pen in hand . . .
While we are far apart . . . To send my love and kisses and . . .
To offer you my heart.

ENCOURAGEMENT

Encouragement is that support . . . Which we can always use
. . . Especially when we have cause . . . To think that we may
lose . . . It lifts us up when we are down . . . And turns our tears
away . . . And proves there is a sunny side . . . To every rainy
day . . . Encouragement is good for us . . . In everything we
do . . . And naturally we ought to be . . . Prepared to give it too
. . . A pleasant word, a kindly deed . . . And just a friendly smile
. . . Are those ingredients that go . . . To make this life worth
while . . . Encouragement is something bright . . . That never
costs a cent . . . And yet it always does so much . . . To make the
world content.

THIS CHRISTMAS DAY

God bless you on this Christmas Day . . . With happiness supreme . . . And may you gather all the gifts . . . Of which you
ever dream . . . May all your friends remember you . . . With
sentiment sincere . . . To add a world of pleasure and . . . To
multiply your cheer . . . God bless you with the courage to . . .
Pursue each noble quest . . . And grant this golden Yule will be
. . . By far your happiest . . . May all the ornaments and lights
. . . Upon the Christmas tree . . . Reflect the peace and comfort
of . . . Your loving family . . . May every moment of your life . . .
Seem wonderful and new . . . And in the year a week away . . .
May all your dreams come true.

73

EQUILIBRIUM

Some people think too seriously . . . About this life on earth
. . . And wonder if they really are . . . Of any solid worth . . .
They worry over how they look . . . And what they do each day
. . . Their faults and inhibitions and . . . What certain people
say . . . While others simply sail along . . . Without a thought or
care . . . Except to find amusement and . . . To take the fullest
share . . . But neither kind is sensible . . . And neither kind is
right . . . And neither is equipped to win . . . Or reach the
greatest height . . . For life must have its smiles and tears . . . Its
light and heavy heart . . . And everybody should accept . . . And
do his equal part.

LOOK UP, MY LOVE

My darling, I could never be . . . Concerned about the past . . .
For you are mine and I am yours . . . As long as we may last . . . I
do not care what you have done . . . Or what you may have been
. . . Or what the world may criticize . . . And label as a sin . . .
And as for that, I have not lived . . . A perfect life on earth . . .
Indeed I ought to be ashamed . . . Of my intrinsic worth . . . But,
darling, it is time for us . . . To put our fears away . . . And trust
in God to help us start . . . A new and brighter day . . . So let us
leave the shadows for . . . The glory of the sun . . . And let us
join our hands and hearts . . . In battles to be won.

GOD IS MY FRIEND

If I had not a single friend . . . To love and comfort me . . . I
know that I would still have God . . . To keep me company . . . I
know that I could talk to Him . . . However far apart . . . And I
would hear His gentle voice . . . If only in my heart . . . And He
would take my hand in His . . . And guide me on my way . . .
Along the path of sunshine where . . . The clouds are never gray
. . . For God is my eternal friend . . . Who never lets me down
. . . Or loses interest when I wear . . . A worry or a frown . . .
And though the flame that lights my soul . . . May grow a little
dim . . . He does not question me as long . . . As I have faith in
Him.

74

TABLE TENNIS

Some people call it ping-pong or . . . The table tennis game
. . . But any way you look at it . . . The rules are still the same
. . . You take a little paddle and . . . You hit a little ball . . .To
make it touch the table-top . . . And bounce against the wall . . .
Of course you may discover your . . . Opponent has some skill
. . . And he may happen to connect . . . And score a perfect kill
. . . Or you may strut around and think . . . That you are pretty
hot . . . And some important moment you . . . May muff an easy
shot . . . But it is fun and it provides . . . A healthy exercise . . .
For mind and muscle and the swift . . . Maneuvering of eyes.

EXCUSES

Excuses are the means by which . . . We satisfy our souls . . .
While we are wasting time on earth . . . Or striving for our goals
. . . They are a kind of cover-up . . . For laziness and play . . .
When we are not concerned about . . . The hour of the day . . .
But also they enable us . . . To keep away from fun . . . When we
are serious about . . . A job that should be done . . . They are the
explanations that . . . Are either strong or weak . . . According to
our actions or . . . The sentences we speak . . . Excuses save
embarrassments . . . And help to make amends . . . For all the
little hurts that try . . . To interfere with friends.

BANKER'S PRAYER

I say this prayer to You, my God, . . . For guidance and for
grace . . . That I may always do my part . . . And I may fill my
place . . . Each day I deal in worldly wealth . . . And watch the
way it mounts . . . In terms of interest on a loan . . . Or bigger
bank accounts . . . But I would be of service to . . . The rich and
to the poor . . . And help them with the problems and . . . The
tasks they must endure . . . And as a banker I would be . . . Their
counselor and friend . . . With all the aid and comfort I . . .
Could possibly extend . . . I want to join my people in . . . The
things they hope to do . . . To make themselves secure and build
. . . A better world for You.

75

SWEETIE PIE

I call my darling "Sweetie Pie" . . . Because she is my wife . . .
And does so much to bless me with . . . The happiness of life
. . . It may not seem so dignified . . . And yet we all play games
. . . And on our dear ones we bestow . . . Some silly-sounding
names . . . And it is not so funny when . . . You think a little bit
. . . For she is sweet as any pie . . . When you have tasted it . . .
Her smile is sweet, her voice is sweet . . . And sweet are all her
ways . . . However haunting are the nights . . . Or troublesome
the days . . . She helps me manage my affairs . . . And keeps my
spirits high . . . And no one else in all the world . . . Can bake a
better pie.

FAMILIAR PATTERN

When I get tired of my work . . . I walk around the block . . .
And look for some familiar door . . . Where I may pause and
knock . . . Where I may find a friendly smile . . . And sip a cup
of tea . . . With cookies made of wishes on . . . A plate of memory
. . . And there I while the time away . . . And watch the sun go
down . . . And talk about the people with . . . Their offices in
town . . . I wonder what they think about . . . And what they
hope to do . . . And if they would be satisfied . . . If all their
dreams came true . . . And then I go back home again . . . And
ponder to myself . . . The wisdom of the ages in . . . The books
upon my shelf.

MIRROR OF LOVE

Your eyes are like a mirror, dear . . . Wherein I see my heart
. . . And what it means to be with you . . . And how it hurts to
part . . . And there I see my foolishness . . . And all my selfish
pride . . . Because your wistful gaze will not . . . Allow my sins
to hide . . . But also, dearest, I behold . . . The love I have for
you . . . And how I long to fill your hopes . . . And make your
dreams come true . . . How I adore you every day . . . And dream
of you at night . . . When silver stars reveal their gleam . . . Of
everlasting light . . . And all the wonders of the world . . . The
oceans and the skies . . . Are beautifully reflected in . . . The mirror of your eyes.

TO BE INVITED

I like the kindly people who . . . Invite me as their guest . . .
With time for entertainment and . . . With friendship of the best
. . . I thank them for the pleasure of . . . Their hospitality . . .
And for each happy moment in . . . Their genial company . . . It
means so much to have some friends . . . Who want to be with
you . . . And who are always interested . . . In everything you do
. . . My friends are my encouragement . . . To reach a higher
goal . . . And live a more enduring life . . . With all my heart and
soul . . . I like to be their special guest . . . And share in every
toast . . . But I am even happier . . . When I can be their host.

TAXI TALK

I like to call a taxicab . . . To take me here and there . . . No
matter what the hour and . . . Regardless of the fare . . . Not just
for transportation or . . . For being in a hurry . . . Or any other
common cause . . . To overcome a worry . . . But just because I
like to hear . . . The cabby speak his mind . . . With everyday
philosophy . . . That is so hard to find . . . He tells me all the
latest news . . . And talks about the weather . . . And why the
people on this earth . . . Should try to get together . . . And in his
friendly company . . . I have a pleasant trip . . . And always I
reward him with . . . An extra special tip.

FLOORWALKER

He is that special gentleman . . . Who strides across the floor
. . . To make you feel more welcome when . . . You come into
the store . . . Who answers all your questions and . . . Directs you
on your way . . . And who approves the checks you write . . .
When it is time to pay . . . He also helps the personnel . . . With
problems that arise . . . And sees that every shelf is stocked . . .
With quality and size . . . And all the while he has to be . . . A
good detective too . . . And watch for sticky fingers and . . . The
tricks they try to do . . . In stylish clothes and gentle gait . . . His
job may look like fun . . . But many are his duties and . . . The
tasks that must be done.

MY CONSTANT LOVE

My love for you is constant as . . . The stars of silver bright . . .
And just as fervent in the day . . . As in the dreamy night . . . It
never struggles in the rain . . . Or wanders in the snow . . . Nor is
it one to change its course . . . Wherever winds may blow . . .
My love is everlasting as . . . The hills where shepherds sleep
. . . And like a sanctuary, it . . . Is spiritual and deep . . . Because your song is in my heart . . . And when you say you care
. . . Your words become the echo of . . . The answer to my
prayer . . . And all the world may melt away . . . Beyond a mist
of blue . . . But there will never be an end . . . To my great love
for you.

FALSE FACE

Of all repulsive people in . . . The widespread human race . . .
I think the worst is one who wears . . . An artificial face . . . Who
gives the greeting and the smile . . . That typify the friend . . .
But who is only interested . . . In trying to pretend . . . The one
who feels that all the world . . . Is just a bunch of fools . . . And
any goal may be attained . . . Without regard to rules . . . It may
be for the money or . . . The influence at stake . . . But always it
is selfish and . . . For no one else's sake . . . And though appear-
ances may give . . . The attitude of grace . . . There is no charm
or beauty in . . . The artificial face.

THE BELL RANG, MOMMY!

Whenever Mommy cooks or bakes . . . She sets the oven clock
. . . So it will run and it will tick . . . Until the final tock . . .
And then the signal sounds and then . . . In voices loud and
clear . . . The children call to her and shout . . . "The bell rang,
Mommy, dear!" . . . And that is very well indeed . . . But
Mommy would prefer . . . That they would turn the burner off
. . . Instead of calling her . . . It gets a little tiresome . . . To
have to jump and run . . . Each time the youngsters holler that
. . . Her recipe is done . . . And yet I think that underneath . . .
She really likes to hear . . . The old, familiar family cry . . . "The
bell rang, Mommy, dear!"

TELEVISION

I like to sit and gaze upon . . . The television screen . . . And
study every football play . . . And every boxing scene . . . To
watch comedians and see . . . The latest style in dress . . . And
take a look at gentlemen . . . Who represent the press . . . I
follow nearly everything . . . The stations televise . . . And I am
never unaware . . . Of what they advertise . . . I think that television is . . . The wonder of today . . . Despite distortions that
distract . . . And take the fun away . . . It is a great accomplishment . . . But may there never be . . . The kind of telecast
that might . . . Invade our privacy.

TO PAY MY DEBTS

Help me, O Lord, to pay my debts . . . However large or small
. . . With promptness and with cheerfulness . . . And gratitude
to all . . . Not just the bills that I receive . . . Or favors that I
owe . . . But more specifically the gifts . . . Their friendly hearts
bestow . . . The little words of kindness and . . . The deeds so
many do . . . To help me face my problems and . . . To see my
struggles through . . . O Lord, enable me to give . . . The best
there is in me . . . Of love and comfort, faith and hope . . . And
boundless charity . . . That I may have no cause to cry . . . Or
reason to regret . . . And I may balance all my books . . . Without a single debt.

HATE NOT THE GREAT

Sometimes we envy and begrudge . . . The people who are
great . . . And wish their glory would have been . . . Our fortune
and our fate . . . We do not know why praise should go . . . To
them instead of us . . . Or why they ride in limousines . . . While
we go on the bus . . . And yet the facts are simple and . . . The
truth is all too plain . . . That it is through their guidance that
. . . We make our greatest gain . . . It is their leadership in life
. . . That paves the golden way . . . To more enduring comfort
and . . . To brighten hopes each day . . . However unintentional
. . . The efforts that they give . . . Somehow they help the world
to find . . . A better way to live.

MADAM PRESIDENT

She is the leader of the group . . . The one who holds the reins
. . . To strive for constant progress and . . . Inspire greater gains
. . . She chooses her committees and . . . Directs them to report . . . And offers them suggestions and . . . Advice of every
sort . . . Although she has her officers . . . And others at her side
. . . Her duties are so many that . . . Her strength is often tried
. . . But when her term is over and . . . She lays her gavel
down . . . Her work is compensated and . . . She well deserves
her crown . . . And then in every flower fair . . . And every
grateful smile . . . She knows that all her time and toil . . . Have
truly been worth while.

ALL THAT YOU ARE

I see the picture of your face . . . Your eyes, your lips, your
hair . . . And in your gentle voice I hear . . . The music of a
prayer . . . I walk beside you on a cloud . . . Of dreams that
never end . . . Because I love you and because . . . You are my
dearest friend . . . In winter when the ground is white . . . In
spring when leaves are green . . . On summer days and autumn
nights . . . You blend with every scene . . . You make each moment memorable . . . By just the way you smile . . . And life, for
all its sorrow, seems . . . A little more worth while . . . I love you
for the glitter that . . . You give to every star . . . And thank
you, dear, with all my heart . . . For everything you are.

THAT DAY IS HERE

Once more that dreaded day is here . . . When no one may
relax . . . Unless he has attended to . . . His U.S. income tax . . .
Of course so many people now . . . Are paying as they go . . .
But always there are certain ones . . . Who are a little slow . . .
They dilly and they dally or . . . They just decline to pay
. . . Until the closing moment of . . . The last accounting day
. . . When it is so much easier . . . To keep the records clear . . .
By sending cash to Uncle Sam . . . Throughout the current year
. . . And if the debt is overpaid . . . There is no cause to wail . . .
For there will be the pleasure of . . . A rebate in the mail.

KRISTINA'S SHOW

Kristina goes to movies with . . . Her brothers now and then
. . . And always she is glad to go . . . And see the show again . . .
And when she tags along with us . . . We do not mind the price
. . . We pay for our Kristina dear . . . To let her see it twice . . .
But always she remembers what . . . She saw the day before . . .
And she insists on telling us . . . The scenes there are in store
. . . And usually quite loud enough . . . For everyone to hear
. . . So all the folks are sure to know . . . What pictures will
appear . . . And that is most embarrassing . . . And disconcerting
too . . . But she is such a darling child . . . We know not what
to do.

TO SERVE MY GOD

I want to serve almighty God . . . Because He gave me life . . .
And by His grace He helps me through . . . Each struggle and
each strife . . . He comforts me when I am sad . . . And calms my
every fear . . . Until at last the faintest cloud . . . Is bound to
disappear . . . And when my heart is happy and . . . I hasten to
rejoice . . . He seems to bless my spirit with . . . His sympathetic
voice . . . And so I try to serve my God . . . And do my humble
part . . . With all my true sincerity . . . And faithfulness of heart
. . . Because I owe so much for all . . . That He has done for me
. . . That all of me belongs to Him . . . For all eternity.

WHO WORK SO HARD

The ones who labor are the ones . . . Who work for you and
me . . . Who lift the mighty cranes and turn . . . The wheels of
industry . . . Who lay the bricks and hammer nails . . . And mix
and pour cement . . . To shape the stores and buildings and . . .
The homes we buy or rent . . . They make our clothes, our cars
and stoves . . . And all that we amass . . . For pleasure or necessity . . . According to our class . . . And for their daily struggle
and . . . Their brave, united ranks . . . We praise and we applaud
them and . . . We give eternal thanks . . . God bless the ones
who toil so hard . . . And may they always be . . . The symbol of
America . . . And our democracy.

TO BE REMEMBERED

It's nice to be remembered when . . . You're sitting home alone
. . . And someone takes the trouble and . . . The time to telephone . . . Or when you have to stay in bed . . . And someone
calls on you . . . To see if there is anything . . . That he or she
can do . . . It's nice to be remembered with . . . A greeting card
or smile . . . When you have reached the marker of . . . Another
happy mile . . . Or when an anniversary . . . Is knocking on your
door . . . And friends are hoping it will be . . . Just one of many
more . . . Whatever reason there may be . . . For merriment
and song . . . It's nice to be remembered and . . . To know that
you belong.

WHEN I AM BUSY

I know I have been busy, dear . . . With many things to do . . .
And little opportunity . . . To spend my time with you . . . My
moments have been occupied . . . With duties to be done . . .
From dawn to dusk and from the stars . . . Until another sun . . .
But you are in my every thought . . . And always in my heart . . .
However still the telephone . . . Or far we are apart . . . You are
forever in my mind . . . And in my every scheme . . . And you are
all the wondrous world . . . Of which I ever dream . . . And
when I have to be alone . . . Whatever I may do . . . Believe me,
dear, each task is one . . . I dedicate to you.

TRUE CHARITY

O Lord, if I do any deed . . . To make this day worth while
. . . I want to be sincere in it . . . And do it with a smile . . . I
hope it will be something that . . . Will be considered good . . .
And that its kindly purpose will . . . Be fully understood . . . Because an act of charity . . . Is like an empty prayer . . . Unless the
highest motive of . . . Unselfishness is there . . . O Lord, I long
to praise Your name . . . In everything I do . . . And out of
humbleness reflect . . . My gratitude to You . . . And so if I do
anything . . . That might be set apart . . . I want it to be something that . . . Will please Your loving heart.

THE BLIND

The human beings who are blind . . . Are those who cannot
see . . . The physical proportions of . . . A person or a tree . . .
They lack the power to behold . . . The picture of a street . . .
The colors of a rainbow or . . . The flowers at their feet . . . But
also they need never look . . . On ugliness or dirt . . . Or face the
scowls that threaten or . . . The sneers that try to hurt . . . They
do not have to check the clock . . . For night to follow day . . .
Or gaze upon the tears that flow . . . When life has passed away
. . . And yet it seems they have their dreams . . . And sometimes
they can see . . . Much more than is apparent to . . . Our visi-
bility.

ALWAYS

I will respect your wishes and . . . I will not call or write . . .
But always when the sun goes down . . . My heart will say good
night . . . And always when the day is done . . . And when the
stars appear . . . I shall remember all the words . . . You ever
whispered, dear . . . And I shall walk in loneliness . . . Along
the silent sea . . . And seek the ship that might have sailed . . .
To bring you back to me . . . I may not ever find your smile . . .
Or hold your hand again . . . But every image will be bright
. . . And beautiful as then . . . And truly as I promised you . . .
The moment that we met . . . I will adore you always and . . .
I never will forget.

LONG HAULER

He hauls the heavy merchandise . . . By truck from coast to
coast . . . And carefully delivers it . . . Where it is needed most
. . . He drives along until his eyes . . . Are just about to close . . .
And then he stops beside the road . . . To slumber or to doze . . .
It does not matter much to him . . . If it is day or night . . . Except that he must satisfy . . . His healthy appetite . . . And also
after sundown he . . . Must move with greater care . . . Where
foolish drivers fail to dim . . . Their headlights' blinding glare
. . . His job is not an easy one . . . For it requires grit . . . To
truck a load of merchandise . . . And take good care of it.

YOU MEAN SO MUCH

There is so much of happiness . . . That you have given me
. . . That I could never pay you back . . . In time or memory . . .
But I would like to have you know . . . I never will forget . . .
And there has been no moment, dear . . . That I could once
regret . . . There has not been a day with you . . . That has not
been complete . . . Or ever any sorrow, dear . . . That has not
tasted sweet . . . You are the echo of my heart . . . In every song
I sing . . . And you are like a miracle . . . That only God can
bring . . . And that is why I love you, dear . . . And from the
very start . . . I have desired you so much . . . And given you
my heart.

THE FRIENDS I HAD

I used to have some special friends . . . I do not have today
. . . And many times I wonder why . . . We had to drift away . . .
I know I left the neighborhood . . . As some of them did too . . .
But that is not a real excuse . . . For friendship to be through
. . . I wrote them letters now and then . . . And some of them
replied . . . Yet gradually and casually . . . The correspondence
died . . . Perhaps it is the way of life . . . That changes everything . . . And what is past is only ours . . . To be remembering
. . . But every time I think of them . . . And hold them in my
heart . . . I wonder why they do not write . . . And why we had
to part.

CHAMBER OF COMMERCE

It is that group of citizens . . . Who loyally unite . . . To make
their city or their town . . . A more inviting site . . . Who publicize its benefits . . . To firms and industries . . . Especially of
taxes low . . . And cheap utilities . . . To swell its population and
. . . Increase its daily bread . . . And help each civic enterprise
. . . To grow and forge ahead . . . The chamber welcomes
visitors . . . And leads the big parade . . . To build the town and
make secure . . . The freedom of its trade . . . It is the wheel
of progress great . . . In culture, work, and play . . . With strength
and courage to defend . . . The democratic way.

DEAR UNCLE

Dear Uncle, you have always been . . . Just like a dad to me . . . And I am truly happy in . . . Your friendly company . . . I thank you for your many gifts . . . Your greetings and your smiles . . . Your telegrams and letters and . . . Your voice across the miles . . . But most of all I thank you for . . . Your generous advice . . . On confidence and courage and . . . The good of sacrifice . . . The blessing of an honest heart . . . And faith to conquer strife . . . The need for certain pride and yet . . . To live a humble life . . . Dear Uncle, you are so sincere . . . And kind in every way . . . That I admire you and grow . . . More grateful every day.

DEAR AUNT

Dear Aunt, of all the things I write . . . I hope these lines will be . . . The very best that could express . . . The gratitude in me . . . My thankfulness for every smile . . . And kindness you have shown . . . And for the hours spent with you . . . Instead of all alone . . . You have not owed me anything . . . And yet in your sweet way . . . You have contributed so much . . . To brighten every day . . . You have encouraged me to dream . . . According to my heart . . . And you have helped me to decide . . . And make the proper start . . . Dear Aunt, each time I think of you . . . I love you more and more . . . And hope you gather everything . . . That you are wishing for.

WHATEVER SERMON

A million sermons fill the air . . . When Sunday comes around . . . And some of them are passable . . . And some of them are sound . . . But most of them are meant to preach . . . The teachings and the truth . . . According to the following . . . Of elders and of youths . . . And we should listen quietly . . . And try to understand . . . That we were born to honor God . . . And keep His least command . . . And we should carry home with us . . . The messages they say . . . And do our level best to live . . . A better life each day . . . A sermon may be wonderful . . . Or it may miss the mark . . . But every word that praises God . . . Will guide us through the dark.

HEART IN OUR WORK

Success does not depend upon . . . A lucky break or quirk . . .
But it is likely if we put . . . Our heart into our work . . . Although sometimes a lazy mind . . . May make a sudden gain . . .
The chances are that finally . . . The stride will be in vain . . . Because the only progress that . . . Is permanent and real . . . Is that
which faithful fortitude . . . And energy reveal . . . We have to
earn our way in life . . . If we would reach the top . . . And there
should be no other place . . . Where we decide to stop . . . So let
us meet the pattern that . . . Is always straight and true . . . And
put our heart in every task . . . We undertake to do.

THE DEADLY FLAME

A flame may be a little one . . . But when it starts to grow . . .
It can be much more damaging . . . Than all the floods that
flow . . . Each sudden spark of fire is . . . A ruthless enemy . . .
That tries to smother human life . . . And ruin property . . . And
yet it is not difficult . . . For people to prevent . . . If only care
is exercised . . . And time is wisely spent . . . If homes are wired
properly . . . And trash is put away . . . And if commercial buildings are . . . Protected every day . . . So let us all be conscious of
. . . This obligation great . . . And guard against the deadly flame
. . . Before it is too late.

MY GUIDING LIGHT

Your friendship is the dearest thing . . . That I have ever had
. . . Because each moment it has done . . . So much to make me
glad . . . It has encouraged me to try . . . To live a better way . . .
And be particular about . . . The things I do or say . . . In many
ways it has become . . . The pattern of my life . . . And given
me the strength to meet . . . Each struggle and each strife . . . I
would not be the same without . . . The friendship you have
shown . . . Because I know I never could . . . Have done so much
alone . . . Your friendship is my guiding light . . . Wherever I
may be . . . And it is all the lasting joy . . . Of every memory.

HANDSOME JIMMIE

Our Jimmie used to be a boy . . . Who did not want to dress
. . . And when the day was Sunday he . . . Was always in distress
. . . Because he liked to bum around . . . In old and sloppy
clothes . . . And he was set against the least . . . Sophisticated
pose . . . But now he primps and polishes . . . And combs his
hair all day . . . And in selecting suits he looks . . . For colors
bright and gay . . . He is a handsome lad and tall . . . Not far
from fifteen years . . . And all the lovely ladies sigh . . . Wherever he appears . . . And while he says he does not care . . . About
a single girl . . . We wonder why he gives his hair . . . That little
fancy twirl.

WE LOVE YOU, LORD

Dear Lord, we bow in reverence . . . Beside Your bed of straw
. . . Where Magi brought their gifts of gold . . . And shepherds
knelt in awe . . . We offer You our humble thanks . . . And we
sincerely pray . . . That we may please Your loving heart . . .
On this Your Christmas Day . . . We long to have good will
toward men . . . And peace upon this earth . . . That we may live
in charity . . . And be of better worth . . . We know that we have
made mistakes . . . And we have failed to be . . . Deserving of
Your blessings and . . . Your great eternity . . . But we adore
You, Lord and God . . . And promise to be true . . . And on this
day we humbly say . . . Our thankfulness to You.

MY HOBBY

Some people like to gather stamps . . . Old coins or bottle tops
. . . Antiques or match book covers or . . . The labels from the
shops . . . Their hobbies are innumerable . . . And show all sorts
of trends . . . But I am always striving to . . . Collect a lot of
friends . . . Because they mean much more to me . . . Than
ordinary things . . . Like photographs and greeting cards . . . Or
lavaliers and rings . . . They comfort me when I am sad . . . They
smile when I am gay . . . And in their company I live . . . A
more exciting day . . . Although they cost me nothing they . . .
Are priceless as can be . . . And that is why my hobby is . . . To
save them carefully.

I AM MYSELF

Sometimes I look around at all . . . The things I left behind
. . . And dream about the outcome if . . . I had not changed my
mind . . . I wonder what I would have been . . . And what I
might have done . . . If I had silently pursued . . . The pattern
of the sun . . . I might have gathered greater wealth . . . In much
more worthy ways . . . And lived a life of happiness . . . For
many nights and days . . . I might have won the highest goal . . .
That one could want on earth . . . And held the fame that marks
a name . . . Of everlasting worth . . . But also, on the other hand
. . . I might have been a sham . . . So why should I complain
about . . . The person that I am?

YOU, ONLY YOU

There may be greater dreams in life . . . And skies of brighter
blue . . . But there is no one else on earth . . . Who means as
much as you . . . Who does so much to comfort and . . . Encourage me each day . . . And give me all the faith I need . . .
To keep defeat away . . . There may be higher mountains than
. . . The ones that I have scaled . . . And more exciting oceans
than . . . The seas that I have sailed . . . There may be sweeter
songs than all . . . The music I have heard . . . And there may
be a thousand goals . . . By other hearts preferred . . . But if I
know from day to day . . . That you are at my side . . . The whole
wide world is wonderful . . . And I am satisfied.

THEIR HALLOWEEN

Tonight the happy youngsters will . . . Go up and down the
street . . . To lean on bells or knock on doors . . . And holler
"trick or treat" . . . They will be wearing funny clothes . . . And
masks of every kind . . . And there will be some boys and girls
. . . Who will be hard to find . . . But they will just be having
fun . . . And we should do our bit . . . To let them have their
Halloween . . . And make the most of it . . . And we should have
some candy or . . . Some other nice surprise . . . When they
would raid our domicile . . . With bright and eager eyes . . . So
let our hearts be happy in . . . The sacrifice we make . . . As much
as we are doing it . . . For all the children's sake.

YOUR LOVING WORDS

My heart remembers all the things . . . You ever said to me . . .
And all of them were wondrous words . . . Of love and sympathy . . . The phrases of affection and . . . The sentences that
sighed . . . And those that gave me comfort and . . . Encouragement and pride . . . The praises and the promises . . . The hopes
that filled the air . . . And every breath of gratitude . . . That
echoed like a prayer . . . Yes, I remember all of them . . . And I
remember too . . . Your generous forgiveness when . . . I brought
some hurt to you . . . And though I know I cannot find . . . The
words I want to say . . . I do adore and love you, dear . . . Each
moment of the day.

CHEATERS

Some people cheat in business deals . . . While some resort to
dice . . . To take unfair advantage and . . . Exact their swindling
price . . . The method does not matter, for . . . The process is
unfair . . . And those who play the game that way . . . Are those
who do not care . . . They are unscrupulous and cold . . . In all
they undertake . . . And every motive they pursue . . . Is for their
selfish sake . . . They are the frauds that fawn upon . . . The
feeble and the blind . . . And all who are not gifted with . . . A
more discerning mind . . . And they are those that crowd the
court . . . And overflow the jail . . . Because the world in which
they live . . . Is always bound to fail.

I LEAVE THE ASHES

When winter fades and welcome spring . . . Appears with smiling face . . . I stir the last cold ashes in . . . My idle fireplace . . .
And then I leave them undisturbed . . . While weeks and months
go by . . . For they are like the gentle ghosts . . . Of dreams that
never die . . . They bring back memories of days . . . When
laughter filled the room . . . And of the bright, enchanting nights
. . . When love began to bloom . . . The ashes in my humble
hearth . . . Are silent souvenirs . . . Of all the whispered promises
. . . And hopes of yesteryears . . . The sweetness of a stolen kiss
. . . The softness of a sigh . . . And every tear that under-
lined . . . The meaning of good-by.

THOMAS ALVA EDISON

To Thomas Alva Edison . . . We give our praise today . . . For
all the many means by which . . . He helped us on our way . . .
The phonograph, the hearing aid . . . The incandescent light
. . . And other great discoveries . . . That ease our daily plight
. . . He was a genius on this earth . . . And yet a simple soul . . .
Who chose the welfare of the world . . . As his unselfish goal . . .
He did not try to gather wealth . . . Or glorify his name . . . And
yet by his accomplishments . . . He gained immortal fame . . . He
understood and he fulfilled . . . His date with destiny . . .
By never flinching from his task . . . To serve humanity.

IN THE PARK

I wandered in the park today . . . And every shade was green
. . . The gentle grass, the trees, and all . . . The bushes in between . . . I felt the innocence of spring . . . When things begin
to grow . . . And I forgot the wilder wind . . . That whirled
around the snow . . . The warbling of a thousand birds . . . Enchanted all the air . . . And everything was peaceful and . . .
Perfection everywhere . . . And then I could not help but think
. . . What fools we are today . . . To strive for wealth and prominence . . . And just to laugh and play . . . When God has given
us the world . . . And all the stars above . . . And all He ever
wants from us . . . Is everlasting love.

GOD LOVES THE YOUNG

God made the earth, the sun, and moon . . . The stars and
you and me . . . And everything that is a part . . . Of His eternity
. . . He fashioned all the flowers fair . . . The rain, the hail, and
snow . . . The rivers and the fields and trees . . . And all the
winds that blow . . . And He must cherish His designs . . . As
very well He may . . . Especially the miracles . . . Of life and
night and day . . . But more than all the wonders of . . . The
world where we abide . . . I think He loves the children who . . .
Are always at His side . . . The little boys and girls whose prayers
. . . Are so sincerely meant . . . Because they are so eager and . . .
So young and innocent.

GOD BLESS YOU, SISTER

God bless you, darling sister, and . . . With all my heart I pray
. . . That all your hopes will be fulfilled . . . On this your special
day . . . I send you birthday greetings, dear . . . Across the many
miles . . . With deep devotion and with all . . . My gratitude
and smiles . . . My thanks for your encouragement . . . And for
your faith in me . . . My admiration for your life . . . In God's
good company . . . Your every day is like a song . . . For all the
world to hear . . . And every message you impart . . . Is filled with
joy and cheer . . . I hope that all your prayers are heard . . . And
all your dreams come true . . . And may God bless you and bestow . . . His richest gifts on you.

MY MYRIAD FRIENDS

I have a friend for every day . . . That I have been on earth
. . . And every one of them has been . . . Of some enduring
worth . . . Each one of them has shown a smile . . . Or said a
word or two . . . To give me faith and courage and . . . To help
my dreams come true . . . Each one has been of timely aid . . .
To keep my tears away . . . And make a golden memory . . . Of
every yesterday . . . I cannot thank them half enough . . . For all
that they have done . . . To multiply the silver stars . . . And
magnify the sun . . . But if they ever need me I . . . Am at their
beck and call . . . With everything my heart can give . . . To
serve them one and all.

TICKET

A ticket is the password to . . . A dinner or a dance . . . That
may include a business deal . . . Or start a new romance . . . It
is an invitation to . . . A party or a show . . . Where social lions
have their fling . . . Or common people go . . . It claims the
laundry or the goods . . . That needed some repair . . . Or promises a trip by land . . . By ocean or by air . . . A ticket is a raffle
card . . . Or piece of paper thin . . . The numerals on which may
be . . . The number that will win . . . It is a special prize that
must . . . Be taken out in trade . . . Or just a summons to the
court . . . Where traffic fines are paid.

KRISTINA'S TRIP

I took Kristina on the train . . . And she was good as gold . . .
And many were the sights she had . . . The pleasure to behold
. . . The cows and horses and the sheep . . . The towns along
the way . . . The river banks and bridges and . . . The skies of
night and day . . . Of course I had to care for her . . . And
entertain her too . . . But that was not so difficult . . . For every-
thing was new . . . She liked the spacious lounge car where . . .
The people sat and read . . . Or smiled at her and listened to . . .
The funny things she said . . . The dining car intrigued her and
. . . She really ate her fill . . . And all in all my four-year-old . . .
Found traveling quite a thrill.

IN MODERATION

In order to achieve the best . . . And gain the fullest measure
. . . We should relax and have a share . . . Of merriment and
pleasure . . . But whether in a group of friends . . . Alone or on
vacation . . . Our self-indulgence should be in . . . The best of
moderation . . . We should not wear our bodies down . . . Or
dull our mental powers . . . By too much love of appetite . . .
Through long and sleepless hours . . . For when the piper must
be paid . . . It is a different story . . . And all too often and too
late . . . We find that we are sorry . . . So let us be intelligent
. . . About our recreation . . . And let us daily strive to do . . .
All things in moderation.

BELIEVE ME, DEAR

There is no word, there is no phrase . . . To make my meaning
clear . . . And tell your heart how sweet you are . . . How lovable
and dear . . . There is no present I could bring . . . To show my
love for you . . . And prove how much you are a part . . . Of
everything I do . . . But in the world there is no one . . . Who
gives me so much bliss . . . And there is no one else, my love . . .
Whose lips I want to kiss . . . You are the image of my dreams
. . . The hope of every prayer . . . And every moment of my life
. . . Is yours alone to share . . . I know I cannot say it well . . .
But please believe me, dear . . . No love could be more lasting
and . . . No promise more sincere.

MY NEW YEAR WISH

I send this special wish to you . . . To start the New Year right
. . . That all your hours will be gay . . . And all your moments
bright . . . I hope the sun will shine on you . . . Wherever you
may go . . . And may you be as carefree as . . . The gentle winds
that blow . . . May you discover many friends . . . You never
knew before . . . And may their happiness in life . . . Be always
at your door . . . I pray that every song you sing . . . Will bring
another smile . . . And all your plans and projects will . . . Be
more than worth your while . . . A most successful New Year is
. . . My heartfelt wish for you . . . And as the weeks and months
go by . . . May all your dreams come true.

WHAT I MUST DO

I do not watch the weather vane . . . Or listen to the clock . . .
For music on the hour or . . . To hear it tick and tock . . . I do
not count the days and nights . . . Or think about the year . . .
Or worry over elements . . . That change the atmosphere . . . I
only know that I shall live . . . As long as God may say . . . And
there are certain things on earth . . . That I must do today . . .
The duties He has given me . . . And I alone can do . . . If I am
to respect His will . . . And keep my promise true . . . For
nothing else can be of weight . . . Or valuate my time . . . Except
as God is in my heart . . . Eternal and sublime.

IN MY HAIR

There are so many folks in life . . . Who get into my hair . . .
That they are just about enough . . . To drive me to despair . . .
The clerk who is discourteous . . . The friends who never write
. . . And certain grumpy neighbors who . . . Are spoiling for a
fight . . . The waitress who forgets the food . . . I ordered long
ago . . . And patrons who distract me while . . . I watch a picture
show . . . Oh, I could go on naming them . . . Until the end
of time . . . And furnish all the copy for . . . A catalogue of crime
. . . But if the pages of that book . . . Were quite complete and
fair . . . They also would reveal how much . . . I get in people's
hair.

IS IT WORTH WHILE?

We go along from day to day . . . To find a tear or smile . . .
And wonder whether after all . . . This life is worth our while
. . . We see so many tragedies . . . That happen here and there
. . . And sufferings that seem much more . . . Than anyone can
bear . . . And there are times when we ourselves . . . Are faced
with problems great . . . And we must have the human strength
. . . To bear our sorrow's weight . . . And yet we know that there
is bound . . . To be a brighter dawn . . . If we just have the
courage and . . . The will to carry on . . . We know that we can
conquer fear . . . If only we will try . . . And every now and then
there is . . . A rainbow in the sky.

FARMER'S PRAYER

These rough and calloused hands, O God . . . That touch the
soil each day . . . I fold in supplication as . . . I bow my head and
pray . . . That You will guide me at my plow . . . And bless the
seeds I sow . . . And grant the rain and sunshine that . . . Will
help my crops to grow . . . Protect my livestock and my barn
. . . And every humble shed . . . That I may pay the mortgage
off . . . And keep my family fed . . . Let not the lightning strike
my house . . . Or any storm prevail . . . And never let me go
astray . . . Along the homeward trail . . . But give me hope and
courage, God . . . And strength in time of stress . . . That I may
cultivate Your love . . . And harvest happiness.

TIDY ATTIRE

I may not be particular . . . About the way I dress . . . But I
must say I am opposed . . . To downright sloppiness . . . I do not
like to look at clothes . . . That seem to hang and slide . . . As
though they have no use except . . . To cover up the hide . . .
The coat or trousers, dress or gown . . . That cause a guy to gape
. . . Because they are not worn with care . . . Or do not fit the
shape . . . I hate to see a dangling tie . . . Or gaze at dirty shoes
. . . And sloppy sox on either sex . . . Are nothing to amuse . . .
I do not favor fashion plates . . . To decorate the street . . . But I
believe we all should try . . . To be a little neat.

TOO MUCH TURKEY

That turkey tasted wonderful . . . And all the trimmings too
. . . But I am still so full of food . . . I know not what to do . . . I
wish I had no mail to read . . . Or business dates to keep . . . I do
not feel like working now . . . I only want to sleep . . . I only
want to dream about . . . The hours that we spent . . . In merriment and laughter and . . . With everyone content . . . And then
I want to dream ahead . . . To joy on Christmas Day . . . When
Santa will be coming with . . . His reindeer and his sleigh . . . I
wish that New Year's, Easter, and . . . Vacation time were here
. . . I wish that every holiday . . . Would be a holiyear.

YOUR NAME

I always like to say your name . . . Wherever we may meet . . .
At home or at a party or . . . Upon a public street . . . It seems
to have an echo soft . . . That lingers in the sky . . . As though it
meant a fond hello . . . But never once good by . . . It rings
above the rafters like . . . A lovely organ song . . . To lift me and
inspire me . . . And keep my courage strong . . . Your name is
something special that . . . I always like to say . . . Because it is
the sun that shines . . . When all the clouds are gray . . . It is the
magic melody . . . That haunts my happy heart . . . And holds me
ever close to you . . . Though we may be apart.

WHEN EVENING COMES

When evening comes I thank my God . . . For one more day of
life . . . And for the patience to endure . . . The struggle and the
strife . . . I thank Him for the flowers fair . . . The sunshine and
the rain . . . And for the silver stars of night . . . That touch my
windowpane . . . His many blessings comfort me . . . And guide
each step I take . . . And they inspire me to live . . . For His beloved sake . . . I long to be His faithful friend . . . And do His
holy will . . . However deep the valley is . . . Or high the distant
hill . . . And so when evening comes and when . . . Another day
is gone . . . I thank my God and pray that He . . . Will grant
another dawn.

AS LONG AS WE LOVE

Dear one, the world belongs to us . . . In every song and sigh
. . . As long as we are faithful and . . . We do not say good-by
. . . As long as you abide with me . . . And I am true to you . . .
And hand in hand we understand . . . And share the old and new
. . . There is no rain or hurricane . . . To foster any fear . . .
While we are honest with ourselves . . . And we are both sincere
. . . There is no snow to lock the door . . . Or wind to rock the
roof . . . Unless we lose our balance and . . . We try to be aloof
. . . The world is ours and life itself . . . Is perfectly divine . . .
As long as I belong to you . . . And you are really mine.

CONFERENCE

A conference is a meeting to . . . Discuss and to decide . . . If
something should be acted on . . . Or gently laid aside . . . It may
be so important that . . . It will affect the fate . . . Of government and human life . . . In nations small or great . . . Or it may
be a waste of time . . . Where people sit around . . . With no
precise objective and . . . No wisdom to expound . . . Where all
they do is ramble on . . . And let the hours pass . . . While smoke
and idle talk unite . . . To form a useless gas . . . A conference
takes our temperature . . . And feels our mental pulse . . . But it
has no significance . . . Unless it gets results.

BUY CHRISTMAS SEALS

When you are getting postage stamps . . . To shower happiness
. . . With Christmas cards and presents wrapped . . . In pretty
packages . . . Be sure to buy the Christmas Seals . . . That help so
much to fight . . . The dread disease that strikes the lungs . . .
And fills the heart with fright . . . Consider those who suffer now
. . . And who must waste away . . . Unless we all cooperate . . .
And do our part today . . . Tuberculosis can be curbed . . . And
victims may be cured . . . But medicine must be obtained . . .
And special care assured . . . So buy and use the Christmas Seals
. . . That serve this worthy cause . . . And in your soul will shine
the light . . . Of God and Santa Claus.

PRAISE BE TO GOD

The Lord has risen from His grave . . . And all the angels sing
. . . O let us praise Him in our hearts . . . And with the gifts we
bring . . . The present of a sacrifice . . . That we have truly made
. . . Our kindness to a neighbor or . . . The prayers that we have
prayed . . . The humbleness to overcome . . . The passion of our
pride . . . The faithfulness that guards the soul . . . Against whatever tide . . . Let us adore the Lord, our God . . . And bow before
His throne . . . And strive to earn the guiding grace . . . That
comes from Him alone . . . For He has risen from the dead . . .
And opened wide the door . . . To joy and peace and glory in . . .
His home for evermore.

TIME FOR SCHOOL

Vacation days are over and . . . The schoolbell rings again . . .
For children and for teachers and . . . Young ladies and young
men . . . The desks and books are dusted off . . . The pens are
filled with ink . . . And it is time for playful minds . . . To settle
down and think . . . From A-B-C and c-a-t . . . To algebra and
Greek . . . And all the secrets of this life . . . That scientists may
seek . . . It is the time to study and . . . Develop new ideas . . .
To weigh the words of scholars and . . . To test their theories
. . . But equally important is . . . The need for voices clear . . .
To greet the football season with . . . An overwhelming cheer.

MY PERFECT DAY

My perfect day is one when I . . . Have many things to do . . .
And yet have time to rest and play . . . And find a friend or two
. . . A day when I am busy and . . . I labor with a will . . . Until
the shadows lengthen and . . . The factories are still . . . When
there are smiles around the hearth . . . And friendly hands to
shake . . . And every thought I think is one . . . For someone
else's sake . . . Nor do I mind if skies are gray . . . And rain is in
the street . . . Or if the wind is wild or if . . . There is a scorching
heat . . . My perfect day is one when I . . . Have lived the hours
through . . . With work and play and time enough . . . To find a
friend or two.

97

I YIELD TO YOU

My heart has yielded to your charms . . . As you must surely
know . . . For when I hold you in my arms . . . I cannot let you
go . . . I have surrendered to your will . . . With every part of me
. . . And every promise I fulfill . . . Becomes your victory . . .
But, oh, it is a sweet retreat . . . And one I most prefer . . . Be-
cause it makes my life complete . . . To be your prisoner . . .
Whatever cloud may shroud the day . . . Or cover us with rain
. . . I never want to run away . . . Or ever break the chain . . . I
want to share your memory . . . Of every dream come true . . .
And in your heart I want to be . . . An endless part of you.

THEY GROW SO FAST

Along about this time of year . . . I get my ruler out . . . And
make some marks upon the wall . . . To settle every doubt . . . I
take the children one by one . . . When we are all alone . . . And
measure them to see how much . . . They actually have grown
. . . And then I check the records and . . . I find Kristina dear
. . . Has grown a great deal taller in . . . The passing of a
year . . . Young Donnie too is getting big . . . As fast as he can
rise . . . While Jimmie merely lacks an inch . . . From reaching to
the skies . . . And as I study every mark . . . That I must wipe
away . . . It always makes me feel that I . . . Get smaller every day.

I TAKE MY TIME

There are so many things in life . . . That I would like to do
. . . To please my loving family . . . And make their dreams come
true . . . But everything requires time . . . And I am quite aware
. . . That patience is a portion of . . . The answer to a prayer . . .
And so I do not hurry and . . . I do not walk too fast . . . Because
I want to make my way . . . And reach my goal at last . . . I try to
take the world in stride . . . And live from day to day . . . As
much as opportunities . . . May come along my way . . . And be
content with what I have . . . To give my family . . . In keeping
with my prospects and . . . With my ability.

TIMELY WEATHER

The wind and rain, the sun and snow . . . Are all my special friends . . . Provided they appear in time . . . To serve my happy ends . . . I like the gentle breeze that blows . . . And whispers in my ear . . . When I am wrapped in thoughts and dreams . . . Of someone very dear . . . I like the rain that splashes down . . . When spring is in the air . . . And all the grass is green again . . . Around the flowers fair . . . The sun that shines in summer when . . . The sea is wide and blue . . . The snow that blankets field and street . . . When winter days are new . . . Each kind of weather seems to give . . . The earth a magic face . . . Provided it appears in time . . . To take its proper place.

WHEN YOU ARE WEARY

When you are weary and when life . . . Seems difficult or odd . . . Look not around for some escape . . . But turn your thoughts to God . . . Be not discouraged or depressed . . . Nor let your wisdom sway . . . But keep tomorrow in your mind . . . To start another day . . . For God is always with you in . . . The morning and the night . . . To comfort and inspire you . . . With everlasting light . . . He is the fount of solace and . . . The vase for every tear . . . He is the dawn of every day . . . The end of every year . . . Give Him your faith, your hope, your love . . . In everything you do . . . And He will carry every cross . . . That tasks and troubles you.

WHEN I AM AWAY

The train is rolling smoothly now . . . The towns are passing by . . . And from my window I behold . . . The stars that light the sky . . . It is a pleasant journey, love . . . And when I go to bed . . . I shall be that much nearer to . . . The goal that lies ahead . . . But, oh, my love, I wish that I . . . Could turn the train around . . . And I could be with you again . . . Where sweeter joys abound . . . I wish I had not had to leave . . . Not even for a day . . . Because I am so lonely, love . . . When I must be away . . . The world is like a stranger and . . . There is no time or space . . . When I have not the happiness . . . To look upon your face.

TWO AND TWENTY YEARS

For two and twenty years, my love . . . You have been true to
me . . . In every triumph, great or small . . . And in adversity . . .
You have been constant as the stars . . . In sickness and in health
. . . And you have honored and obeyed . . . In poverty and
wealth . . . You have consoled me in my tears . . . Rejoiced in
every smile . . . And in a thousand ways your words . . . Have
made my life worth while . . . How can I ever thank you, love . . .
Sufficiently to say . . . How much you really mean to me . . .
Each moment of each day? . . . But, oh, I do adore you and . . .
I pray to God above . . . That I shall always strive to be . . . Deserving of your love.

MIRACLE OF BIRTH

The seed becomes a flower fair . . . The acorn sprouts a tree
. . . And in its time a tiny child . . . Assumes reality . . . It is a
miracle of God . . . That there is life on earth . . . Of bird and
fish and animal . . . And in the human birth . . . But higher is
our heritage . . . And greater is our goal . . . For God has given
each of us . . . Our own immortal soul . . . And it is ours to save
from sin . . . Or one that we may lose . . . According to the virtue
or . . . The evil that we choose . . . So let us guard it jealously . . .
And magnify its worth . . . And let us praise and thank Him for
. . . The miracle of birth.

JOY IN NORWAY

Today in Norway there is joy . . . And all her people play . . .
Because it is their national . . . And most important day . . . The
hour in their memory . . . When Norway first became . . . The
freedom-loving nation that . . . Has gained enduring fame . . .
Her heartaches have been many and . . . Her struggles have been
long . . . But always her devoted sons . . . Have kept their courage
strong . . . The beauty of her winding fjords . . . Reflects her
peaceful soul . . . Where mountains rise to meet the skies . . .
And fertile valleys roll . . . God bless Norwegians everywhere . . .
On this important day . . . And may their country always have
. . . The best in every way.

USED CAR

We all would like an auto new . . . To take us here and there
. . . And one that would not cost so much . . . To drive or to
repair . . . But when we do not have the cash . . . To buy the
latest fad . . . There always is the motorcar . . . That someone
else has had . . . The car that has been traded in . . . And now is
advertised . . . As being quite a bargain and . . . An asset to be
prized . . . It may not be as fancy or . . . As elegant to see . . . As
one assembled lately and . . . Delivered F.O.B. . . . But if we
choose it carefully . . . It may be good as new . . . And when we
pay the purchase price . . . We save some money too.

MY DEBT TO YOU

You make no claim on anything . . . That I possess or do . . .
And yet there is so much, my friend . . . That I am owing you . . .
I owe you for the courage and . . . The sunshine in my heart . . .
And every inspiration that . . . Imbues my daily art . . . I owe you
something for your smile . . . And for your words of cheer . . .
And for the joyful memories . . . That fill my yesteryear . . . My
every hope has been your wish . . . My every dream your prayer
. . . And you have shown a thousand times . . . How much you
really care . . . I thank you for your friendship and . . . The happiness you bring . . . And constantly I tell myself . . . I owe you
everything.

IT MUST BE SPRING

There is a mildness in the air . . . A softness in the soil . . .
And there is less of weariness . . . In struggle and in toil . . . The
sun is somewhat warmer now . . . The sky a brighter blue . . .
And something seems to tell the heart . . . That life is fresh and
new . . . It must be time for spring again . . . And time to look
around . . . For greener grass and flowers fair . . . To decorate the
ground . . . The snow and ice have disappeared . . . Where now
the rivers flow . . . And fertile fields are stirring in . . . Their
eagerness to grow . . . The soul is filled with faith and hope . . .
And joy in everything . . . It must be time to live again . . . It
must be really spring.

VERSATILE JIMMIE

Our Jimmie is as versatile . . . As any lad can be . . . For he can cook and shine his shoes . . . And iron expertly . . . When he is hungry he will make . . . Some gingerbread or toast . . . Or he will boil or fry the food . . . That pleases him the most . . . He polishes his footwear in . . . The morning and at night . . . Until it has the sparkle of . . . The brightest beacon light . . . And when his shirt is rumpled, it . . . Receives his special press . . . To guarantee perfection in . . . The manner of his dress . . . These traits should come in handy when . . . He starts his married life . . . And they should help a lot to ease . . . The burden on his wife.

BEYOND THE SEA

Some day my ship will touch the bay . . . And I shall leave the sea . . . To take you in my arms again . . . And hold you close to me . . . Beyond the whipping of the wind . . . The lashing of the waves . . . And all the haunting images . . . Of deep and sodden graves . . . No more will there be loneliness . . . Along a distant shore . . . With empty streets and hollow sounds . . . That echo through a door . . . But I shall sit beside you when . . . The fireplace is warm . . . Surrounded by the walls of love . . . Against whatever storm . . . And I shall whisper all the hopes . . . And dreams that sailed with me . . . Beyond the blue horizon and . . . The reaches of the sea.

JUST A SMILE

There are a lot of other things . . . That seem to be worth while . . . But I would rather have the joy . . . And comfort of a smile . . . To hold the golden picture of . . . A kind and gentle gaze . . . And hear the friendly words that lips . . . Express in silent ways . . . And I would rather see a glance . . . Of sentiment sincere . . . Than shake the hand of anyone . . . Without a meaning clear . . . Because a smile means more to me . . . Than bright and sunny skies . . . And all the satisfaction of . . . A triumph or a prize . . . A smile is my umbrella and . . . My roof against the rain . . . And all the medicine I need . . . To conquer every pain.

JUST FOR TODAY

If I can overcome myself . . . For just a single day . . . Then
there will be no obstacle . . . I cannot put away . . . There will be
no despair of heart . . . Or softness of the soul . . . To conquer
and imprison me . . . And keep me from my goal . . . But I shall
walk with courage strong . . . And with my head raised high . . .
And I shall see the sun shine through . . . The clouds that shroud
the sky . . . Whatever happened yesterday . . . Is over now and
gone . . . And there is no assurance that . . . Another day will
dawn . . . So let me strive and fight to keep . . . The promise that
I say . . . Not for tomorrow or a year . . . But only for today.

PRAYER FOR GRACE

This morning, God, we ask Your help . . . With humble hearts
and true . . . That we may be more honest and . . . Acceptable to
You . . . Give us this day the grace we need . . . To do our very
best . . . And when temptation faces us . . . To pass our every
test . . . To be considerate and kind . . . And do some lasting
good . . . For family and government . . . And for our neighborhood . . . Be with us every moment, God . . . Before the sun is
gone . . . And then protect us through the night . . . Until another dawn . . . We want to walk the righteous path . . . With
faith and hope renewed . . . And by the way we serve You, God
. . . To show our gratitude.

WANT AD

The want ad is a little thing . . . To catch the public eye . . .
When people have some goods to sell . . . Or when they hope to
buy . . . Or when they try to trade a mule . . . An auto or a house
. . . Or introduce a better trap . . . To catch the lowly mouse . . .
Some persons use it to describe . . . The sort of work they seek
. . . And some to advertise the jobs . . . That pay so much per
week . . . The want ad tells of rooms to rent . . . And what is lost
or found . . . And begs the one who disappeared . . . To write or
drop around . . . It has a hundred uses in . . . The paper every
day . . . And well is worth the little sum . . . The buyer has to
pay.

MY FLOWERS

My flowers do not come from shops . . . Or near my garden
wall . . . Because my flowers are the friends . . . Who take the
time to call . . . They are the living lilacs and . . . The roses red
and white . . . The tulips and forget-me-nots . . . Of every day
and night . . . They are the folks who ring my bell . . . Or write
me from afar . . . To offer me their services . . . And tell me how
they are . . . Who somehow always seem to have . . . A little time
to spare . . . To fill my vases with their smiles . . . And let me
know they care . . . They are the gentle souls with whom . . . I
never want to part . . . Because they are the flowers fair . . . That
blossom in my heart.

TRAFFIC TICKET

The traffic ticket is a thing . . . We do not like to get . . . But
now and then we make mistakes . . . And so we have to fret . . .
And now and then policemen seem . . . A little bit unfair . . .
In handing out the summonses . . . That get into our hair . . . We
may appear impatient for . . . The light to show up green . . .
And sometimes we may disobey . . . A sign we have not seen
. . . But whether we feel justified . . . Or know that we are wrong
. . . We should not try to fix the rap . . . Or do a dance and
song . . . Because the traffic laws are made . . . To help us mortals
live . . . And most policemen hate to write . . . The tickets they
must give.

PATRIOT'S PRAYER

I want to serve my country, God . . . In time of peace and war
. . . That freedom and equality . . . May live for evermore . . . I
want to wear a uniform . . . When there is cause to fight . . . And
fire gun and hand grenade . . . For every human right . . . And
when our banner is secure . . . And there is calm at sea . . . I want
to help our nation keep . . . Its true democracy . . . To vote in
each election for . . . A better government . . . And to abide by
all the laws . . . Of popular consent . . . I ask You, God, to give
me strength . . . And courage every day . . . That I may serve my
country in . . . The patriotic way.

104

BLESS YOU, AUNT BERTA

Happy birthday, dear Aunt Berta! . . . May this be your lucky
day . . . May your dreams and your desires . . . Be fulfilled in
every way . . . May the sunlight kiss your doorstep . . . May the
sky be bright and blue . . . And with joy and peace and comfort
. . . May this life be good to you . . . You deserve the best, Aunt
Berta . . . For the kindness you bestow . . . For your smiles and
words of welcome . . . With their warm and friendly glow . . .
For the faith and love and courage . . . You inspire us to hold
. . . And the constant, deep devotion . . . In your gentle heart of
gold . . . We are grateful, dear Aunt Berta . . . And with all our
love we say . . . Happy birthday and God bless you . . . Every
moment of each day.

SALES MANAGER

He supervises all the men . . . Whose job it is to sell . . . And
lets them know when they are slow . . . Or they are doing well
. . . He hires and he fires with . . . The sanction of his boss . . .
And regularly he reports . . . The profit or the loss . . . But also he
must draw and watch . . . The charts on business trend . . . And
figure out what he can do . . . With what he has to spend . . . He
has to work up new ideas . . . And keep a weather eye . . . On
ways to stimulate the sales . . . And send them soaring high . . .
He seems to be a man who just . . . Tells others what to do . . .
But actually he struggles and . . . His task is never through.

PRAYER FOR HEALTH

O gracious Father, bless my mind . . . And keep my body well
. . . That I may glorify Your name . . . And constantly excel . . .
Bestow on me the wisdom and . . . The courage that I need . . .
To give a good example by . . . My every word and deed . . .
Allow me all the human strength . . . And health of limb and
heart . . . That I must have to do my best . . . In every daily art
. . . Because I want to serve You well . . . As long as I am here
. . . And carry out successfully . . . A virtuous career . . . O gra-
cious Father, favor me . . . With mind and body sound . . . To
help me earn a humble place . . . Where peace and joy abound.

WASHINGTON, D.C.

I like the streets of Washington . . . The flowers and the trees
. . . The little parks and quaint cafés . . . Endeared with memories . . . The Tidal Basin and the Mall . . . The cherry blossoms
bright . . . The White House and the Capitol . . . Resplendent in
the night . . . I like to stroll in Rock Creek Park . . . And wander
through the zoo . . . Or walk along Connecticut . . . To shop for
something new . . . And then there are the embassies . . . The
churches and the homes . . . Of grandeur that is greater than . . .
The glory that was Rome's . . . The monuments, the heroes'
graves . . . The ghosts of yesteryears . . . The long parades of stars
and stripes . . . And freedom-loving cheers.

KEEP IN STEP

No generation ought to try . . . To live its life again . . . Because the world will never be . . . The same as it was then . . .
There have to be some changes for . . . The good of all concerned . . . And we can profit only by . . . The lessons we have
learned . . . However queer and cruel or . . . Considerate and
kind . . . The past is gone forever and . . . We should not
look behind . . . Except to be reminded of . . . The failures we
have known . . . And of the sins for which we should . . . Endeavor to atone . . . But otherwise we ought to try . . . To keep in
step today . . . With every generation new . . . In all its work and
play.

BUT YOU WERE GONE

There is so much I wish that I . . . Had had a chance to say
. . . Before your heart decided and . . . Before you went away
. . . I wanted to remind you of . . . The days we used to know
. . . When summer smiled in sunshine and . . . The winter
walked in snow . . . When spring bestowed its flowers on . . . The
joy of every dance . . . And autumn lingered in the leaves . . . Of
beautiful romance . . . But you were gone before the stars . . .
Had faded from the sky . . . Before I could explain to you . . . Or
kiss your lips good-by . . . And now I fear it is too late . . . To find
another dawn . . . Our magic moon has disappeared . . . And
what is past is gone.

HOME ECONOMY

As long as I remember now . . . My wife has preached to me
. . . About the value and the good . . . Of home economy . . .
Not just to clear the mortgage on . . . The house we want to own
. . . But also to be frugal with . . . The light and telephone . . .
To pay insurance premiums and . . . To hold our spending down
. . . On food and clothes and furniture . . . And happy times in
town . . . And many are the times that I . . . Have found it quite
a strain . . . And I have been inclined to sigh . . . Or murmur and
complain . . . But as I watch our progress I . . . Am grateful as
can be . . . To her whose wifely wisdom is . . . Our best security.

MY FRIEND

My friend is one who never scolds . . . Or criticizes me . . .
But whose example wakes me up . . . To what I ought to be . . .
Whose kindly soul is obvious . . . In every word and deed . . .
And who is always eager to . . . Fulfill the smallest need . . . Who
carries on unselfishly . . . For every human heart . . . Until I cannot help but feel . . . I ought to do my part . . . My friend is one
who brings the sun . . . And takes the rain away . . . For everything of happiness . . . To decorate the day . . . The one who
seeks no glory but . . . Who gladly takes the blame . . . Whenever
anything goes wrong . . . In life's important game.

WELCOME WAGON

The kindly Welcome Wagon is . . . A most exciting car . . .
That carries gifts and friendly smiles . . . To houses near and far
. . . To mothers with their babies new . . . To girls of sweet six-
teen . . . And her whose heart has promised to . . . Become her
lover's queen . . . To families that pack their things . . . And find
a new address . . . And those who come from other towns . . . In
search of happiness . . . The Welcome Lady calls on them . . . In
best of hostess style . . . With presents from the merchants that
. . . Are very much worth while . . . She gives advice and renders
aid . . . And everything is free . . . For friendship and good will
throughout . . . The whole community.

MY WISHFUL PRAYER

God made you good and wonderful . . . In every noble way
. . . And there is nothing I can add . . . To bless your special day
. . . But all my birthday wishes now . . . Are knocking on your
door . . . To bring you wealth, the best of health . . . And joy
for evermore . . . I hope you will be happy and . . . Your life
will be complete . . . With friendships all around you and . . .
With flowers at your feet . . . May sorrow never find you or . . .
A teardrop touch your eye . . . But may the sunlight and the
stars . . . Adorn your every sky . . . I know that God is in your
heart . . . And He is proud of you . . . And on this day I pray that
He . . . Will make your dreams come true.

CUSTOMER

A customer is one who buys . . . The merchandise for sale . . .
In person or by telephone . . . By telegraph or mail . . . He may
be quick in purchasing . . . Or he may take his time . . . And he
may spend quite lavishly . . . Or try to save a dime . . . He may
be very critical . . . Of all that he inspects . . . Or casually indifferent towards . . . The item he selects . . . But he is just as
mighty and . . . Important as can be . . . For he is indispensable
. . . To our economy . . . And when there is a question or . . .
An argument in sight . . . The merchant wise is he who says . . .
The customer is right.

BUT NEVER PART

There will be moments to regret . . . And little tears to cry . . .
But may it never be a fact . . . That we have said good-by . . .
And there will be some lonely nights . . . And disappointing days
. . . But, darling, let us never reach . . . A parting of the ways . . .
Our love has been too wonderful . . . For it to disappear . . . And
have each memory become . . . A ghost of yesteryear . . . My
dreams would languish in the dust . . . Without your soft caress
. . . And all the world would soon become . . . A tomb of emptiness . . . Because I live each hour, dear . . . For your beloved
sake . . . And if you ever went away . . . I know my heart would
break.

KEEP OCCUPIED

There is no joy in idleness . . . Or good in foolish fun . . . But only in the knowledge that . . . Our work is being done . . . The certainty that we discharge . . . Our duty well and true . . . Without complaining of the things . . . That we are asked to do . . . It fills the heart with happiness . . . And satisfies the soul . . . While giving greater confidence . . . To reach a higher goal . . . The busy hand and thoughtful mind . . . Are never dull and bored . . . But they will cultivate success . . . And harvest great reward . . . And then when we decide to rest . . . And contemplate our score . . . We know our pride is justified . . . And means a whole lot more.

NEVER LONELY

The night is never lonely when . . . I see the stars above . . . And when I give my heart to God . . . And His eternal love . . . I do not mind the darkness and . . . I entertain no fear . . . As long as I remind myself . . . That He is always near . . . I merely tell myself again . . . That He designed the night . . . As surely as He shaped the sun . . . And every candlelight . . . I know that He is with me when . . . The shadows touch the ground . . . And He is every breath of life . . . And part of every sound . . . He made the moon and universe . . . And He created me . . . To dwell in His companionship . . . For all eternity.

WEDDING WORRY

A wedding invitation is . . . A joy for me to get . . . And yet it is the very thing . . . That makes me frown and fret . . . Because I know I ought to buy . . . A present for the bride . . . As one more feather for the nest . . . Where lovers will abide . . . And so I have to scratch my head . . . And search my fuzzy mind . . . For something that is suitable . . . In quality and kind . . . Perhaps a mirror, lamp, or vase . . . A picture or a chair . . . A piece or two of silver or . . . Attractive chinaware . . . And when I finally decide . . . On what I think will do . . . Invariably some other guest . . . Makes that selection too.

NEVER TO FAIL YOU

I hope I never fail You, God . . . However far I stray . . . With
all the human weaknesses . . . That follow me each day . . . I
hope in spite of all my sins . . . I may fulfill my place . . . And
so at least to that extent . . . Appreciate Your grace . . . Let me
repent my every wrong . . . And strive to make amends . . . To
You, my God, and unto all . . . My enemies and friends . . .
But if my heart is careless and . . . I frequently forget . . . And
if at times I go my way . . . Without sincere regret . . . I hope
and pray that in the end . . . My deeds will prove their worth
. . . And justify Your faith in me . . . For all my days on earth.

BREAKING THINGS

So many things are broken in . . . Our house from day to day
. . . It worries and it frightens us . . . And fills us with dismay
. . . The children drop a looking-glass . . . A picture or a
plate . . . And though they try to stop the fall . . . It always is
too late . . . They may not be expensive things . . . And yet they
all add up . . . The table lamp, the radio . . . The window and
the cup . . . We stretch our weekly budget to . . . Replace them
one by one . . . And find it quite impossible . . . To get the
project done . . . But we are confident our home . . . Will never
fall apart . . . Because we drop no promise and . . . We never
break a heart.

THE APATHETIC

Some people go to work each day . . . To earn their daily bread
. . . With never any special thought . . . To grow and get ahead
. . . They have no real ambition or . . . The eagerness to learn
. . . And midnight oil, except for play . . . Is never theirs to
burn . . . They are the blind who do not see . . . The world's im-
portant needs . . . They are the deaf who do not hear . . . The
call to greater deeds . . . They are the lazy-minded and . . . The
smug and selfish too . . . Who do no more for others than . . .
They ever have to do . . . And yet they want the world to be . . .
Magnificent and strong . . . While they proclaim their grievances
. . . When anything goes wrong.

BUSY DON

Our Don enjoys the movies and . . . A story book or two . . .
And there is not sufficient time . . . For all he wants to do . . . He
goes for football, basketball . . . And baseball in the spring . . .
He has a stamp collection and . . . Is fond of everything . . .
Except he has no interest in . . . A single daily chore . . . Like
washing dishes, making beds . . . Or going to the store . . . He
does not want to clean his room . . . Or sit with sister Kris . . .
And sometimes he is much too big . . . To bother with a kiss
. . . But when he brings report cards home . . . Each one reflects
an A . . . And then we smile and thank him and . . . What else
is there to say?

SPORTSMANSHIP

However pleasant people are . . . Or friendly is their grip . . .
There is no stronger bond than that . . . Of honest sportsman-
ship . . . Of playing fair in every game . . . No matter what the
stakes . . . And being quietly resigned . . . When others get the
breaks . . . There is no need to sacrifice . . . Or throw the ball
away . . . Or give the least assistance to . . . The rival in a fray
. . . The only thing is not to cheat . . . By any means at all . . .
Or take undue advantage of . . . A fumble or a fall . . . But just
to struggle onward with . . . A true and steady aim . . . And earn
the letters that will spell . . . A good and worthy name.

NATIONAL FREEDOM DAY

Today we pause to celebrate . . . Our National Freedom Day
. . . With equal rights for everyone . . . In struggle and in play
. . . We cherish the protection of . . . Our Constitution great . . .
And of the independence that . . . Belongs to every State . . . A
people proud, united, and . . . Prepared to work and fight . . .
For liberty and justice and . . . For every human right . . . A land
where all may speak their thoughts . . . And read authentic news
. . . And citizens may cast their votes . . . And worship as they
choose . . . God bless America and keep . . . Our enemies away
. . . That every dawn may hold for us . . . Another freedom day.

NOW BOW IN PRAYER

Let now our heads be bowed in prayer . . . And everlasting praise . . . To God Who is so bountiful . . . Despite our worldly ways . . . In every home, on every street . . . Throughout the human ranks . . . Let there be songs of gratitude . . . As well as silent thanks . . . For God is He Who gave us life . . . And He Who helped us grow . . . To comfort and security . . . In sunshine and in snow . . . To liberty and justice and . . . The right of all to share . . . With freedom of expression in . . . The press and public square . . . Then let us fill our place on earth . . . With humble heart and true . . . And pray that some day all the world . . . Will thank and praise Him too.

DAY BEFORE PAYDAY

In any week or any month . . . There is no other day . . . As awful as the one that comes . . . Before I get my pay . . . My pocketbook is empty and . . . My change is very small . . . In fact there are occasions when . . . I have no cash at all . . . And usually that is the time . . . When bills are falling due . . . And items on the pantry shelf . . . Are dangerously few . . . I always fervently resolve . . . To keep enough on hand . . . To get along and satisfy . . . Each family demand . . . But as each payday comes around . . . I like to celebrate . . . And by the time I start to save . . . I find it is too late.

WHEN APRIL COMES

When April comes I take a walk . . . And look up at the sky . . . And silently I count the clouds . . . That seem to pass me by . . . I know the winter days are gone . . . And spring is here at last . . . While cold and frosty memories . . . Are melted in the past . . . I dream of parks and flowers and . . . The sunlight all around . . . Where lovers lean against a tree . . . But never touch the ground . . . Where everything is wonderful . . . And perfect as can be . . . And every sound that fills the air . . . Is like a melody . . . I wish my April fairyland . . . Would last for evermore . . . With gentle thoughts and loving dreams . . . Of happiness in store.

MY FRIENDS BY MAIL

I form my friendships through my work . . . At home or on the
street . . . On plane and train and trolley and . . . Wherever
people meet . . . In elevators and upon . . . The benches at the
zoo . . . At private parties and in stores . . . Along the avenue
. . . And then there are the friends I find . . . But whom I never
see . . . For they are only in the mail . . . The postman brings to
me . . . And yet I know them just as well . . . As if I met them
here . . . Because they tell me all their thoughts . . . And they
are so sincere . . . And they are just as welcome to . . . And just
as much a part . . . Of every dream where others seem . . . To
captivate my heart.

DREAMS AT SUNDOWN

I dream of you at work and when . . . I wander through the
town . . . But mostly in the evening as . . . The sun is going
down . . . For then the day is ending in . . . A blaze of red and
gold . . . And everything is beautiful . . . And peaceful to behold
. . . The farmer puts his plow away . . . The merchant locks his
store . . . And fishing boats with weary men . . . Are coming
back to shore . . . It is the time when supper starts . . . For children to be fed . . . While flowers nod and silver stars . . . Are
getting out of bed . . . And in that magic hour I . . . Can see my
dreams come true . . . For when the sun is going down . . . I
hurry home to you.

SALUTATORIAN

Selected for his scholarship . . . He is the honored one . . .
Who greets his fellow students when . . . Their senior year is done
. . . Who speaks his words of welcome warm . . . On graduation
day . . . With hopes and wishes of the best . . . For those who
go away . . . He is among the men who serve . . . Their alma
mater well . . . For he inspires others to . . . Advance and to
excel . . . His good example fosters faith . . . And eagerness to
win . . . The glory of a fruitful life . . . And happiness within . . .
And through the ivy-covered years . . . His name will ever be . . .
A tablet in the study hall . . . Of timeless memory.

SHOE SALESMAN

The one whose job is selling shoes . . . Has quite a heavy task
. . . If just to answer all the things . . . The ladies like to ask . . .
He has to compliment the feet . . . Of more than average size
. . . And when the shoe is much too small . . . He has to show
surprise . . . The leather, suède and rattlesnake . . . The closed
and open toe . . . And heels that manufacture height . . . Are
part of every show . . . He has to be attentive and . . . Polite
as he can be . . . To all the customers who think . . . They know
much more than he . . . And though at times his salesmanship
. . . Appears to score a hit . . . It generally is only he . . . Who
really gets a fit.

O GOD IN HEAVEN

O God in Heaven, I am Yours . . . With all my heart and soul
. . . Because You do so much for me . . . To help me reach my
goal . . . Because You grant my happiness . . . And take away
my tears . . . And when I have a troubled mind . . . You quiet
all my fears . . . You do not scold me when I sin . . . But You
are always there . . . In all Your mercy and Your love . . . To
hear my every prayer . . . O God in Heaven, I will try . . . To do
my humble part . . . With every thought and every breath . . .
To please Your gentle heart . . . I promise You I will not rest
. . . Until I reach the end . . . Because I love You and because
. . . You are my dearest friend.

KIND OF A DOG

A dog can be a gentle pet . . . And quite a faithful friend . . .
And often it is worth the cash . . . It causes you to spend . . . It
entertains you with its tricks . . . It joins in every game . . . And
tries to keep you guarded well . . . From burglary and flame . . .
It hounds the fleeing convict and . . . It helps the blind to see
. . . And gallantly in time of war . . . It fights the enemy . . .
But on the other side of it . . . A dog can be a pest . . . And
whine or bark the whole night through . . . To interrupt your
rest . . . It can be very ill-behaved . . . Or wander out of sight
. . . Or, worst of all, it may display . . . The tendency to bite.

OLD MAID

We cannot always reach and take . . . The treasures that we want . . . And sometimes there are empty dreams . . . And memories that haunt . . . And sometimes there is someone sweet . . . Who might have been a bride . . . Except for too much bashfulness . . . Or possibly her pride . . . She may have walked in fairy tales . . . That never could be real . . . Or lacked the courage of the love . . . She wanted to reveal . . . And yet the life she lives alone . . . Need never be in vain . . . For every moment may become . . . An everlasting gain . . . It matters not how fair the face . . . Or dignity of birth . . . But only what the human soul . . . Contributes to the earth.

DINING THE BOSS

Whenever I inform the wife . . . My boss will come to dine . . . I tell her not to bake a cake . . . Or make the silver shine . . . I say that he is just a guy . . . Who likes an Irish stew . . . And who prefers an apple pie . . . To something slick and new . . . But always she will buy the best . . . And flavor everything . . . As though our guest amounted to . . . A president or king . . . And while I struggle to achieve . . . An easy-going air . . . My wife is calmly dignified . . . About the whole affair . . . But then I guess it does no harm . . . Because it seems to me . . . The boss enjoys his dinner and . . . He likes our company.

LET US GIVE

In every town and city now . . . A drive is under way . . . So Santa Claus will not forget . . . The poor on Christmas Day . . . A drive for clothes to keep them warm . . . And food to help them live . . . According to the quantity . . . That we decide to give . . . Their happiness depends upon . . . Whatever we may share . . . Of groceries or garments or . . . The money we can spare . . . So let us be as generous . . . And kindly as we can . . . And do as much as possible . . . For every fellow-man . . . Each bit of clothing, food, or cash . . . Will warm a humble heart . . . And God will bless us many times . . . For having done our part.

STEPPING ON TOES

When people bump us on the street . . . Or step upon our toes
. . . Our first reaction is to scowl . . . And punch them on the
nose . . . We feel we are insulted and . . . No matter what they
say . . . We think it was on purpose that . . . They got into our
way . . . But usually a thing like that . . . Is just an accident . . .
And there is no excuse at all . . . To start an argument . . . Of
course when we are guilty and . . . We hear the others cuss . . .
We think they have a lot of gall . . . To get provoked at us . . .
And so we ought to be more kind . . . In what we do or say
. . . Whenever people bother us . . . By getting in our way.

MAGICIAN

He entertains a watching world . . . With tricks of every kind
. . . And does it all so cleverly . . . We think that we are blind . . .
He pulls the rabbits out of hats . . . And makes things disappear
. . . And what we think is over there . . . Is really over here . . .
A handkerchief becomes a rose . . . A dollar turns to ten . . . And
when a girl is sawed in half . . . She comes to life again . . . His
fingers move with lightning speed . . . As he performs his task
. . . And answers every question that . . . His audience may ask
. . . He is the able artist who . . . Can almost change the sky . . .
To prove that, after all, the hand . . . Is quicker than the eye.

LIFE INSURANCE

Insurance is a splendid thing . . . For everyone to own . . .
Especially to care for those . . . Who may be left alone . . . To
guard against the tragedy . . . That gives no warning sign . . .
But comes with speed and suddenness . . . To take us out of
line . . . Insurance is security . . . For children and a wife . . .
To comfort them for months and years . . . And possibly for life
. . . It takes the husband's place on earth . . . As though he still
were here . . . To bring his earnings to the door . . . Of those he
held so dear . . . And it is such a small expense . . . Compared
to other things . . . When we consider all the good . . . And
happiness it brings.

TACTLESS

Some people never seem to know . . . They give themselves
away . . . By merely raising eyebrows or . . . By something that
they say . . . They simply lack diplomacy . . . Or what is called
finesse . . . And they are not concerned about . . . Their neighbor's happiness . . . They figure they are smarter than . . . The
smartest in the land . . . And everyone should recognize . . . The
wisdom they command . . . But they are neither wise nor great
. . . And all their neighbors know . . . That they are only acting
up . . . And putting on a show . . . And though they may succeed
at times . . . In getting pretty far . . . Eventually they all find out
. . . How dumb they really are.

HORSESHOE DONNIE

My Donnie is an expert at . . . The horseshoe pitching game
. . . And though I struggle valiantly . . . I cannot match his fame
. . . His tosses always hug the stake . . . When he declares a
war . . . While ringers are the specialty . . . That multiplies his
score . . . He gets a leaner now and then . . . But he will knock
it down . . . Before I have a chance to throw . . . In challenging
his crown . . . And if I make a ringer or . . . I manage to get two
. . . His shoes are always right on top . . . To cancel all I do
. . . It does not matter how I try . . . Each time I play my son . . .
He always is the first to reach . . . That score of 21.

OLD FRIENDS

Each golden friendship I have known . . . Is like a guiding star
. . . That leads me through the yesteryears . . . Of places near
and far . . . The large and little cities and . . . The streets of long
ago . . . Where life was merely part of all . . . The winds that
used to blow . . . Each helping hand and loving smile . . . Is
like a song of old . . . Imbued with all the melody . . . I wish
that I could hold . . . And though the hours still to come . . .
May be a million more . . . I dream about the happiness . . . That
filled my heart before . . . I see the faces young and bright . . .
That meant so much to me . . . And their endearing friendship
is . . . My fondest memory.

O GOD, REMEMBER ME

Remember me, O God, when I . . . Am troubled in my heart
. . . And when it seems that You and I . . . Are sort of far apart
. . . When I am feeling lonely and . . . Discouraged over strife
. . . And everything is difficult . . . According to this life . . .
Remember me and help me, God . . . For I am weak and frail
. . . And when my lamp of faith goes out . . . I falter and
I fail . . . I want to walk beside You and . . . To hold Your guid-
ing hand . . . Because there are so many things . . . I do not
understand . . . I love You, God, with all my soul . . . Wherever
I may be . . . And humbly I petition You . . . To please remem-
ber me.

DOUBLE DUTY

With people on vacation, there . . . Is little time for play . . .
Around the busy office where . . . I have to work each day . . . It
seems that I am weighted down . . . With twice as much to do
. . . And in those hours spent in town . . . I never quite get
through . . . The summer heat is bad enough . . . Without the
extra toil . . . That makes me gruff and makes me puff . . . And
sometimes start to boil . . . It is the most unpleasant part . . . Of
all the office year . . . And there is nothing in my heart . . . Of
solace or of cheer . . . Except the thought that when I go . . .
On my vacation spree . . . I may bestow my every woe . . . On
some minority.

THEIR TRUST IN ME

Much more than praise for fame or wealth . . . Or expert competence . . . I long for friends and to enjoy . . . Their utmost
confidence . . . Their confidence that I shall strive . . . For someone else's sake . . . And that I shall in time fulfill . . . Each promise that I make . . . That I shall never once betray . . . The trust
they put in me . . . However strong temptation is . . . Or great
the urge may be . . . I long to live a loyal life . . . And prove that
I am true . . . In every little thought and word . . . And everything I do . . . I want them to believe in me . . . And trust me
to the end . . . And praise me not for glory but . . . Because I
am their friend.

LUCKY 12TH

The 12th day of the month appears . . . To bring good luck to
me . . . And therefore holds a special place . . . In my life's his-
tory . . . I do not mean that every month . . . It is a golden day
. . . That brings me extra happiness . . . In business or at play
. . . But when my fortunes rise above . . . The normal mark and
when . . . I look up at the calendar . . . It is the 12th again . . .
And so around that time each month . . . I wonder and I wait
. . . To see if there will be some cause . . . To sing and celebrate
. . . Because without the least approach . . . Or effort I may
make . . . Invariably that is the day . . . I get a lucky break.

ON CALVARY'S CROSS

They crucified my Lord and God . . . And pierced His gentle
heart . . . And though it happened long ago . . . I know I played
a part . . . My every pride and passion and . . . My selfishness
and greed . . . Contributed the nails that caused . . . His hands
and feet to bleed . . . Each sinful deed became a thorn . . . Upon
the crown He wore . . . And every cruel word I said . . . Increased the rabble's roar . . . I made Him walk and stumble on
. . . His way to Calvary . . . And there I raised Him on a cross
. . . For all the world to see . . . And there in agony He died . . .
That we might live anew . . . In His divine, forgiving words . . .
"They know not what they do."

GRUMBLING GUEST

Some people simply have to get . . . Their troubles off their
chests . . . But they should never do it when . . . They are invited guests . . . It is all right to talk in tears . . . And now and
then complain . . . About a seeming tragedy . . . Or just a cloud
of rain . . . To be dissatisfied with life . . . Or feel a wrong is done
. . . When others get their wishes or . . . The prizes that are
won . . . But misery and mournful moods . . . Are not the things
to share . . . When those who think they have them are . . . Invited anywhere . . . Such conduct cannot ever be . . . Becoming
to the guest . . . For it reveals the invitee . . . As somewhat of a
pest.

KRISTINA STUDIES

Kristina is a pupil now . . . And she is mighty proud . . . And
when the teacher calls on her . . . She answers right out loud . . .
She is so very glad that she . . . Is six years old at last . . . And
infancy and babyhood . . . Apparently are past . . . Because she
always wanted to . . . Be studious and wise . . . And learn to read
and write and spell . . . And how to memorize . . . And now she
knows her room in school . . . And how to find the way . . .
And where to eat and what to do . . . When it is time to play . . .
Kristina loves to go to school . . . And we are sure that she . . . Is
on the road to glory in . . . Some university.

GETTING FIRED

When we get fired from a job . . . It always seems to be . . . A
bitter disappointment and . . . A sort of tragedy . . . We may
have had it coming or . . . We may not be to blame . . . But we
should not be overwrought . . . Or ever quit the game . . . It may
be possible that we . . . Have gotten quite a break . . . Although
the boss did not intend . . . To do it for our sake . . . There may
be opportunities . . . That never would have been . . . If we had
not been fired from . . . The job that we were in . . . So let us
keep our courage high . . . And let us strive each day . . . To
take advantage of the breaks . . . That come along our way.

TAKING A WALK

I like to take a walk at dawn . . . Or in the afternoon . . . And
sometimes when the stars are out . . . Around a golden moon . . .
To wander over field and hill . . . Or down a country lane . . .
Unless the day is freezing or . . . The clouds are filled with rain
. . . I like to roam the city streets . . . And look in windows bright
. . . And gaze at all the lighted signs . . . That decorate the night
. . . To contemplate the features of . . . The people on their
way . . . From factory and office at . . . The closing of the day
. . . And wonder how they live and if . . . Their houses large
and small . . . Are empty dreams or cozy homes . . . That wel-
come one and all.

DUSTY DREAMS

I look back over all the skies . . . To every day we knew . . .
And yellow is the calendar . . . Of hours spent with you . . . And
heavy is the cobweb of . . . The long and lonely years . . . Since
you and I agreed, my love . . . To share our smiles and tears . . . I
shall remember how we walked . . . Across the crystal snow . . .
And how the spring was everywhere . . . When winds began to
blow . . . The gentle winds that kissed your hair . . . As I would
touch your lips . . . While we were dreaming of the stars . . . And
sailing magic ships . . . But now the stars are faded and . . . The
ships have gathered rust . . . And all the dreams we dreamed, my
love . . . Are nothing more than dust.

SPECIAL TREAT

If I had lots of money I . . . Would like to give a treat . . . To
all the little boys and girls . . . I see along the street . . . Especially the eager tots . . . Who look so hungry for . . . The candies
and the cookies in . . . The window of a store . . . With noses
pressed against the panes . . . And little lips apart . . . They stir
up all the feeling in . . . My sympathetic heart . . . I want to
hustle them inside . . . And let them take their pick . . . And
satisfy their appetites . . . Without becoming sick . . . I only wish
I had the cash . . . To give a special treat . . . To every little boy
and girl . . . I see along the street.

IF NO ONE HAD A FRIEND

What dreary place this world would be . . . From origin to end
. . . If no one knew his neighbor well . . . And no one had a
friend . . . If no one gave a cheerful smile . . . And no one said
hello . . . Or ever moved a finger small . . . To help a flower grow
. . . Our life is only beautiful . . . As long as we are glad . . . And
there are those who sympathize . . . Whenever we are sad . . . As
long as there is someone who . . . Is kind enough to care . . . With
comfort and encouragement . . . And now and then a prayer . . .
Our time would all be wasted and . . . The money we might
spend . . . If everybody lived alone . . . And no one had a friend.

ONE MORE YEAR

I thank You, God, for giving me . . . Another year to spend . . .
I thank You for it from its start . . . Unto this very end . . . I
know the many promises . . . I made and said to You . . . And all
the ones I overlooked . . . And what I failed to do . . . Forgive
me, God, for being frail . . . Forgive the fool in me . . . And help
my soul to serve You now . . . With more sincerity . . . Give me
another year on earth . . . And help me to fulfill . . . My pledges
and my promises . . . To do Your holy will . . . Give me the
courage and the faith . . . To keep my word with You . . . That
every prayer may speak my soul . . . And every vow be true.

NEW CITIZEN

There is no greater cause for joy . . . Or any prouder day . . .
Than his who takes that sacred oath . . . To serve our U.S.A. . . .
Who swears allegiance to our flag . . . And whom the court de-
crees . . . A citizen with all our rights . . . And all our liberties
. . . No more is he a foreigner . . . Or needs to feel alone . . .
Because we have adopted him . . . Among our very own . . . He
is a true American . . . In every sense we hold . . . And we are
confident he will . . . Be worth his weight in gold . . . And so we
wish the best for him . . . In all that he may do . . . And pray
that he will honor well . . . Our great red, white, and blue.

MANICURIST

The manicurist cuts your nails . . . And trims the edges right
. . . And polishes until your hands . . . Are beautiful and bright
. . . She uses special scissors and . . . A buffer and a file . . . And
wears a dainty apron and . . . A captivating smile . . . You may
appear quite suddenly . . . Or you may telephone . . . But while
you sit and talk with her . . . You never feel alone . . . She listens
to your troubles or . . . Your story of success . . . And when you
leave she wishes you . . . A world of happiness . . . She may not
quite agree with you . . . Or fully understand . . . But she will
always sympathize . . . And hold your friendly hand.

LIGHT ON THE PORCH

I like a cozy little home . . . A neat and pretty lawn . . . But most of all I like at night . . . To see the porch light on . . . It seems to lend a friendly and . . . A warm, inviting touch . . . As though to whisper please come in . . . And thank you very much . . . It means the house is lived in and . . . The folks may be inside . . . And like as not, in love and peace . . . They happily abide . . . The porch light is a beacon light . . . To guide the welcome guest . . . And greet the children of the house . . . When they come home to rest . . . I like its kindly gleam but when . . . I see it in the dawn . . . I know it is the careless sign . . . That someone left it on.

THANK YOU—I'M SORRY

There are two things that we should not . . . Be hesitant to say . . . According to our conduct and . . . The gifts that come our way . . . And one of them is "thank you" for . . . The favors we receive . . . Our happiness, our true success . . . And all that we achieve . . . The other is "I'm sorry" for . . . The blunder or mistake . . . That stepped upon another's toes . . . Or caused some heart to ache . . . We should be grateful for our joys . . . And sorry for each sin . . . If we are eager to deserve . . . The goal we strive to win . . . So let us set aside our pride . . . And say "I'm sorry, friend" . . . And "thank You, God, for life and all . . . The blessings You extend."

MY HEART IS YOURS

My heart belongs to you, my love . . . As long as I may live . . . And I have any happiness . . . Or sympathy to give . . . As long as there is sunlight and . . . A single star above . . . And just as long as any song . . . Will echo words of love . . . I offered you my heart and all . . . That I might ever be . . . If only every hour you . . . Would share your life with me . . . And when you took my promise, love . . . And you declared your own . . . I knew that I would never cry . . . Or ever feel alone . . . And that is why I strive each day . . . To make your dreams come true . . . And why in every way, my love . . . My heart belongs to you.

THE BEST IN ME

I gather up the yesteryears . . . And weigh them one by one . . .
My actual accomplishments . . . And what I might have done . . .
I wonder where I would have gone . . . And what I would have
gained . . . If I had turned the other way . . . And never once
complained . . . If I had never longed to rise . . . Above the
common life . . . With all the heavy burden of . . . Its struggle
and its strife . . . I might have had a brighter world . . . With
happiness supreme . . . And then again it might have been . . . A
most unpleasant dream . . . But in the end I tell myself . . .
Whatever else might be . . . At least my humble heart has tried
. . . To give the best in me.

MY HOPE FOR YOU

When you are somewhat older and . . . Your dreams are more
mature . . . I hope you will be wiser and . . . Your heart will be
more sure . . . Because the future holds a day . . . When you are
bound to find . . . That you have chosen and it is . . . Too late to
change your mind . . . Real love is not a plaything, dear . . . That
you can throw away . . . And instantly pick up again . . . Wherever you may stray . . . Each person has an equal right . . . To
happiness on earth . . . And all the world is judged by what . . .
Its promises are worth . . . And so I hope as time goes by . . .
Your heart will have more sense . . . And you will not divide
yourself . . . By sitting on the fence.

PRESIDENT'S PRAYER

God, help me guide this country well . . . And do the best I
know . . . That every loyal citizen . . . May benefit and grow . . .
Let me appreciate the bills . . . The Congress sends to me . . .
And weigh each one with wisdom and . . . With true integrity
. . . Let me be conscious of the words . . . The highest court may
say . . . To state the final ruling of . . . Our democratic way . . .
In agriculture, industry . . . And every kind of tax . . . Let me
ignore all politics . . . In favor of the facts . . . But most of all I
ask You, God . . . To listen to my prayers . . . For lasting peace
and fruitfulness . . . In all our world affairs.

CUB SCOUT DONNIE

Our Donnie likes to be a Cub . . . And does his very best . . .
To learn his scouting lessons and . . . Excel in every test . . . He
goes to all the meetings and . . . Enthusiastically . . . He strives
for all the honors and . . . The prizes there may be . . . We think
the world of him and we . . . Are proud of his success . . . And
all the worthy deeds he does . . . For human happiness . . . But
here at home he seems to be . . . Opposed to any chore . . . Like
washing dishes, making beds . . . Or going to the store . . . And
so although we want our boy . . . To have his share of fun . . . We
feel a Cub Scout ought to have . . . More HOMEwork to be done.

I LIKE TO TRAVEL

I like to travel far and wide . . . And see the friends I know . . .
And make a thousand other friends . . . Wherever I may go . . .
They say that travel broadens one . . . And that is surely right
. . . And meeting many people is . . . A wonderful delight . . .
Of course I do enjoy my town . . . And all the folks at home . . .
But now and then I drift in dreams . . . And get the urge to
roam . . . To visit places and to see . . . How other people live
. . . And sort of share the happiness . . . That their surroundings
give . . . And everywhere I go it seems . . . Our thoughts and
feelings blend . . . And every human being likes . . . To find
another friend.

MY NEW YEAR'S PRAYER

This New Year's Day I ask You, God . . . For all the aid I need
. . . To honor You in every thought . . . And every word and
deed . . . To cherish and protect my wife . . . And help our chil-
dren grow . . . In grace and goodness and in all . . . The things
they ought to know . . . To serve my church and country and . . .
Extend the best in me . . . For every high and worthy cause . . .
In my community . . . I ask You, God, to give me strength . . .
That I may not complain . . . Or strive with greed and jealousy
. . . For any selfish gain . . . Bestow Your blessing on my soul
. . . And keep me in Your care . . . And let each day I live this
year . . . Become another prayer.

WHY SEEK REVENGE?

Why do we struggle for revenge . . . When someone makes us sore? . . . Why do we always feel impelled . . . To even up the score? . . . An eye for eye, a tooth for tooth . . . Why does it have to be . . . That we demand this pattern of . . . Exact equality? . . . For that is not the will of God . . . And not the way to live . . . When we should try to understand . . . And in our hearts forgive . . . Too many times we overlook . . . The sins that we possess . . . And think of nothing else beyond . . . Our selfish happiness . . . We ought to see our weaker selves . . . With reason to regret . . . And be resigned and willing to . . . Forgive and to forget.

LUNCHEON CLUB

I like the kind of luncheon club . . . That gathers once a week . . . To laugh and sing, report on things . . . And hear some person speak . . . It makes for good companionship . . . Promotes a happy mood . . . And nourishes the body with . . . A plate of tasty food . . . Sometimes it sponsors projects for . . . The needy and the poor . . . Or backs a civic enterprise . . . That surely will endure . . . I like the club where pleasure is . . . Of primary concern . . . And visitors are welcomed and . . . Invited to return . . . Its door to equal membership . . . Is easy to unlock . . . And every smile is worth a share . . . Of friendship's priceless stock.

WANDERING WIVES

Some wives are never satisfied . . . To spend the day at home . . . But they are rather restless and . . . They are inclined to roam . . . They go to clubs and meetings and . . . They search for other fun . . . And many are the errands that . . . They simply must get done . . . Of course there are some ladies who . . . Have nothing else to do . . . And who can very well afford . . . The hobbies they pursue . . . But there are those who wander off . . . And are inclined to shirk . . . Their sewing and their cooking and . . . A lot of other work . . . And who perhaps have children and . . . Whose husbands cannot pay . . . For hired help to take the place . . . Of wives who like to play.

MARCH OF DIMES

With all the rhythm in my heart . . . I write these little rhymes
. . . That everyone will join the ranks . . . To help the March of
Dimes . . . To scatter sunshine and to lift . . . The spirits that are
low . . . By being soldiers in the fight . . . To conquer polio . . . I
pray that all may take the time . . . To turn around and look . . .
And charity may be the key . . . To every pocketbook . . . For
God is always good to those . . . Who are prepared to give . . .
That other souls may not despair . . . Or suffer as they live . . .
And so I hope with all the rhymes . . . And rhythm in my heart
. . . That everybody's extra dimes . . . Will do their worthy part.

HAPPY BOSS

When I wake up at dawn and when . . . I raise my sleepy head
. . . I always try to get up from . . . The right side of my bed . . .
But more importantly I hope . . . My boss will do it too . . . So
he will not be grouchy when . . . He marches into view . . . Because when he is out of sorts . . . It is not very long . . . Before
the office is upset . . . And everything goes wrong . . . Each working day I hope and pray . . . He had a restful night . . . His breakfast coffee tasted good . . . And everything looked bright . . . For
nothing so inspires me . . . Or makes my job worth while . . . As
just to hear his friendly voice . . . And see his cheerful smile.

OUR BANNER BRIGHT

Our banner is the symbol bright . . . Of freedom unto all . . .
At work, at play, at home, and in . . . The packed convention hall
. . . It represents our right to speak . . . And worship as we please
. . . To choose our leaders and to shape . . . Our own communities . . . Our flag consists of stars and stripes . . . In red and white
and blue . . . That tell our stirring history . . . Of faith and
courage true . . . A stripe for every colony . . . A star for every
state . . . To signify the unity . . . That makes our nation great
. . . And so we sing our praises and . . . Salute our flag today . . .
And may Old Glory guard our shores . . . And always guide the
way.

KRISTINA'S BLUE JEANS

Kristina loves her blue jeans and . . . She wears them every day . . . Regardless of the weather or . . . What anyone may say . . . In school, at play, to parties, and . . . Wherever you may search . . . Except of course on Sunday when . . . Kristina goes to church . . . She thinks no other article . . . Is quite so much in style . . . And when she puts those blue jeans on . . . She always wears a smile . . . She has a dozen dresses and . . . Perhaps a dozen more . . . But they just rest on hangers or . . . They sleep upon the floor . . . The blue jeans are her favorite . . . As she has often said . . . And if she could, I know she would . . . Be wearing them to bed.

REJOICE IN HIM

The heavy stone was rolled away . . . The sepulcher was bare . . . But in that early morning light . . . The angels lingered there . . . Behold! The Lord has risen from . . . The grave where He was laid . . . That life eternal may be ours . . . And death forever stayed . . . He gave His life that we might rise . . . Above a world of sin . . . To glory in His kingdom and . . . The holiness therein . . . Where lonely sorrows disappear . . . And fears forever cease . . . In perfect union with The Prince . . . Of everlasting peace . . . Let us rejoice in Him today . . . With love and gratitude . . . And let us walk with courage and . . . With faith and hope renewed.

MODERN MARKET

The grocery store of long ago . . . Was quite a homey place . . . Where every customer possessed . . . A kind, familiar face . . . Where cracker barrels, pickles, and . . . The glow of candlewicks . . . Inspired conversation to . . . The best of politics . . . It was a great tradition but . . . Today we have the store . . . Where everything is better than . . . We ever had before . . . The sanitary market where . . . The people help themselves . . . And vitamins are guaranteed . . . On all the handy shelves . . . And we are truly grateful for . . . The changes time has made . . . To give us quicker service and . . . The foods of finer grade.

IMPORTANT FRIEND

I like the influential friend . . . Who does so much for me . . .
And who is there to help in time . . . Of real necessity . . . Who
has the magic power and . . . The strength to turn the tide . . .
When I am faced with promises . . . Of charity or pride . . . But
even more important is . . . The influential friend . . . Who looks
beyond the clouds and sees . . . A rainbow at the end . . . Who
lifts me up when I am down . . . And tries to urge me on . . .
Whenever I am dubious . . . About another dawn . . . Who uses
every influence . . . To get my lips to smile . . . And makes me
feel that after all . . . My life is worth the while.

MUSIC BOX

I like to hear piano tunes . . . And organ melodies . . . And
when a violin is played . . . It brings back memories . . . I like all
kinds of instruments . . . Including chiming clocks . . . But most
of all my heart enjoys . . . The little music box . . . It may be in
the open or . . . In some secreted place . . . As when you lift the
cover on . . . The powder for your face . . . It may be in a drink-
ing mug . . . Or cake of special size . . . Or in some other way it
may . . . Provide a nice surprise . . . But best of all I like to hear
. . . The notes of "Silent Night" . . . That carol from a Christmas
crib . . . When all the stars are bright.

SIGN PAINTER

He may not be a Rembrandt or . . . A Michelangelo . . . But
with his humble brush he paints . . . An entertaining show . . .
He makes the letters large and small . . . In colors bright and gay
. . . And all the pictures that attract . . . Our eyes from day to
day . . . The household goods, the food we eat . . . The coffee,
milk, and tea . . . The clothes we wear, the cars we drive . . . And
every luxury . . . Sometimes he climbs to dizzy heights . . . To
start a special sign . . . And do his neat and perfect job . . . On
every scene and line . . . He may not be a master in . . . The
world of finer art . . . But oft his advertising brush . . . Will win
the human heart.

MY FISHING LUCK

Somewhere the fish are biting now . . . For those who cast and
troll . . . And those who use the lowly worm . . . To gain their
sporting goal . . . And somewhere in this country there . . . Are
boats that churn the lake . . . As they are heading for the shore
. . . With their enormous take . . . The perch, the bass, and sun-
fish, and . . . The mackerel and trout . . . And those the deep-sea
fishermen . . . Forever talk about . . . Somewhere the fish are
biting now . . . For all who sit and wait . . . But not for those who
are compelled . . . To use my kind of bait . . . Whose flies and
minnows and whose worms . . . Are figments of the mind . . .
Because like me they are not free . . . To leave their daily grind.

MY LOVE, MY VALENTINE

I send this greeting card to you . . . With love in every line . . .
And with the hope that you will be . . . My darling valentine
. . . Because I offer you my heart . . . And every promise true
. . . That I will honor and obey . . . And always cherish you . . . I
will be yours to have and hold . . . Beyond the farthest shore . . .
Today, tonight, tomorrow, and . . . Forever, evermore . . . Your
every dream will be my hope . . . Your faith will be my prayer . . .
And all I do will prove to you . . . How much I really care . . .
And when I hear you whisper that . . . Your loving heart is mine
. . . I will rejoice in having won . . . The sweetest valentine.

THE COMMON WORDS

Some correspondents never seem . . . To find a better way . . .
To send their many addressees . . . The things they want to say
. . . They try to use the biggest words . . . That they can put in
ink . . . To draw the written pictures of . . . Whatever they may
think . . . It may be just a social note . . . Or else a business deal
. . . In either case it does not help . . . To tell the way they feel
. . . Because no person likes to get . . . A message in the mail . . .
That sounds the least ambiguous . . . Or does not hit the nail . . .
It is the common words that count . . . And faithfully convey . . .
The thoughts and the desires that . . . We really want to say.

MY MEMORIES

My memories are all the words . . . That you have said to me
. . . And all the happiness of your . . . Delightful company . . .
The pleasure of each evening in . . . The gleam of candlelight
. . . The picture of a mystic moon . . . And silver stars at night
. . . They are the morning glories and . . . The hills that seem to
rise . . . When dawn is like a dreamland and . . . The sun adorns
the skies . . . My memories remember you . . . The moment that
we met . . . And all the songs and kisses that . . . I never can forget . . . The hours and the flowers and . . . The times we had to
part . . . And every little secret that . . . I whispered to your heart.

RESIGNATION

As God may give so God may take . . . And life must come and
go . . . Whatever weather may prevail . . . Or how the rivers flow
. . . It is not ours to question Him . . . To murmur or complain
. . . Or criticize Him for the tears . . . That mingle with the rain
. . . Our sorrow and our tragedy . . . Are his divine command . . .
And in the deepest darkness we . . . Must try to understand . . .
God rules the whole wide world and all . . . The universe He
made . . . And if we love and honor Him . . . We need not be
afraid . . . And if He wants us to be sad . . . And undergo a loss
. . . Then let us do His holy will . . . And let us bear our cross.

MY OFFERING

This day is just a particle . . . Of all I offer you . . . To fill your
heart with happiness . . . And make your dreams come true . . . I
dedicate each day and night . . . Of every year to be . . . To loving you and giving you . . . The best there is in me . . . I promise
you a rainbow bright . . . For every drop of rain . . . And your
abiding faith in me . . . Will never be in vain . . . Your every wish
or fancy is . . . My deep desire now . . . And every word you
whisper is . . . My everlasting vow . . . I offer you my very self
. . . For what I may be worth . . . To honor you and multiply
. . . Your happiness on earth.

IN EVERY WAY

I want to be your special friend . . . In every way I know . . .
And do the most I can for you . . . Wherever you may go . . . To
comfort you in sorrow and . . . To praise you in success . . . And
multiply the moments that . . . Provide your happiness . . . I
want to change your sky of gray . . . To one of gold and blue . . .
And in so many other ways . . . To help your dreams come true
. . . For that is what a friendship means . . . To those who are
sincere . . . Beyond the portion of a day . . . Or part of any year
. . . To be unselfish in our hearts . . . And by each word and
deed . . . To recognize each glory and . . . To serve in every need.

SODA JERKER

He slings the sodas and prepares . . . The sundaes and frappés
. . . That satisfy the appetite . . . And please the hungry gaze . . .
With chocolate or vanilla and . . . A squirt of whipping cream
. . . Combined with syrup, fruit, or nuts . . . He fashions quite a
dream . . . He makes the milk shake and the malt . . . The lemonade and such . . . And strives to give each special dish . . . His
super-duper touch . . . In apron white and jaunty cap . . . He
keeps the counter clean . . . But now and then around the gills
. . . He looks a little green . . . And that is when he samples
drinks . . . Or reaches on the shelf . . . And goes a trifle over-
board . . . To satiate himself.

SOME GOOD IN ALL

Some people always criticize . . . Our faults and our mistakes
. . . Instead of praising virtue and . . . The courage that it takes
. . . Instead of giving credit for . . . The deeds that we have done
. . . And helping to inspire us . . . In battles to be won . . . There
is some good in all of us . . . If only folks will look . . . And try to
skip the pages that . . . Are faded in our book . . . It is so easy to
condemn . . . And tear a structure down . . . With hate or jealousy or wrath . . . Or just to play the clown . . . But it requires
character . . . And wisdom in this life . . . To lift the spoon of
kindness and . . . To put away the knife.

MY ONLY LOVE

If all the treasures of the world . . . Belonged to me, my sweet
. . . My only use for them would be . . . To lay them at your feet
. . . To offer them along with all . . . The love I have for you . . .
That all your hopes might be fulfilled . . . And all your dreams
come true . . . And that would still be not enough . . . To tell
your loving heart . . . How lonely and how sad I am . . . When we
must be apart . . . I want you more than anything . . . The
world can ever give . . . Because you are the only one . . . For
whom I truly live . . . You are the sun that lights the dawn . . .
The silver stars above . . . And all around the clock you are . . .
The only one I love.

MAD MOTORIST

The highways now are crowded with . . . A million cars or more
. . . And many are the motorists . . . Who get real good and sore
. . . They blame the other fellow for . . . The slowness of their
stride . . . While they would like to speed and push . . . All other
cars aside . . . The restless driver is the one . . . Who has but little
sense . . . And whose indifferent carelessness . . . Accounts for
accidents . . . He does not heed the warning signs . . . That mark
a hill or curve . . . And if there is no room to pass . . . He will
not budge or swerve . . . But if the vehicles collide . . . He knows
that he is right . . . And with his temper uncontrolled . . . He
wants to start a fight.

OUR FLAG OF SYMPATHY

When there is tragedy at home . . . Or war across the sea . . . It
is a comfort to behold . . . Our flag of sympathy . . . The banner
bright with field of white . . . Behind a cross of red . . . To aid the
injured living and . . . Identify the dead . . . The Red Cross of
America . . . Is built on sacrifice . . . Without a wish for glory and
. . . Without a thought of price . . . Except the cost of charity . . .
That we may think is worth . . . Some sort of contribution to
. . . The welfare of this earth . . . So let us all be grateful now
. . . That we are still alive . . . And give as much as we can spare
. . . To help the Red Cross drive.

TIME FOR OTHERS

The measure of a man's success . . . And his enduring worth
. . . Is whether he can really keep . . . His feet upon the earth
. . . If he can put his work aside . . . One minute of the day . . .
To telephone or drop a line . . . To someone far away . . . If he
can take the time to talk . . . And give a bit of cheer . . . If only
to be thankful for . . . A word of praise sincere . . . The measure
of a man's success . . . Is not his wealth or fame . . . But how he
treats his fellowman . . . In life's important game . . . How much
he thinks of others and . . . How much he strives to be . . . A
neighbor and a leader in . . . His own community.

KRISTINA'S CAP

Kristina is supposed to wear . . . A stocking cap all day . . .
When it is cold and when the wind . . . Is blowing every way . . .
But many times she runs outside . . . Or hurries off to school . . .
Without the least intention of . . . Remembering this rule
. . . And many times when she comes home . . . We have to ask
her where . . . She left the fancy stocking cap . . . She had around
her hair . . . Or else she dashes in the house . . . And tosses it
around . . . Until it is a miracle . . . If ever it is found . . . But
now and then we laugh because . . . She looks beneath her bed
. . . When all the while her stocking cap . . . Is on her pretty
head.

SO GOOD IS GOD

Almighty God is good to me . . . Wherever I may go . . . With
many times the blessings that . . . I ask Him to bestow . . . He
helps me every morning and . . . Protects me in the night . . .
And guides me through the wilderness . . . With everlasting light
. . . In every undertaking He . . . Is always at my side . . . To
counsel and to caution me . . . Against whatever tide . . . And if I
do not hear His voice . . . And if I go astray . . . He brings me
back and teaches me . . . To live a better way . . . Almighty God
is wonderful . . . And He is good to me . . . And I desire to
deserve . . . His great eternity.

FRIENDLY FAVOR

A favor is a special thing . . . That may not mean so much . . .
But it is something that reflects . . . A kind and worthy touch . . .
However little or how large . . . The deed may seem to be . . . It
is the perfect cornerstone . . . Of love and sympathy . . . Because
it is a sacrifice . . . That rises from the soul . . . To help another
human reach . . . Some all-important goal . . . A favor is a
friendly act . . . For those in need of aid . . . If only to encourage
them . . . When they would feel afraid . . . It is the least that we
can do . . . To show we really care . . . For relatives and neighbors and . . . For people everywhere.

LOST SHEEP

Sometimes I leave the beaten path . . . And go my way alone
. . . And many are the sins for which . . . Some day I must atone
. . . I know I should not do it but . . . I let my wisdom stray . . .
And then the sunlight disappears . . . And all the skies are gray
. . . And then my thoughts become confused . . . My soul is
filled with fear . . . And every smile that might have been . . . Is
turned into a tear . . . I wander in a wilderness . . . That seems to
have no end . . . And I am lost without a light . . . And never any
friend . . . But somehow in the darkest night . . . Wherever I may
roam . . . My Shepherd reaches out His hand . . . And leads me
gently home.

MY MEMO BOOK

I keep a memorandum book . . . That faithfully relates . . .
The many things ahead of me . . . Including dinner dates . . . I
make a note of pending deals . . . And people I must see . . . As
well as certain business friends . . . Who should be calling me . . .
The letters to be written and . . . Some goods I ought to get . . .
And when to file my tax return . . . And try to pay the debt . . .
It is a daily record of . . . The things I have to do . . . The places
where I ought to go . . . And who is really who . . . Indeed I
could not do without . . . The memorandum book . . . That
guides my every step except . . . When I forget to look.

LOOK THEM UP

Whenever I go on a trip . . . Someone will say to me . . . Be
sure to get in touch with Joe . . . Or telephone Marie . . . Of
course I never in my life . . . Have heard of either one . . . But I
am told that they are grand . . . And always full of fun . . . And
so when I arrive in town . . . I give those folks a ring . . . And say
hello and ask them how . . . Is every little thing . . . Well, sometimes they are quite polite . . . And fairly patient but . . . Invariably they answer me . . . As though I were a nut . . . And that is
why whenever I . . . Invade another town . . . I do not care to
call the names . . . That I have written down.

IRONING BOARD

Its folding legs support the top . . . On which the iron stands
. . . When Mother finishes a job . . . Or has to rest her hands . . .
It is the table where a shirt . . . A handkerchief or dress . . . Is
made to look like new again . . . Beneath an expert press . . . The
napkins and the luncheon cloths . . . The towels bright and gay
. . . The blue jeans and the little pants . . . That hurry out to
play . . . It has a special padding to . . . Provide a softer touch
. . . And keep the wash from scorching and . . . From creasing
overmuch . . . It plays a most important part . . . Wherever people
meet . . . Because it helps the world to be . . . Immaculate and
neat.

NEW CAR

Of all the pleasures and the thrills . . . That come from near
and far . . . Not many match the glory of . . . A new and shiny
car . . . The joy of giving up the bus . . . That nearly fell apart
. . . And getting in an auto that . . . Is always quick to start . . .
It looks just like the limousines . . . That serve the millionaires
. . . And certainly it will not need . . . Those everyday repairs
. . . It gives much better mileage on . . . The highway and the
street . . . And every bright accessory . . . Is just an added treat
. . . From streamlined top to tires and . . . From spacious trunk
to hood . . . In style and in performance it . . . Is marvelously
good.

BEYOND THE GLITTER

God does not frown on worldly wealth . . . And He does not complain . . . About the prominence in life . . . That some of us attain . . . But He expects us to be fair . . . And to appreciate . . . The many earthly blessings that . . . Appear to make us great . . . He wants each one of us to walk . . . With humble heart and true . . . And to be good and generous . . . In everything we do . . . For gold is not an evil thing . . . And fame is not a curse . . . Unless we cover up our faults . . . And we conceal our purse . . . God does not care how wealthy or . . . Successful we may be . . . As long as we obey His laws . . . And live unselfishly.

FRIENDLY GUEST

I like to visit every friend . . . The old, the new, the best . . . But even more than that I like . . . To have him as my guest . . . I want to entertain him and . . . To share my few possessions . . . To serve him food and listen to . . . His thoughts and his impressions . . . To dream with him of other days . . . And those that still may be . . . And casually compare my own . . . With his philosophy . . . I wish him all the best of luck . . . In every undertaking . . . And hope his goal and purpose he . . . Will never be forsaking . . . And when he leaves my humble home . . . I say a special prayer . . . That God will bless and favor him . . . And keep him in His care.

SOLDIER OF FORTUNE

A soldier sought his fortune in . . . The days of long ago . . . And he was quite a character . . . For anyone to know . . . He wandered forth from town to town . . . And knocked on every door . . . Or sailed the seven seas in search . . . Of some enchanting shore . . . But now there is no fortune on . . . The highway or the sea . . . Except as one inherits cash . . . Or gains monopoly . . . And even then the road is rough . . . Considering the tax . . . And antitrust officials who . . . Refuse to turn their backs . . . Today the searching soldier must . . . Accept his fortune small . . . According to his pension or . . . A bonus unto all.

BE CAREFUL

Be careful when you work today . . . In factory or store . . .
More lives are lost through accidents . . . Than men are killed in
war . . . Be careful at the office, in . . . Your home, and on the
street . . . For only as you stay awake . . . Will you stay on your
feet . . . Be sober when you drive your car . . . Be cautious where
you step . . . And don't go dashing here and there . . . With too
much zip and pep . . . Watch out at railroad crossings and . . .
Don't burn that match too long . . . Don't overestimate your
strength . . . (You know, you might be wrong) . . . Let not your
story be the one . . . The tragic headlines tell . . . You only have
one life to live . . . So live it long and well.

BLESS US FOREVER

Bless us, O Lord, and all the gifts . . . We gratefully receive . . .
And let us always have the strength . . . And courage to believe
. . . Look lovingly and favorably . . . Upon our way on earth . . .
And help us do our best to be . . . Of everlasting worth . . . We
thank You for the kindness and . . . The mercy You have shown
. . . And in the knowledge of Your love . . . We never feel alone
. . . Be with us every moment, Lord . . . Wherever we may go . . .
Help us appreciate the rain . . . And all the winds that blow . . .
Inspire us to saintliness . . . And bless our every breath . . . And
guide our way each night and day . . . To joy in life and death.

NEW PAGES

The pages of this book are new . . . And they are ready now
. . . As are the fields of time before . . . The turning of the
plow . . . And they are waiting eagerly . . . As are the watchful
hills . . . For dawn to wake the sleeping earth . . . And still the
whippoorwills . . . There will be kings to challenge and . . . A
thousand walls to scale . . . And dreams will melt to memories
. . . Along a lonely trail . . . But always opportunity . . . Will
knock upon the door . . . And ships that brave the higher wave
. . . Will find another shore . . . So let there be no lingering . . .
While sun and candle burn . . . But let the pen begin to write . . .
Before the pages turn.

NORTHWEST CORNER

I like to get behind the wheel . . . About this time of year . . .
And travel to Tacoma in . . . The land of Mount Rainier . . . To
climb the path to paradise . . . Where flowers kiss the snow . . .
And say a fond hello again . . . To all the friends I know . . . To
cross the narrows, swim, and fish . . . And stroll along the bay . . .
Or visit in Seattle for . . . The portion of a day . . . The wondrous
state of Washington . . . Has all the atmosphere . . . Of true
democracy and of . . . The mighty pioneer . . . Where no one
ever asks your name . . . And no one makes demands . . . But
everyone is helpful and . . . Believes in shaking hands.

FRIENDSHIP FLOWERS

For every flower in my vase . . . I have a special friend . . .
With favors for the asking and . . . With storybooks to lend . . .
With sympathy and kindness and . . . Encouragement to give
. . . And all the happy sunshine that . . . A flower needs to live
. . . They are my summer roses and . . . My iris of the fall . . . My
lilacs in the springtime and . . . My holly in the hall . . . I treasure
them and tend to them . . . As they would care for me . . . And
when they fade I put them in . . . My book of memory . . . I fold
their gentle petals as . . . A loving work of art . . . And with the
pages of my dreams . . . I press them to my heart.

TONE OF VOICE

The only real importance of . . . Whatever words we say . . . Is
how we use them to express . . . The thoughts we would convey
. . . The way we make our meaning known . . . By just our tone
of voice . . . Instead of by the sentences . . . And phrases of our
choice . . . For we may stop to shout hello . . . Or we may yell
good night . . . Or we may even whisper it . . . And still not be
polite . . . A friendly message may be cold . . . And it may hurt
or sting . . . Because our vocal cords may have . . . A most sar-
castic ring . . . And so whatever greeting or . . . Remark we pass
around . . . We ought to be more careful of . . . Our slightest oral
sound.

WIFE IN THE MUD

My wife is always telling me . . . The way to drive a car . . .
And how to back the buggy up . . . And not to go too far . . . She
is a careful driver and . . . An expert at the wheel . . . And all her
special knowledge she . . . Is happy to reveal . . . But yesterday
she started out . . . And skidded off the drive . . . And I am glad
and grateful that . . . My wife is still alive . . . She missed the
nearest tree but when . . . She landed with a thud . . . Our car
was most emphatically . . . And firmly stuck in mud . . . I had to
call the towing truck . . . To get it out somehow . . . And what
I called my darling wife . . . I don't remember now.

CHILDREN OF GOD

When little children go to church . . . It always seems to me
. . . That they are holding hands with God . . . In sweet tran-
quillity . . . That there is music in the wind . . And incense in
the air . . . And there are angels at their side . . . To guard them
everywhere . . . They listen to His every word . . . And somehow
they can feel . . . That Paradise is something that . . . Is beautiful
and real . . . Their little eyes look up to Him . . . With innocence
and love . . . And they belong to Him as much . . . As all the stars
above . . . And when they fold their hands and pray . . . It always
seems to me . . . They are His most enduring hope . . . To save
humanity.

STAMP COLLECTOR

He gathers stamps from near and far . . . And saves both old
and new . . . Especially the very rare . . . And those first issues
too . . . He puts them in an album where . . . There is a separate
space . . . For every color, shape, and price . . . And every famous
face . . . Uncanceled stamps are preferable . . . But canceled ones
will do . . . Although he must be certain they . . . Are genuine
and true . . . He buys them from a dealer or . . . He gets them in
a trade . . . Or dashes to the postal clerk . . . As soon as they are
made . . . His title of philatelist . . . May sound a little strange
. . . But stamp collections can produce . . . A handsome piece of
change.

FRIENDS IN CHURCH

The time we spend with loving friends . . . Is filled with joy
and pleasure . . . And so much more than ever when . . . We go
to church together . . . There is a lot of happiness . . . In putting
on a party . . . With food and drink, some games to play . . . And
laughter hale and hearty . . . There is a world of cheerfulness . . .
In visiting our neighbors . . . And helping to console them in
. . . Their troubles and their labors . . . But how much more inspiring . . . And more inviting is it . . . To walk into the House of
God . . . And pay The Lord a visit . . . To share our friendship
with His own . . . While reverently expressing . . . Our gratitude
and fervent prayers . . . To gain His wondrous blessing.

SONG IN THE RAIN

The song that I remember best . . . Is one that brings me tears
. . . And leads me gently by the hand . . . To all the yesteryears
. . . The melancholy melody . . . That mingles in the rain . . .
And wistfully reminds me with . . . Its sad and sweet refrain . . .
Of days that brought me happiness . . . And nights of silent bliss
. . . When all my dreams of beauty bright . . . Were blended with
a kiss . . . The music lingers in the air . . . And in my broken
heart . . . But there is only emptiness . . . Where lovers had to
part . . . And though each flower in the spring . . . May offer me
a friend . . . I know the sun must slip away . . . And every song
must end.

OLD THINGS

I like old houses and old streets . . . The tree that shows its
age . . . And that familiar color of . . . The fading printed page
. . . I like old shoes and battered hats . . . The wrinkles in a brow
. . . And fields that have not felt for years . . . The turning of a
plow . . . Each month and moon of long ago . . . And every smile
and tear . . . Become the music of a song . . . That leaves a
souvenir . . . The world goes on from day to day . . . With love
and flowers fair . . . And many are the hands that reach . . . For
newness everywhere . . . But in my heart I treasure all . . . The
things that used to be . . . And I am really happy when . . . I
dream in memory.

OUR WASHINGTON

George Washington was truly great . . . And we give thanks today . . . That he began the country that . . . Is now the U.S.A. . . . He led the way to Valley Forge . . . And all throughout the war . . . That we might live in liberty . . . And peace for evermore . . . And ever since he raised the flag . . . To guide his valiant force . . . Our nation has endeavored to . . . Pursue his prudent course . . . He was a mighty statesman and . . . An able president . . . The symbol of democracy . . . And equal government . . . We give our praise to Washington . . . And thank almighty God . . . That one so great belonged to us . . . And walked upon this sod.

KRISTINA'S BIKE

Kristina has a bicycle . . . And she is proud and glad . . . Because it is the very first . . . That she has ever had . . . She used to ride a tricycle . . . But then she grew so tall . . . That she decided it was much . . . Too childish and too small . . . So now she tours the neighborhood . . . On just a couple wheels . . . And anyone at all can see . . . How wonderful she feels . . . She swings into her saddle and . . . She grips the handlebars . . . And she is always careful of . . . Pedestrians and cars . . . Kristina loves her bicycle . . . In colors blue and white . . . And everywhere she pedals it . . . She is a pretty sight.

LOVERS' PRAYER

Almighty God, we join our hands . . . And lift our eyes to You . . . As we beseech Your blessing on . . . Our promise to be true . . . Give us the sunshine of the day . . . And let us have the light . . . Of every moon and silver star . . . To keep our courtship bright . . . Help us to plan the days ahead . . . With prudence and with care . . . And with the fervent constancy . . . To sympathize and share . . . Let virtue guide our every step . . . And teach our souls to live . . . In readiness to sacrifice . . . And promptness to forgive . . . And when our lips pronounce the vows . . . That bring us heart to heart . . . Let there be nothing on this earth . . . To draw our love apart.

CIRCLE OF FRIENDS

Old friends are always wonderful . . . And some are priceless too
. . . But we should look around and try . . . To cultivate the
new . . . Because the circle that is formed . . . By all the hands
we shake . . . Surrounds the height and margin of . . . The prog-
ress that we make . . . And if our friends of years ago . . . Are
all we have today . . . Then surely we have slowed our stride . . .
And walked an idle way . . . Whereas each new one helps to ease
. . . Our struggle and our strife . . . And every larger circle is . . .
A longer lease on life . . . So let us keep the gentle friends . . .
That we have come to know . . . But also let us do our best . . .
To make the circle grow.

ON THE BUS

There may be faster ways on earth . . . To reach a certain place
. . . But on the bus we seldom think . . . In terms of time or space
. . . Because we know that we behold . . . A prettier terrain
. . . Than we could see above the clouds . . . Or from the average
train . . . Among our fellow passengers . . . We never feel alone
. . . And somehow all the countryside . . . Appears to be our own
. . . We stop at spots along the way . . . To stretch our weary
legs . . . And get a drink of water or . . . To order ham and eggs
. . . The bus belongs to rich or poor . . . Wherever they may be
. . . With tickets punched for pleasure and . . . For real economy.

LET'S STAY AHEAD

It is a very easy thing . . . To have a lazy mind . . . To dilly-
dally and to let . . . Our duties fall behind . . . And it may seem
quite wonderful . . . To sit around and rest . . . Without a single
worry or . . . A problem on our chest . . . But trying to make up
for it . . . Is not a simple thing . . . And finally there has to be
. . . A day of reckoning . . . Each hour that is wasted is . . . A
golden hour lost . . . And in the ledger of our life . . . Is debited
the cost . . . The moments that have vanished are . . . Impossible
to find . . . So let us strive to stay ahead . . . And never fall
behind.

OUR COMMUNITY CHEST

If there is kindness in our heart . . . And goodness in our soul
. . . Then let us do our part to help . . . Our Chest attain its goal
. . . Let us contribute all we can . . . To make it a success . . .
And thereby lend a helping hand . . . To life and happiness . . .
That faith and courage may endure . . . And those who need may
share . . . In greater opportunities . . . For people everywhere
. . . There is no more inspired task . . . Or project that could be
. . . More beneficial than the Chest . . . In our community . . .
So let us all be generous . . . And do our very best . . . To help
our worthy neighbors who . . . Depend upon the Chest.

TO LIVE FOR OTHERS

When there is sadness in my heart . . . And tears invade my
eyes . . . I look upon the flowers and . . . The beauty of the skies
. . . I contemplate the blessings that . . . My God has given me
. . . And all the comfort and the joy . . . Of every memory . . .
And if the clouds are dark and if . . . The rain is on the street . . .
I think of other people in . . . Their hour of defeat . . . And I
compare my lot with theirs . . . And what they have in store . . .
And always it appears to me . . . That I have so much more
. . . And then I see my failure and . . . The courage that I need
. . . To live my life unselfishly . . . In thought and word and deed.

REMEMBER NOW

Pearl Harbor glistens in the sun . . . With armament and might
. . . The sirens wait in silence and . . . The searchlights roam the
night . . . The sea is calm and quiet now . . . And there are peaceful stars . . . But there are still the hearts that hurt . . . And still
the ugly scars . . . No hourglass can bury grief . . . No tide can
wash away . . . The tragedy of error and . . . The price we had to
pay . . . So may these memories remain . . . With prayers upon
our lips . . . And may no rusty fingerprints . . . Identify our ships
. . . Remember now the anguish and . . . The misery we shared
. . . And let our military be . . . Forevermore prepared.

WE LOVE OUR BOSS

The boss looks mighty tough at times . . . But now and then it seems . . . His heart is sentimental and . . . He does enjoy his dreams . . . Especially when we recall . . . The day he started life . . . Or mark the years that he has shared . . . With his beloved wife . . . A sudden birthday party or . . . An anniversary . . . Will make him just as gentle and . . . As sweet as he can be . . . And so we keep a record of . . . The dates that mean the most . . . And always we are quite prepared . . . To drink a healthy toast . . . And always we are happy and . . . We do not mind the price . . . Because the boss who looks so tough . . . Is really very nice.

GRADUATE'S PRAYER

My days in school are over, God . . . And now I go my way . . . To make my fortune in the world . . . According to my clay . . . I have acquired knowledge from . . . The books that I have read . . . And from my many teachers and . . . The wisdom they have said . . . But I am fully conscious, God . . . That this is just the start . . . And there is much that only time . . . And living can impart . . . And that is why I fold my hands . . . And say this prayer to You . . . To help me solve my problems and . . . To see my struggle through . . . I need Your strength and guidance and . . . Your everlasting grace . . . To meet the many troubles and . . . The trials I must face.

LETTER WRITERS

Some people write long letters in . . . The time they have to spare . . . Because they think their views on life . . . Are wonderful to share . . . They tell the President how he . . . Should run the U.S.A. . . . What legislation he should sign . . . And which to throw away . . . They keep the governor informed . . . On what he ought to do . . . And they would guide the mayor in . . . His problems old and new . . . But most of all they spend their time . . . In writing to the press . . . To teach the world the only way . . . To lasting happiness . . . They may be quite sincere and yet . . . Their letters seem to hint . . . That all they really want is just . . . To get their names in print.

MY TOAST TO YOU

I wish with all my heart today . . . The things that you want
most . . . And to the dreams that fill your heart . . . I drink a
special toast . . . I hope that every day will bring . . . The joys
that you desire . . . And you will gain the glories and . . . The
virtues you admire . . . I hope your every morning will . . . Be
beautiful and bright . . . And you will always have the stars . . .
To light your way at night . . . May everything be perfect, dear
. . . And in the fullest measure . . . With all the future in your
hand . . . And memories to treasure . . . Because I love you and
because . . . Whatever I may do . . . I want your loving heart to
know . . . That I belong to you.

STORE MANAGER

He has to be the early bird . . . Who opens up the store . . .
Unless he has the help he needs . . . To let him sleep and snore
. . . But when he does arrive for work . . . He has to count each
face . . . And see that all the merchandise . . . Is in its proper
place . . . The cash must be accounted for . . . And checks must
be okayed . . . The inventory has to jibe . . . And workers must
be paid . . . It is the manager who must . . . Dispose of each
complaint . . . And when the customer is wrong . . . To exercise
restraint . . . Indeed his job is difficult . . . And he may gripe and
groan . . . But some day if he perseveres . . . The store may be
his own.

KIND OF A PARTY

I do enjoy a party if . . . It is not staid or dowdy . . . And if
it does not last too long . . . And does not get too rowdy . . . I
mean I like a party if . . . The people all are nice . . . And if in
perfect decency . . . Variety is spice . . . But all too often there
is one . . . Who has to be a smarty . . . And strive relentlessly to
be . . . The life of all the party . . . Who wants to draw attention
and . . . To be a comic star . . . And usually is someone who
. . . Will carry things too far . . . I do not like the kind of time
. . . Where people get too merry . . . And make remarks or swing
an ax . . . They later wish to bury.

HOUSE IN A MESS

When Christmas Day has passed away . . . Our house is in a mess . . . But nothing more effectively . . . Could speak of happiness . . . The toys around the living room . . . The footprints on the stair . . . The dishes in the kitchen sink . . . And boxes everywhere . . . The children have not made their beds . . . Their clothes are on the floor . . . And all the atmosphere is like . . . The aftermath of war . . . These are the testimonials . . . That Santa Claus was here . . . These are the silent evidence . . . Of merriment and cheer . . . And so it does not matter that . . . Our house is in a mess . . . Because it means our Christmas was . . . A wonderful success.

COMMUNITY PRAYER

Dear Lord, my fervent prayer today . . . Is not a prayer for me . . . But for the people young and old . . . Of my community . . . The ones who live a mile away . . . Or just across the street . . . The proud and humble, rich and poor . . . Wherever they may meet . . . May they be happy in their homes . . . And everywhere they go . . . And may they share forever in . . . The blessings You bestow . . . Dear Lord, protect their families . . . From tragedy and plight . . . And otherwise make certain that . . . They get along all right . . . Inspire them with faith and hope . . . And help their dreams come true . . . And surely they will always give . . . Their gratitude to You.

STREET SANTA

He stands all day and rings his bell . . . For everyone to hear . . . And thus awakens in our hearts . . . The song of Christmas cheer . . . In his familiar suit and beard . . . He braves the snow and sleet . . . To gather dimes and nickels from . . . The folks along the street . . . The little coins that mean so much . . . To those who are so poor . . . That there is never any meal . . . Of which they can be sure . . . Who look to Santa on the street . . . For all the clothes they wear . . . And wonder if our hearts will hear . . . Their soft and humble prayer . . . We do not owe him anything . . . And we may pass him by . . . But if we do we may regret . . . And God may ask us why.

MY WISH ON A STAR

The moon is watching you tonight . . . Wherever, dear, you are
. . . And when you look up at the sky . . . You see a silver star
. . . Perhaps the one on which my heart . . . Is wishing we would
be . . . Together in the pleasure of . . . Each other's company
. . . But anyway I hope your heart . . . Will always hear my
prayer . . . And you will know and understand . . . How much I
really care . . . That you are every thought I have . . . And every
song I sing . . . And when the winter wanes you are . . . The
harbinger of spring . . . You are the golden glory of . . . The sunlight and the moon . . . And every moment, dear, I hope . . .
That I may see you soon.

CHOOSING FRIENDS

I do not choose my friendships by . . . How wealthy they may
be . . . But only by what they can do . . . To serve and comfort
me . . . The willingness of friendly hearts . . . To hear me when
I call . . . To soothe my soul and lift me up . . . Whenever I
may fall . . . I may not ever need them and . . . I may not ask
their aid . . . But if I do, I want to feel . . . That they will make
the grade . . . That they will never let me down . . . And leave
me to my plight . . . When thundershowers sweep the day . . .
Or wash away the night . . . The same as I would give my all
. . . When they have need of me . . . Or just to share the happiness . . . Of friendly company.

OUR INCOME TAX

The poor are really wealthy and . . . The wealthy ones are poor
. . . According to the income tax . . . Our country must endure
. . . For if we earn a little bit . . . The tax is rather small . . .
While otherwise our Uncle Sam . . . Will ask for nearly all . . . It
may not seem so fair to some . . . And yet what else could be . . .
A better democratic plan . . . Of true equality? . . . Each citizen
should do his part . . . And pay his proper share . . . For unity
and happiness . . . And freedom everywhere . . . To overcome
the greedy and . . . To conquer every strife . . . And try to give
this world of ours . . . A better way of life.

EACH DAY ON EARTH

Each day I live is one more day . . . That God is giving me . . .
Before my soul is summoned to . . . Begin eternity . . . Another
day to work and pray . . . And try to make amends . . . If only
by devotion to . . . My family and friends . . . To praise Him and
to honor Him . . . And give my gratitude . . . For comfort and
security . . . In shelter and in food . . . Then let me linger not in
bed . . . Beyond the morning sun . . . But let this be a day for
God . . . That I have well begun . . . And when tomorrow comes
I hope . . . That it will be for me . . . Another day to work and
pray . . . Before eternity.

LIVING IN CIRCLES

Some people walk in circles or . . . They seem to talk that way
. . . And they discover every dawn . . . Is just like yesterday . . .
They do not try to get ahead . . . And nothing matters much
. . . Without the special flavor of . . . That old, familiar touch
. . . They dream about their future but . . . They carry not a
care . . . And they are not at all concerned . . . With getting
anywhere . . . Because of course their circles have . . . That uniform design . . . That never shows a starting point . . . Or any
finish line . . . They merely go around and round . . . And bring
them back once more . . . To all the simple thoughts and things
. . . That they have known before.

IDLE KEYS

The summer is a lazy time . . . For folks to while away . . .
And that is when we seldom see . . . Or hear our Donnie play
. . . He takes piano lessons and . . . He practices real well . . .
But when vacation comes around . . . It seems to cast a spell
. . . Our Donnie swims and fishes and . . . Has baseball on the
brain . . . And he is never in the house . . . Except when there
is rain . . . He dashes out each morning now . . . As soon as skies
are bright . . . And keeps his locomotion up . . . As long as there
is light . . . And so his good piano stands . . . And gathers dust
each day . . . While Donnie searches here and there . . . For
something else to play.

MAN WITH PUSHCART

He wends his way along the street . . . To sell his sundry wares
. . . And offers inexpensively . . . To lighten people's cares . . .
A gadget for the kitchen or . . . The lace to tie a shoe . . . A
special wax or polish that . . . Will make your things look new
. . . His prices are adjustable . . . Within a certain range . . .
And usually he is prepared . . . To barter and exchange . . .
There is no prospect in his rank . . . For fortune or for fame . . .
And few in number are the ones . . . Who know him by his
name . . . His place in life is humble but . . . He has a kindly
heart . . . And he is satisfied to plod . . . And push his lowly cart.

MY HUMBLE BEST

I often wish that I had kept . . . The path that beckoned me
. . . Because I know it would have meant . . . A greater victory
. . . I would not have the worldly things . . . That now I call my
own . . . And possibly I would have been . . . Forgotten and
alone . . . But I would not be worrying . . . About a cloud of
gray . . . And I would not have had the sins . . . That weigh my
soul today . . . And yet there are accomplishments . . . Of which
my heart is proud . . . And there are even praises that . . . The
people say out loud . . . And while I might have done much more
. . . To gain eternal fame . . . At least I have the comfort of . . .
A good and worthy name.

SALUTE OUR SONS

Let us salute our valiant sons . . . Who lie beneath the sod . . .
And pray that they are happy now . . . Eternally with God . . .
Let us salute them for their fight . . . By air and land and sea
. . . And for the swift and steady deeds . . . That showed their
bravery . . . We are forever thankful for . . . Their loyal hearts
and true . . . And for their faith in freedom and . . . Our great
red, white, and blue . . . Their sacrifice was glorious . . . And
theirs will ever be . . . The names that fill our hall of fame . . .
And bless our history . . . Unselfishly they gave their all . . . To
bring a brighter dawn . . . So let us honor them today . . . And
stanchly carry on.

EXCEPT THE TEARS

Whatever memories I find . . . Are yours to have and keep . . .
Including all my happy dreams . . . When I am sound asleep
. . . Including every perfect day . . . And night that we have
known . . . And every kiss that we have shared . . . When we
have been alone . . . But not including any tear . . . That ever
left your eye . . . Or any part or syllable . . . Of whispering good-
by . . . Because I do not want your heart . . . To feel the least
regret . . . And anything that made you sad . . . I want you to forget . . . I want to give you every thought . . . And every dream in
me . . . But never any sorrow or . . . Unpleasant memory.

OUR KIND OF JOB

A job is only good or bad . . . According to the way . . . We
feel about our duties and . . . Our present rate of pay . . . If we
are quite dissatisfied . . . With what we have to do . . . We ought
to look for something else . . . To sort of change our view . . .
And if our wage or salary . . . Is giving us a fit . . . We ought to
ask the boss for more . . . Before we ever quit . . . But if we
really try to take . . . An interest in our work . . . We probably
will never sigh . . . Or be inclined to shirk . . . And we should
know that every goal . . . We struggle to achieve . . . Is seldom
gained unless we give . . . Much more than we receive.

MY SECRET DIARY

I keep a secret diary . . . Of everything I do . . . The different
places where I go . . . And all the faces new . . . My sorrow and
my happiness . . . And every little song . . . Of beauty and of
ugliness . . . And what is right and wrong . . . The people who
befriend me and . . . The ones who pass me by . . . And those
who get my letters and . . . Who promise to reply . . . I keep a
secret diary . . . Of each and every debt . . . So I will not be
negligent . . . And I will not forget . . . And it is really secret
and . . . I hold it far apart . . . Because the only words I write
. . . Are written in my heart.

LET US BE THANKFUL

Let us pursue our special task . . . And go our separate way
. . . But let us all give gratitude . . . On this Thanksgiving Day
. . . Our heartfelt gratitude to God . . . For blessings small and
great . . . Including warmth and comfort and . . . The food upon
our plate . . . For life and health and knowledge and . . . Our
family and friends . . . And for the chance to right our wrongs
. . . And try to made amends . . . Let us be thankful for the
sun . . . And every rainbow bright . . . The fertile field, the
factory . . . And quiet in the night . . . And let it be remembered
now . . . That God is always here . . . And we should thank Him
every day . . . And not just once a year.

INFORMALLY YOURS

The formal dance and dinner and . . . The perfect spot of tea
. . . May please the social set but they . . . Do not appeal to
me . . . For I adore a barbecue . . . Or hot dog on a bun . . .
And just a juke box in a joint . . . To have a lot of fun . . . I
have no fault to find with those . . . Who seem to swim in cash
. . . Or who prefer filet mignon . . . To ordinary hash . . . But
I am just a common guy . . . Who wanders here and there . . .
With nothing formal on the floor . . . Or on the bill of fare . . .
Who merely looks around the world . . . And tries to play his
part . . . By adding to the happiness . . . Of every human heart.

GOODS RETURNED

Enclosed please find one broken heart . . . In need of much
repair . . . And please remit some damages . . . For all the wear
and tear . . . I do not want a refund or . . . The finest substitute
. . . But just the mere assurance that . . . You really give a hoot
. . . Of course there was no guarantee . . . That it would stay
intact . . . And yet I think this item could . . . Be more securely
packed . . . And even if you do not feel . . . You owe the slightest
debt . . . You could at least be courteous . . . And say that you
regret . . . So please inspect this broken heart . . . And see what
you can do . . . And give me credit or accept . . . My humble
I.O.U.

IN SECOND GRADE

Kristina now can hardly wait . . . To be in school once more
. . . And be with all her friends again . . . And all the joys in
store . . . To read and write and be polite . . . When teacher calls
her name . . . And do her part in every task . . . And play in
every game . . . She is so very proud that now . . . She is in
second grade . . . And nothing seems to worry her . . . And she
is not afraid . . . In fact she wants to get ahead . . . By studying
at home . . . And crowding facts and figures new . . . Inside her
little dome . . . She wants to get a star of gold . . . For every
special page . . . More bright than both her brothers got . . .
When they were just her age.

NEEDLING

There is no need to needle folks . . . In earnest or in fun . . .
But there are some who constantly . . . Belittle everyone . . .
Who like to poke at people for . . . The things they do or say
. . . And try repeatedly to push . . . Their prominence away . . .
They either want to show how smart . . . They think they really
are . . . Or else they just are jealous of . . . Another rising star
. . . In any case they have no right . . . To pick on other folks . . .
And ridicule them with remarks . . . Or ill-considered jokes . . .
Indeed there is no surer way . . . To start a bitter strife . . . And
in the last analysis . . . To lose a friend for life.

FOR ALL THE YEARS

I wish you every happiness . . . For all the years ahead . . .
And hope that I may always help . . . To keep you comforted
. . . To be your friend in trouble and . . . Your counselor in
strife . . . And take away whatever tears . . . May try to touch
your life . . . I hope the sun will shine on you . . . Wherever you
may be . . . And may each silver star reflect . . . Some pleasant
memory . . . And whether I am near you or . . . We have to be
apart . . . May love and faith and courage blend . . . A rainbow
in your heart . . . There are no sentiments that I . . . Could more
sincerely say . . . May God protect and cherish you . . . And bless
you every day.

HARBOR OF MY DREAMS

I dream of starlight in the sky . . . And moonlight on the sea
. . . And of a ship that sails tonight . . . To bring you back to
me . . . I dream about a garden where . . . The honeysuckle grew
. . . And where I called you sweetheart and . . . I gave my love
to you . . . The ermine of a winter night . . . The hunter-green
of spring . . . The russet robe of autumn days . . . And summer's
golden wing . . . The city street, the open field . . . The mailman
at the door . . . And all the happy promises . . . We pledged forevermore . . . And, oh, I pray your ship will sail . . . A calm and
quiet sea . . . To reach the harbor of my dreams . . . And bring
you back to me.

WE DO REMEMBER

Their graves are not forgotten and . . . They did not die in vain
. . . But every act of bravery . . . Became another gain . . . We
still remember every deed . . . And every gun that roared . . . The
ships and submarines that sailed . . . And every wing that soared
. . . They were the gallant heroes of . . . That fateful yesterday
. . . When every hope was pinned upon . . . The mighty U.S.A.
. . . And in this hour we recall . . . And we salute each name . . .
And promise there will never be . . . The slightest cause for shame
. . . For we will keep the stars and stripes . . . Forever at the
mast . . . And there will be democracy . . . As long as life will last.

NEVER ENOUGH

Some people never seem to know . . . How much they really
own . . . And why it is important to . . . Leave well enough alone
. . . They keep on reaching for the things . . . To which they
have no right . . . Until they get their fingers in . . . An argument
or fight . . . They are not satisfied to have . . . Sufficient for their
needs . . . But they demand publicity . . . For more important
deeds . . . And in the process they permit . . . No crossing of
their path . . . However much their method may . . . Incur their
neighbors' wrath . . . They force their way ahead despite . . .
How selfish it may be . . . And then they always wonder why
. . . They meet with tragedy.

PAYDAY TO PAYDAY

Each time I get my salary . . . I work my budget out . . . And by my calculation there . . . Is never any doubt . . . I have enough to pay the rent . . . And buy a bunch of food . . . And liquidate the other bills . . . That constantly intrude . . . And so I should not hesitate . . . Or ever worry then . . . About how soon my salary . . . Will come around again . . . But as the days and nights go by . . . I always seem to find . . . That I am just a little bit . . . Financially behind . . . And so my budget never is . . . As big as it should be . . . And it is never equal to . . . My meager salary.

ENTIRELY FOR YOU

O Lord, I want to live this day . . . Entirely for You . . . With everything I think or say . . . And everything I do . . . I want to give the best in me . . . Of heart and soul and mind . . . And glorify You constantly . . . By being good and kind . . . Because each hour that I live . . . And all that I possess . . . Are priceless presents that You give . . . To bring me happiness . . . You comfort me in every task . . . And help my heart to win . . . And You are lenient when I ask . . . Forgiveness for a sin . . . And so the least I can afford . . . Or undertake to do . . . Is just to live this day, O Lord . . . Entirely for You.

RADIO ANNOUNCER

The radio announcer is . . . That member of the staff . . . Who does not try to make you cry . . . Or generate a laugh . . . He merely tells in measured tones . . . The words he has to say . . . About the news or weather or . . . To give the time of day . . . Of course there are occasions when . . . He reads commercials too . . . And then he does his best to sell . . . Some merchandise to you . . . And when events are sudden or . . . Emergencies arise . . . He gets a bit excited and . . . He strives to dramatize . . . But generally his voice is calm . . . And cool as it can be . . . And he is just reporting to . . . His radio family.

SPRING IN THE CITY

I like to walk along the street . . . And watch the children play . . . And listen to their laughter and . . . The happy things they say . . . Or take a stroll around the park . . . And see them gathered there . . . For games and picnics on the grass . . . With never any care . . . I like to look at lovers young . . . Who saunter hand in hand . . . With now and then a bashful sign . . . To show that love is grand . . . Or gaze upon the couples with . . . Their buggies bright and new . . . As they parade so proudly while . . . Their babies smile and coo . . . And I enjoy the picture of . . . The folks along in age . . . And try to read the gentle lines . . . Upon their facial page.

WHO HAVE NO CHILD

There are the wife and husband who . . . Are justly proud and glad . . . When of an hour they become . . . A mother and a dad . . . They have a little baby who . . . Means all the world to them . . . A miracle from Heaven and . . . A really priceless gem . . . But also there are spouses good . . . Who are not ever blest . . . With God's fulfillment of their prayer . . . And their sincere request . . . They linger in a land of hope . . . Where every thread is bare . . . And where the only pattern is . . . The dream that they may share . . . And though they may not ever have . . . A bundle bright and new . . . They well deserve God's blessing for . . . Their love so dear and true.

NO DIFFERENT NOW

The world is not so different now . . . From what it used to be . . . When other people on the earth . . . Were making history . . . They used to worry long ago . . . About the wicked way . . . In which their generation lived . . . And how they liked to play . . . Their futuristic fashions and . . . Their politics and strife . . . And all the other tendencies . . . That permeated life . . . They thought the world was full of sin . . . And almost held their breath . . . While waiting for humanity . . . To meet the doom of death . . . But we are still in business at . . . The same successful stand . . . And virtue still is common to . . . The code of every land.

ETERNAL THANKS

I thank You, God, with all my heart . . . For being good to me
. . . And for the chance to gain a place . . . In Your eternity . . .
I know the sins that weigh my soul . . . Are more than I can
count . . . And I could never expiate . . . Or purge the whole
amount . . . But I can ask forgiveness and . . . I know my soul
may rise . . . Above the wondrous beauty of . . . The everlasting
skies . . . I know that if I love You, God . . . I cannot lose the
way . . . For You will lead me through the dark . . . And guide
me through the day . . . And that is why I promptly choose . . .
The path I know is true . . . And why I love You, God, and give
. . . Eternal thanks to You.

MESSENGER

The messenger delivers notes . . . And cables from afar . . . As
well as telegrams that state . . . Whatever facts there are . . . He
carries cash and stocks and bonds . . . A package large or small
. . . And news of victory in war . . . Or of a city's fall . . . His
pouch or pocket may contain . . . A greeting warm and gay . . .
Or tearful information that . . . Will cloud the brightest day . . .
He travels on a motorbike . . . Or pedals with his feet . . . Enjoys
the comfort of a car . . . Or walks along the street . . . Whatever
be his message in . . . The daytime or the night . . . He helps
the world to do the things . . . It wants to expedite.

TAKE CARE

Are you as careful as you think? . . . Are you prepared today
. . . To fight a sudden fire and . . . To keep the flame away? . . .
Have you considered all the means . . . To have your home protected . . . And had the wires in your store . . . Officially in-
spected? . . . Well, how about the daily trash . . . That gathers
at your door . . . And how about the matches and . . . The ashes
on the floor? . . . You cannot be too cautious of . . . That instant
conflagration . . . That might destroy the smallest toy . . . Or
sweep the widest nation . . . So look around with greater care
. . . And do your best to be . . . A guardian of human life . . .
And costly property.

NO OTHER WAY

There simply is no other way . . . To say I love you, dear . . .
And that is why I use those words . . . To make my meaning
clear . . . The same as when I talk to God . . . In glory or despair
. . . With old, familiar phrases of . . . A universal prayer . . .
Perhaps they sound mechanical . . . And commonplace at times
. . . And yet they speak as much as prose . . . Or any perfect
rhymes . . . They are the words that tell your heart . . . How
much I think of you . . . And why my every deed is one . . . To
help your dreams come true . . . There is no substitute in life
. . . For sentiment sincere . . . Or any other way to say . . . How
much I love you, dear.

BLESS YOU, SON

Your birthday, Jimmie, is a day . . . We treasure and remember
. . . And not to merely celebrate . . . The 14th of November
. . . You were a baby beautiful . . . The first we ever had . . .
And many were the ways in which . . . You made us proud and
glad . . . Of course you were no angel and . . . You gave your
share of trouble . . . But no one else could charm us so . . . Or
ever be your double . . . And nobody could brighten more . . .
Our happy family scene . . . Than you, our Jimmie dearest, at
. . . The age of seventeen . . . And so we wish you all the best
. . . In every good endeavor . . . God bless you on this special day
. . . And bless you, son, forever.

CHRISTMAS FOR ALL

God bless old jolly Santa Claus . . . And speed him on his way
. . . With presents for the young and old . . . To brighten
Christmas Day . . . With pretty dolls and Teddy bears . . . For
little girls and boys . . . And luxuries for older folks . . . Who
look for larger joys . . . May Christmas bring good will to men
. . . And peace to every land . . . With faith and hope and charity
. . . And love on every hand . . . Let everyone help Santa
Claus . . . To be a real success . . . And decorate each Christmas
tree . . . With perfect happiness . . . And may the spirit ling
through . . . The year about to start . . . That God may
His blessing great . . . To every human heart.

PRIDE IN LABOR

I used to work in factories . . . When I was just a boy . . . And I can tell you frankly now . . . It wasn't any joy . . . The jobs were tough, the hours long . . . And there was little pay . . . And every morning of my life . . . Was just another day . . . But there was one impelling thought . . . That always stayed with me . . . And made me proud to be a part . . . Of growing industry . . . The simple fact that I could clothe . . . And keep my body fed . . . With these two hands that God bestowed . . . To help me earn my bread . . . The knowledge that I had the health . . . The wisdom and the brawn . . . To do the labor of a man . . . And bravely carry on.

CIRCUS COMING

It will not be too long until . . . The circus comes to town . . . Because the billboards bright display . . . The picture of a clown . . . And there are posters that present . . . The lion in his lair . . . The bareback riders and the ones . . . Who swing so high up there . . . The tiger and the elephant . . . The camel and the seal . . . And cowboys fighting Indians . . . As though it all were real . . . I seem to smell the popcorn and . . . To taste the lemonade . . . And hear the children clap their hands . . . To greet the big parade . . . Oh, I can hardly wait until . . . The circus comes to town . . . So I can be a kid again . . . And giggle at the clown.

FOR YOU THIS YEAR

May you be blessed with perfect health . . . And all the best of cheer . . . Throughout the days and weeks and months . . . And seasons of this year . . . May you enjoy the comfort and . . . Companionship of friends . . . And may your wishes be fulfilled . . . Where every rainbow ends . . . In every call by telephone . . . And every letter new . . . May there be hope, encouragement . . . And happiness for you . . . In every song may love and faith . . . Provide the melody . . . And may your life be filled with peace . . . And with prosperity . . . Without a disappointment and . . . Without the smallest tear . . . And no misfortune or remorse . . . To mar a perfect year.

ETERNITY

I have not seen eternity . . . Or talked to one who knows . . .
Because it is intangible . . . As any wind that blows . . . I have
not walked among the dead . . . Or heard the angels pray . . .
Nor do I have the magic sight . . . That goes beyond today . . .
And yet as I may feel the wind . . . And find it warm or cold
. . . I know that death is never all . . . The future has to hold . . .
I know there must be something more . . . Than merely smiles
and tears . . . And more than just the calendars . . . That mark
the passing years . . . As surely as I tell myself . . . I have a lasting
friend . . . And there must be a God above . . . Forever without
end.

SWITCHBOARD GIRL

She answers all the calls that come . . . From near and far away
. . . And listens carefully to what . . . Each caller has to say . . .
And then she promptly plugs the board . . . And pulls a certain
key . . . To ring the phone on someone's desk . . . With joy or
sympathy . . . She dials local numbers and . . . She places distant
calls . . . And patiently replies to him . . . Who whispers or who
bawls . . . Of course sometimes she blushes and . . . She fears her
job is lost . . . Because in spite of everything . . . She gets the
wires crossed . . . But usually she manages . . . To do her duty
right . . . And generally is known to be . . . Congenial and polite.

IN SIMPLE WORDS

I search the corners of the world . . . Each hour of the day . . .
To find the words that might express . . . The things you want to
say . . . I scan the dictionary and . . . I look into your heart . . .
For phrases that are suitable . . . To make a fitting start . . . And
then I take my pen in hand . . . And I begin to write . . . About
the thoughts that come to you . . . When stars adorn the night
. . . I try to analyze your mind . . . And understand your soul
. . . And help you all I can to reach . . . Your most important
goal . . . But finally it seems to me . . . There is no better way
. . . Than just to tell in simple words . . . The things you want
to say.

WHO'S CUCKOO?

Our cuckoo clock is valuable . . . And fancy as can be . . . But every time that bird appears . . . He seems to look at me . . . From 1 to 12, and 12 to 1 . . . Each hour on the dot . . . His cuckoo seems to pick me out . . . And put me on the spot . . . I like to show our timepiece and . . . I point to it with pride . . . But when the cuckoo starts to chirp . . . I try to run and hide . . . Perhaps if I would rest a bit . . . Or walk around the block . . . I would not be inclined to feel . . . As cuckoo as the clock . . . And yet each time the hour strikes . . . At 1 or 2 or 3 . . . That crazy bird comes out the door . . . And cuckoos right at me.

ESPECIALLY NOW

The words I long to whisper now . . . Are all the ones that say . . . I wish good health and happiness . . . For you on Christmas Day . . . And all the words that help to tell . . . How much I love you, dear . . . Each moment of the days and months . . . And seasons of the year . . . I kiss you and I cherish you . . . Whatever time or place . . . Above the brightest glory and . . . Beyond the greatest space . . . I want your lips to share with me . . . Each morsel and each drink . . . And have you be a part of me . . . In every thought I think . . . I love you with my heart and soul . . . Far more than I can say . . . And treasure you especially . . . When it is Christmas Day.

NO LUCK IN LIFE

We always look for luck in life . . . And yet we know The Lord . . . Requires everyone on earth . . . To earn his own reward . . . In other words there is no way . . . To get a lucky break . . . Except as we are meant to have . . . The happiness we take . . . At times it may appear that some . . . Have found an easy way . . . And yet the facts may never match . . . What other people say . . . For only he who makes his mark . . . Can tell the story true . . . Of what he did from day to day . . . To see his struggle through . . . And after all we ought to know . . . The only true reward . . . Is given for the way we work . . . And try to please The Lord.

LET'S NOT BE LATE

If we are looking for success . . . However small or great . . .
We should avoid the habitude . . . Of being always late . . . Of
being tardy every time . . . We start our working day . . . Or when
we go to classes or . . . The places where we pray . . . We should
not disappoint the friends . . . Whom we agree to meet . . . At
some specific hour in . . . A house or on the street . . . Because
repeated tardiness . . . Is laziness of mind . . . And it is inconsid-
erate . . . Improper and unkind . . . It takes so little effort to . . .
Be prompt in what we do . . . And proves that when we promise
things . . . We are sincere and true.

FOR ALL MY FRIENDS

I thank You, God, for all my friends . . . Wherever they may be
. . . For all their gentle words and for . . . Their hospitality . . .
For every letter in the mail . . . And every fond hello . . . And for
the blessing and the warmth . . . They constantly bestow . . .
Because in each and every friend . . . And every true address . . .
I have a guardian against . . . The sea of loneliness . . . I have
encouragement and faith . . . And hope that never ends . . . And
all the inspiration, God . . . On which my life depends . . . And
whether I have known them long . . . Or whether they are new
. . . I cherish them and humbly say . . . My gratitude to You.

HOW LONG, MY LOVE?

How long will you remember me . . . When I am gone away?
. . . How many thoughts will fill your heart . . . Or prayers that
you will say? . . . Will you remember, darling, that . . . I loved
you more than life . . . Whatever tears and troubles and . . .
Whatever storm or strife? . . . Will you recall the happiness . . .
And all the hopes we shared . . . And how you whispered in my
ear . . . To tell me that you cared? . . . And what of all our kisses
and . . . Each wonderful caress . . . And of the sentiments we
tried . . . So deeply to express? . . . How far will you be true to
me . . . Beyond the stars above? . . . Beyond the blue how long
will you . . . Remember me, my love?

OUR BROWNIES

Each week our home becomes the place . . . Where happy
Brownies meet . . . With giggles and with laughter and . . . The
sound of running feet . . . Before their meeting they enjoy . . . A
period of play . . . And then they settle down to do . . . Their
project of the day . . . They learn to dress their pretty dolls . . .
To paint and cook and sew . . . And all the other helpful things
. . . A little girl should know . . . Kristina's mother leads them
and . . . Kristina beams with pride . . . And all the Brownies
struggle hard . . . To learn and keep in stride . . . Because they
like it and they all . . . Look forward eagerly . . . To serving as the
Girl Scouts that . . . They hope some day to be.

FOR ALL THE SICK

O God, consider all the sick . . . Around the world today . . .
The mental sufferers and those . . . Whose bodies waste away
. . . The feeble-minded and the lame . . . And those who are
diseased . . . That they may gather comfort and . . . Their torture
may be eased . . . But most of all consider those . . . Who are so
weak and ill . . . That they do not believe in You . . . Or try to do
Your will . . . Who wander in the wilderness . . . Of selfishness
and pride . . . With no respect for virtue and . . . With only sin
to hide . . . Have mercy on their souls, O God . . . And give them
light to see . . . That life on earth is just a door . . . To Your
eternity.

NO GREATER GOAL

No goal is more important to . . . The husband or the wife . . .
Than bringing little children to . . . The beauty of this life . . .
Than this majestic miracle . . . That God Himself designed . . .
Beyond the comprehension of . . . The scientific mind . . . The
glory of creation and . . . The joy of taking part . . . In nature's
noble plan to shape . . . Another human heart . . . No dream on
earth is sweeter than . . . That day of happiness . . . When there
will be a baby dear . . . To cuddle and caress . . . A little boy or
girl to share . . . The parents' smiles and tears . . . A son or
daughter to adore . . . And cherish through the years.

WHILE THERE IS TIME

Sometimes I get discouraged, God . . . About the debts I owe
. . . And everywhere I try to turn . . . My burden seems to grow
. . . I do not mean my promises . . . To pay financially . . . But
my indebtedness to You . . . And to society . . . The obligations
of my soul . . . For blessings small and great . . . To live a life of
love and not . . . Of selfishness and hate . . . I get discouraged
when I think . . . Of all I might have done . . . And my indifferent attitude . . . In battles to be won . . . And yet I know that if
my soul . . . Is sorry and sincere . . . I still have time to make
amends . . . As long as I am here . . . So give me grace and
wisdom, God . . . And do not let me wait . . . Until at last You
call me and . . . The hour is too late.

WE TALK OF PEACE

We talk of peace at home and in . . . The lands across the sea
. . . And promulgate the principles . . . Of our democracy . . .
We feel there is no other way . . . To put an end to war . . . Than
that of giving all the world . . . The key to freedom's door . . .
And surely none can criticize . . . Or boast a better way . . . To
conquer selfishness and solve . . . The problems of today . . . We
are prepared to argue and . . . To settle every doubt . . . And
there are certain nations we . . . Are willing to help out . . . But
in the last analysis . . . We draw our lines with chalk . . . And
much of what we do toward peace . . . Is little more than talk.

FRIEND FOR TODAY

Some friends remember birthdays or . . . An anniversary . . .
And some will send a Christmas card . . . In faithful memory . . .
And there are those who sometimes write . . . Or use the telephone . . . To see that no familiar soul . . . Is lonely or alone
. . . But all too often there is one . . . Who suddenly pretends
. . . That he has always been among . . . Your most devoted
friends . . . Who has not written you in years . . . Or ever said
your name . . . But who will sing your praises when . . . You gain
the slightest fame . . . And surely and as swiftly as . . . Your star
may fade and fall . . . He will deny he ever knew . . . Or heard of
you at all.

KEY TO THE CITY

The mayors of America . . . Are always giving keys . . . That
symbolize a welcome to . . . Their own communities . . . And
that is very good of them . . . And it is quite unique . . . And
flowery are all the words . . . The mayors like to speak . . . It is a
great tradition in . . . The city and the town . . . And in our
democratic land . . . It is a sort of crown . . . We do not take the
titles of . . . The noble ranks there are . . . But now and then we
do promote . . . Some person as a star . . . And that is when the
gentleman . . . Or lady plays the part . . . That earns our recognition true . . . And wins the public's heart.

YOUR WISH IS MINE

If there is anything you wish . . . Tomorrow or today . . . You
merely have to speak the words . . . That you would like to say
. . . For they are bound to be the words . . . That I would like to
hear . . . So I may know your slightest whim . . . And I may serve
you, dear . . . I want to do whatever you . . . Could ever ask of
me . . . To please your heart with all my love . . . And all my
sympathy . . . I long to bring you happiness . . . Each morning
and each night . . . And polish up the sun and stars . . . To keep
them ever bright . . . So tell me now whatever words . . . Your
lips would like to say . . . And I will light your lamp of joy . . .
And take your tears away.

SELF-SERVICE

Sometimes I think that I would like . . . A servant at my side
. . . To lavish me with comforts and . . . To satisfy my pride . . .
To drive my car, arrange my room . . . And keep my garments
pressed . . . Remind me of my dinner dates . . . And help me to
get dressed . . . A servant who would buy my things . . . And pay
the bills for me . . . And always be prepared to wait . . . On any
company . . . But if I had a servant I . . . Would worry day and
night . . . For fear that some important plan . . . Might not turn
out all right . . . And so I tackle all the tasks . . . And do them
one by one . . . And there is never any doubt . . . About their
being done.

TEACHING PIANO

It is no easy task to teach . . . The music of the keys . . . And
guide the fingers that would play . . . Celestial melodies . . .
Piano-playing is an art . . . That calls for special skill . . . And
endless patience for the dreams . . . The pupil would fulfill . . .
The closest of instruction goes . . . With every number new . . .
But practicing the score at home . . . Is quite important too . . .
It is a long and weary grind . . . And yet it is a joy . . . If there is
any promise in . . . A little girl or boy . . . And when there are
recitals for . . . The hands that really tried . . . The teacher cannot help but feel . . . A deep and lasting pride.

SHARING OUR JOY

What good is any happiness . . . Unless we try to share . . . Its
beauty and simplicity . . . With people everywhere? . . . There is
no joy in selfishness . . . Or going on alone . . . Or any lasting
comfort that . . . Is all our very own . . . We have to walk with
others in . . . This world in which we live . . . And we are never
better than . . . The fellowship we give . . . So let us work together as . . . A strong and friendly team . . . To make each other
happy and . . . Fulfill our fondest dream . . . For only in the
peaceful bliss . . . Of every other soul . . . Can we expect to be
content . . . And gain our greatest goal.

WITH FAITH IN GOD

I may survive for many years . . . Or I may die today . . . And
people may forget me or . . . Remember what I say . . . And I
may shower happiness . . . On those who hear my song . . . Or
magnify the thunderstorm . . . By doing something wrong . . .
But whether there are hopes to share . . . Or any tears to hide
. . . I shall be certain in my heart . . . That I have really tried
. . . And that is all that matters in . . . The face of joy or fear . . .
To give the best there is in me . . . And always be sincere . . . To
serve my neighbor faithfully . . . While I am on this sod . . . And
persevere unselfishly . . . With faith and trust in God.

ALWAYS FORGIVE

My darling, we have made mistakes . . . And we have both been wrong . . . But somehow we have always had . . . The grace to get along . . . And that is the important thing . . . When all is said and done . . . Because we love each other and . . . There is no other one . . . When you are sorry and the tears . . . Are trembling on your cheek . . . I love you so intensely that . . . I cannot even speak . . . And when I whisper to your soul . . . That I am sorry, dear . . . I hear your heart forgiving me . . . With sentiment sincere . . . So let us go through life and give . . . The sacrifice it takes . . . And let us always be prepared . . . To overlook mistakes.

NO ONE MAN

No man is indispensable . . . To any job or trade . . . No matter how remarkable . . . May be his mental grade . . . Because there are so many men . . . With special qualities . . . That there are always substitutes . . . To fill the vacancies . . . There may be some abilities . . . That are considered rare . . . And there may be those geniuses . . . We think we cannot spare . . . But when we find we have to do . . . Without a certain one . . . There still is some successful way . . . To get the project done . . . No man is so important or . . . So clever and so strong . . . That no one else could take his place . . . To help the world along.

NO HANDYMAN

I wish I were a handyman . . . Prepared to do each task . . . Especially the ones my wife . . . Is always there to ask . . . The job of making house repairs . . . Or waxing floors and such . . . And giving parties for our friends . . . With that exacting touch . . . I never seem to have the knack . . . To please my loving wife . . . And that is why we often have . . . A bit of storm and strife . . . But I have this consoling fact . . . When all is said and done . . . That every jack of all the trades . . . Is masterful at none . . . And I would so much rather be . . . An expert in my line . . . If only I could manage to . . . Convince that wife of mine.

WRAPPED IN LOVE

Our hands are very busy now . . . Before and after meals . . .
With boxes and with ribbons and . . . With pretty Christmas seals
. . . For we are sending packages . . . To people far and near
. . . To share with them our sentiment . . . Of happiness and
cheer . . . Our gifts are not expensive and . . . They may not fill
a need . . . But each reflects the gentle thought . . . That prompts
a kindly deed . . . With green and red and silver and . . . A touch
of gold and blue . . . We hope that every addressee . . . Will find
a dream come true . . . We hope each parcel that we ship . . . Will
make somebody glad . . . And help this Christmas be the best . . .
That person ever had.

ALWAYS AT HOME

On Sunday I go visiting . . . And walk right in the door . . .
Where I am always certain that . . . A welcome is in store . . . I
do not have to knock or ring . . . Or telephone ahead . . . Or feel
despair for anything . . . That I have done or said . . . Because it
is the House of God . . . Where I go visiting . . . And where my
soul is filled with peace . . . In prayer and worshiping . . . My
God is never "not at home" . . . But He is always there . . . To
comfort and encourage me . . . And lighten every care . . . As
long as I regret my sins . . . And I sincerely pray . . . With faith in
Him to help me live . . . The true and only way.

SALESWOMEN

Some people think that men alone . . . Can sell the things we
buy . . . But there are women who can talk . . . And catch the
public eye . . . Not just the ladies in a store . . . Where goods are
on display . . . But those who call on customers . . . And know
just what to say . . . Who sell insurance, beauty hints . . . And
magazines to read . . . Appliances, a sewing course . . . And
everything we need . . . They are immensely capable . . . And do
a splendid task . . . Prepared for every problem and . . . Whatever people ask . . . They surely earn their money and . . . The
progress they achieve . . . And they deserve more credit than . . .
They generally receive.

BLACKSMITH

The blacksmith had a busy time . . . In days that used to be
. . . And as the poet aptly said . . . A mighty man was he . . .
From early dawn till late at night . . . He labored at his trade . . .
And many were the horseshoes and . . . The implements he made
. . . But nowadays the nags are few . . . And scattered everywhere
. . . While plows and such are seldom his . . . To fashion or repair
. . . Today the blacksmith takes his tools . . . And goes from town
to town . . . To keep alive the legend of . . . His earlier renown
. . . Unless he serves the cavalry . . . Or dignifies the place . . .
Where thoroughbreds are trained to run . . . In some important
race.

LAWYER'S PRAYER

I ask You, God, to help my cause . . . Whatever it may be . . .
For prosecution or defense . . . For wealth or poverty . . . In
criminal or civil suit . . . However great or small . . . As long as I
am honest when . . . I wear my legal shawl . . . I want to save
the innocent . . . And try to do my share . . . To see that each
defendant will . . . Receive a trial fair . . . I do not ask for riches
or . . . The glory of a star . . . But just to do my duty as . . . A
member of the bar . . . To study and prepare each case . . . And
quietly excel . . . In praise of my profession and . . . To serve my
client well.

RAISE IN PAY

It is a happy feeling when . . . You get a raise in pay . . . And
life itself is wonderful . . . In quite a perfect way . . . You have
more cash with which to buy . . . The things you want to get . . .
And you are not so much inclined . . . To worry or to fret . . .
But it must be the sort of raise . . . That you have well deserved
. . . Because of how efficiently . . . And ably you have served . . .
And not because you know the boss . . . And have a special pull
. . . Or just because his eyes are weak . . . And cannot pierce the
wool . . . The greatest satisfaction and . . . The only kind that
pays . . . Is that of being certain that . . . You do deserve the raise.

BEYOND ALL TIME

No matter what the stars may tell . . . Or what the world may
say . . . I shall belong to you, my love . . . Forever and a day . . .
Forever through the years that reach . . . Beyond the farthest sun
. . . And when the hourglass is still . . . And all the sands have run
. . . I shall belong to you as long . . . As there is any tide . . . And
after all our dreams are gone . . . And every wind has died . . .
When earth and air are melted and . . . The sky alone remains
. . . With idle snows and shadows and . . . With unavailing rains
. . . Because I love you with a love . . . That will not pass away
. . . And I belong to you, my love . . . Forever and a day.

FLY OUR FLAG

Raise high our glorious flag today . . . For all the world to see
. . . And let each mighty gun salute . . . Our stanch democracy
. . . Today is Flag Day and the time . . . To show how proud we
are . . . And reaffirm our loyalty . . . To every stripe and star . . .
Old Glory is the banner bright . . . Of our United States
. . . The symbol of equality . . . And freedom from all hates . . .
Its beauty has inspired us . . . To struggle and to win . . . From
Bunker Hill to Tokyo . . . And Yorktown to Berlin . . . So let us
fly our flag today . . . With spirit brave and true . . . And ask
almighty God to bless . . . The great red, white, and blue.

KRISTINA CRIES

Sometimes Kristina plays with friends . . . Who do not treat her
right . . . And sometimes there are arguments . . . That turn into
a fight . . . And then she hurries home to us . . . To suffer and
complain . . . With tears upon her little cheeks . . . As big as any
rain . . . Of course she may have had a bump . . . Or rolled
around in dirt . . . But usually it seems to be . . . Her feelings that
are hurt . . . Because she holds her sorrow back . . . And keeps
her tears away . . . Until she comes up close and we . . . Can hear
what she would say . . . She always saves her outburst for . . . Her
mother or for me . . . Because she figures she can get . . . Our
loving sympathy.

KICKOFF TIME

The autumn days are here again . . . The leaves begin to fall
. . . And on the college football field . . . We hear the coach's call
. . . We watch the cleats that dig the turf . . . The arm that throws
a pass . . . And here and there the expert toe . . . That leads the
kicking class . . . The quarterback is warming up . . . The center's
head is down . . . And all the players on the team . . . Are set to
go to town . . . The seats are sold for weeks ahead . . . In stadium
and bowl . . . To follow every kickoff and . . . The struggle for a
goal . . . It is the time when bets are made . . . And hopes are
mixed with fears . . . While loyal lungs get exercise . . . In lusty
yells and cheers.

NO RANK OR WEALTH

Each time I hear or read about . . . Some friend who passed
away . . . I live in loneliness throughout . . . The hours of the
day . . . Because I add each one to all . . . The others who have
gone . . . And who provided so much joy . . . To help me carry
on . . . And then I realize more and more . . . How brief the
time we live . . . And how important are the smile . . . And solace
we can give . . . I see the sheer futility . . . Of prejudice and wrath
. . . And why they reach a shallow goal . . . Who take the selfish
path . . . There is no worldly rank so high . . . Or any wealth so
great . . . That it can find a way to turn . . . The key to Heaven's
gate.

PERSONNEL MAN

A most important post in which . . . A person should excel . . .
Is that of looking over and . . . Selecting personnel . . . It takes
a lot of study and . . . Some expert judgment too . . . To choose
the applicants who will . . . Be competent and true . . . He may
be called director or . . . The manager or such . . . But no amount
of title should . . . Affect him very much . . . For his responsibility . . . Must answer every need . . . And he must bear at least a
part . . . Of any wrongful deed . . . And so the task he has to do
. . . Is not exactly fun . . . But he must really get results . . .
Before his job is done.

GIVE ME YOUR FEARS

If there is anything, my love . . . That ever worries you . . . I hope that you will let me know . . . Whatever I can do . . . Because you know it hurts my heart . . . To see the slightest trace . . . Of trouble in your gentle eyes . . . Or fear upon your face . . . I want your problems to be mine . . . And always mine alone . . . For they are more important, love . . . Than any of my own . . . I want to comfort you each day . . . And hold you close at night . . . And make your every moment more . . . Enjoyable and light . . . So rest your anxious head upon . . . The shoulder of my heart . . . And in the shelter of my love . . . Let every doubt depart.

ORDER TAKER

He is the one who goes around . . . With pencil or with pen . . . To take another order for . . . The same old thing again . . . He is no salesman in the sense . . . Of selling more and more . . . Nor is he really interested . . . In any higher score . . . He merely serves the common needs . . . Of all his customers . . . With some attractive product that . . . The public quite prefers . . . It is a somewhat lazy way . . . To make a livelihood . . . And one that will not make him rich . . . Or do him too much good . . . And yet someone must do that job . . . And measure to that size . . . And that may be the only task . . . For which he qualifies.

ALL TRUST IN GOD

The sun moves calmly on its way . . . The shadows walk the night . . . And silently the stars give forth . . . Their everlasting light . . . The trees are swaying in the breeze . . . Their branches gently nod . . . And all of nature seems to place . . . Its confidence in God . . . Why do not human beings do . . . The same upon this earth . . . And give their utmost faith and trust . . . To Him Who gave them birth? . . . For He is always present to . . . Console and comfort all . . . To feed the hungry, heal the sick . . . And lift the ones who fall . . . God knows our problems and our cares . . . And when our hopes grow dim . . . And He will help if only we . . . Will put our trust in Him.

ROOM SERVICE

The good hotel is one where rooms . . . Are comfortable and clean . . . And where the tongue is treated to . . . An excellent cuisine . . . But more than any other way . . . Its reputation zooms . . . If perfect service is conveyed . . . Directly to the rooms . . . The breakfast, luncheon, dinner, and . . . The mixes and the ice . . . The laundering and tailoring . . . And everything so nice . . . The telegrams and letters and . . . The late or early call . . . The barber and the doctor and . . . Just anything at all . . . Of course it is expected that . . . You will provide a tip . . . But you receive quick service and . . . Without the slightest slip.

HAPPY CHRISTMAS, MOTHER

Dear Mother, may your Christmas Day . . . Be filled with happy hours . . . And may your thoughts be young and gay . . . And beautiful as flowers . . . I hope the sun will shine on you . . . And make each moment brighter . . . And as your sweetest dreams come true . . . May all your cares be lighter . . . Because you are my mother dear . . . And in the fullest measure . . . You are the one from year to year . . . I cherish and I treasure . . . And so God bless you, darling, and . . . Reward your each endeavor . . . And bless you for your guiding hand . . . And bless you, dear, forever . . . I hope that Santa Claus will bring . . . His very nicest present . . . And in the New Year everything . . . Will be ideal and pleasant.

BRICKLAYER

He is the humble laborer . . . Who makes a garden wall . . . A presidential palace or . . . An office building tall . . . His trowel pats the mortar down . . . And puts each brick in place . . . To give the outer crust of life . . . A more attractive face . . . The square, the level, and the plumb . . . Are tools that mark his trade . . . But only honest effort can . . . Design his higher grade . . . He shapes the happy chimney and . . . The friendly fireside . . . Where visitors are welcome and . . . Where faith and love abide . . . And though at times he may be slow . . . Or ask for better pay . . . We thank him for the skillful hands . . . That build the U.S.A.

RUBBER BALL

I like a rubber ball because . . . A little girl or boy . . . Can always be so gay with such . . . An inexpensive toy . . . They merely bounce it up and down . . . Or toss it here and there . . . And as they catch it or they miss . . . Their laughter fills the air . . . Of course there are occasions when . . . It breaks a window pane . . . Or messes up the house because . . . Of dust or muddy rain . . . And then there is the tragic ball . . . That rolls into the street . . . Where speeding traffic stills the sound . . . Of happy little feet . . . But when it gets the proper care . . . The rubber ball is fun . . . And helps to pass the time away . . . For daughter and for son.

NO THANKS SUFFICE

If I should say a thousand thanks . . . I know they would not be . . . Sufficient words for all the joy . . . That you have given me . . . They could not start to tell how much . . . Your company has meant . . . And all it has contributed . . . To keep my heart content . . . How happy you have made me with . . . Your understanding smile . . . And how the very thought of you . . . Has made my life worth while . . . My only moments that are sad . . . Are those when you are gone . . . Because your presence does so much . . . To help me carry on . . . And that is why a thousand thanks . . . However sweet and true . . . Would never be enough to give . . . My gratitude to you.

DRY CLEANER

He cleans the slacks and dresses and . . . The skirt and blouse and such . . . And gives the raincoat and the suit . . . That new, refreshing touch . . . The curtains and the neckties and . . . The more expensive shirt . . . And every special item that . . . Has gathered dust and dirt . . . And when the articles are clean . . . They get that perfect press . . . Before they are delivered to . . . The owner's home address . . . Sometimes a spot will linger or . . . A belt will slip away . . . And now and then some cloth will shrink . . . Or colors will not stay . . . But generally the cleaner is . . . An expert in his line . . . And spruces up his customers . . . To keep them feeling fine.

FOREVER GOD

Let us remember God today . . . And let us say a prayer . . .
That He will always keep us in . . . His kind and loving care
. . . Let us give praise and thanks to Him . . . For all His wondrous deeds . . . And His consideration of . . . Our troubles and
our needs . . . Because He never fails us when . . . The day is dark
or dim . . . As long as we have faith and hope . . . And confidence
in Him . . . As long as we are joined to do . . . The good that He
demands . . . And we repose our destiny . . . In His divining
hands . . . For only God can heal our hearts . . . And only God
can be . . . The fullness of our happiness . . . For all eternity.

SHOPPING DILEMMA

When I go window shopping and . . . I have no cash to spare
. . . I see a dozen articles . . . That I would like to wear . . .
I look at all the items that . . . Comprise the luxury line . . .
And silently I tell myself . . . I wish that they were mine . . .
But when I have some money and . . . I hold my head up high
. . . I seldom gaze at store displays . . . Or feel the urge to buy
. . . I weigh the matter carefully . . . To settle every doubt . . .
And finally inform myself . . . That I can do without . . . It seems
my mind and pocketbook . . . Are never in accord . . . And all I
ever want are things . . . That I cannot afford.

A LIMIT TO LABOR

Some people worry while they work . . . Because they have the
fear . . . That life will vanish in a day . . . Or in another year . . .
They want to do their utmost and . . . Acquire all they can . . .
Before they meet the limit of . . . Their temporary span . . . And
it is very possible . . . That in their daily grind . . . They only
have the welfare of . . . Their fellowmen in mind . . . But in their
eagerness to be . . . The winner in the race . . . Too often they
are tempted to . . . Pursue a killing pace . . . And then they lose
and then too late . . . They learn the other side . . . And see the
sense of resting and . . . Of taking life in stride.

IN SCHOOL

The youngsters are in class again . . . To learn their ABC's . . .
Or climb the steps that take them through . . . The universities
. . . They bring their lunches with them or . . . They buy them
at the school . . . And crowd the gym for exercise . . . Or use the
swimming pool . . . They go to plays and dances and . . . They
try to make the team . . . They visualize their goals in life . . . Or
merely sit and dream . . . Their minds are taught the healthy way
. . . To live and grow on earth . . . And day by day they gradually
. . . Become of better worth . . . So they may fill their places
when . . . Their hour is at hand . . . Prepared to take the reins
and be . . . The leaders of the land.

LET ME REPENT

How many scourges have I laid . . . Upon His flesh and bone?
. . . How often have I gone my way . . . And left Him all alone?
. . . How many are the cruel thorns . . . That crown His humble
head . . . To expiate the sins of all . . . The living and the dead?
. . . I crucified my God upon . . . A place called Calvary . . . As
much as all the populace . . . That now is history . . . He gave
His life that I might live . . . And my immortal soul . . . Might
gain the golden glory of . . . Its everlasting goal . . . Then let me
kneel in penitence . . . And hang my head in shame . . . And let
me now sincerely ask . . . Forgiveness in His name.

FLAG OF FREEDOM

The mighty flag of freedom is . . . The flag that flies today . . .
For every citizen and home . . . Throughout the U.S.A. . . .
With stars that represent the states . . . And all their liberties . . .
And thirteen stripes in honor of . . . The gallant colonies . . . We
bare our heads and we salute . . . Old Glory on the mast . . . And
we are justly glad and proud . . . Of our victorious past . . . For
enemies have come and gone . . . And while we paid the cost . . .
There has not been a single war . . . That we have ever lost . . .
And though the world may challenge us . . . We will be stanch
and true . . . To every star and every stripe . . . Of our red, white,
and blue.

BELATED GREETING

My greeting may be somewhat late . . . But still it is sincere . . .
And I am wishing you the best . . . Of happiness and cheer . . . I
wanted to remember you . . . Right on that very day . . . But
other things surrounded me . . . And took my time away . . . I
hope you will forgive me for . . . The fact that I am late . . . And
understand how much I longed . . . To help you celebrate . . .
And if your heart will hear me now . . . I hope that you will find
. . . That all your laughter lies ahead . . . And all your tears behind . . . I wish you everything that life . . . Could ever hold for
you . . . And all the magic you may need . . . To make your
dreams come true.

BASEBALL UMPIRE

Of all the thankless jobs on earth . . . Wherever duty calls . . .
The worst is his who must decide . . . Between the strikes and
balls . . . Who always has to say at once . . . If it is foul or fair . . .
When some determined player hits . . . The horsehide in the
air . . . The man whose eyes must rove the field . . . And cover
every base . . . And figure if the infield or . . . The runner won
the race . . . He is the baseball umpire who . . . Must be prepared
to talk . . . When there is any argument . . . About a run or walk
. . . But whether crowds stand up and cheer . . . Or impolitely
shout . . . He is the one the baseball world . . . Can never do
without.

HER CUP OF COFFEE

I like a cup of coffee and . . . The dreams that go with it . . .
But in the hands of my dear wife . . . It gives me quite a fit . . .
Because she drinks it all day long . . . From morning until night
. . . And when the children are asleep . . . And out of sound and
sight . . . She wants her coffee when the sun . . . Is barely in the
sky . . . And after every dish is washed . . . And I must wipe it
dry . . . Before and after lunch and all . . . Throughout the afternoon . . . From early spring to autumn and . . . December into
June . . . And that would be all right except . . . I have to warm
the pot . . . And always I must wait on her . . . When it is steaming hot.

SO LET US LIVE

As there is God, so there is life . . . And there is light on earth
. . . And every living creature has . . . Its own important worth
. . . However large or small its size . . . However weak or strong
. . . However brief the span of time . . . Or yet however long . . .
For God created everything . . . And everything must be . . .
According to his Holy will . . . For all eternity . . . So let us live
our life for Him . . . With every thought and deed . . . And try to
help our neighbor in . . . The hour of his need . . . Let us be
mindful of His word . . . And let each moment bring . . . The
best that we can offer Him . . . For every living thing.

SIREN

I hate to hear a siren wail . . . Along a busy street . . . Because
so many times it means . . . That life and death must meet . . . It
signifies the tragedy . . . Of someone who is hurt . . . Or of a
human body that . . . Is quiet and inert . . . Or else it sounds the
hurried call . . . To fight a roaring flame . . . And makes me fearful for the home . . . Of some familiar name . . . The siren is a
signal of . . . Some unexpected fate . . . Where rescue workers
may succeed . . . Or help may come too late . . . I do not like to
hear it wail . . . But I am glad that we . . . Are wakened by its
warning sound . . . In our community.

CALLING ALL BOOKS

Dear friends of mine, please look around . . . Your crannies and
your nooks . . . And see if you still have on hand . . . Some old
and borrowed books . . . And see if any of them are . . . The ones
that came from me . . . One day when you and I enjoyed . . .
Each other's company . . . One pleasant day or evening when
. . . You visited my shack . . . And promised that the book you
took . . . Would soon be coming back . . . For there are spaces
here and there . . . On nearly every shelf . . . That should be
filled with volumes that . . . I treasure to myself . . . So please
return them now and please . . . Be not afraid to say . . . That
you intended all the while . . . To bring them yesterday.

BEING THE BOSS

Before I got to be the boss . . . I thought it was a cinch . . . And
all I ever had to do . . . Was not to budge an inch . . . To be the
king of everything . . . And keep an iron rule . . . Where everyone who worked for me . . . Was just another tool . . . But when
I got to be the boss . . . I learned that I was wrong . . . And telling people what to do . . . Was not a simple song . . . I realized
I could not control . . . The human heart and mind . . . Unless
I tried and meant to be . . . Considerate and kind . . . And now
I know each hired hand . . . Is quite a priceless gem . . . And any
glory I may gain . . . Is just because of them.

SUNDAY SERMON

We listen to the lesson or . . . The sermon of the day . . . And
sometimes it is wonderful . . . And we are swept away . . . But
then again the tone is tough . . . And we are told that we . . . Are
sure to be condemned to tears . . . For all eternity . . . The picture of the world is sad . . . And just the slightest glance . . . Is
all we ever need to know . . . We do not have a chance . . . The
Sunday sermon ought to speak . . . Of brighter things in store
. . . And give us hope to gain the goal . . . That we are striving
for . . . It ought to foster faith and strength . . . And all the love
we need . . . To be more persevering and . . . Eventually succeed.

FURNISHING A HOME

The task of furnishing a home . . . Is not a simple one . . .
Indeed it seems to be the kind . . . That never quite gets done
. . . Because a home is more than just . . . A place to sleep and
cook . . . And it should have the things to lend . . . That most
inviting look . . . The curtain, rug, and radio . . . The table,
lamp, and chair . . . Some bric-a-brac, a vase or two . . . And
pictures here and there . . . It takes much more than just a stove
. . . A dresser and a bed . . . A box to cool the meat and milk
. . . Or keep the beans and bread . . . The home should be a nest
of love . . . Where tears are reconciled . . . And where two hearts
are wound around . . . The laughter of a child.

NO TRICK OR MAGIC

So many times we come across . . . Some story of success . . .
And how that person reached the road . . . To wealth and happi-
ness . . . And usually it sounds as though . . . It were a fairy tale
. . . And we are all the more convinced . . . That we are doomed
to fail . . . But if we read it carefully . . . And stop to analyze
. . . There is no trick or magic and . . . There is no sudden rise
. . . It is a long and weary way . . . That winds up to the top . . .
And there is never any time . . . To hesitate or stop . . . And if
we work and if we keep . . . Our shoulder to the wheel . . . Our
chances will be just as good . . . And every bit as real.

PRISONER'S PRAYER

When I have served my sentence, God . . . I pray that I will be
. . . A credit to my country and . . . To my community . . . That
I may not do wrong again . . . And I may never stray . . . Beyond
Your Ten Commandments or . . . What any law may say . . .
For I have learned my lesson, God . . . And I would start anew
. . . To walk in good society . . . And live my life for You . . . I
want to put away my past . . . And build a future bright . . . With
honesty and decency . . . And all I know is right . . . That I may
gain Your blessing, God . . . And my eternal goal . . . And by
my good example I . . . May save another soul.

NOT ANY RAIN

The rain may come in showers and . . . A thunderstorm may
start . . . But nothing can disturb the dream . . . I carry in my
heart . . . The little drops may multiply . . . And lakes and rivers
swell . . . And yet inside of me I feel . . . That everything is well
. . . Because I know that you are mine . . . And you will always
be . . . The happiness of every dawn . . . And every memory . . .
Because you are my guardian . . . Against whatever storm . . .
And in the comfort of your arms . . . I am secure and warm . . .
Not all the downpours and the floods . . . The darkest sky may
send . . . Can ever touch my dream of you . . . Or bring it to an
end.

SMOKE

There is the smoke that signifies . . . A pipe or cigarette . . .
And all the sad or happy dreams . . . That no one can forget . . .
There is the smoke of burning leaves . . . When autumn fills the
air . . . And that of fragrant incense in . . . The fervor of a prayer
. . . And then there is the kind that clouds . . . The battle on a
sea . . . Or spells the sudden signal of . . . Domestic tragedy . . .
It marks the mill where steel is made . . . The train that meets the
dawn . . . And forest camps where embers fade . . . While friendship lingers on . . . But more important is the smoke . . . That
leaves the oven door . . . Or climbs the happy chimney-place . . .
With love forevermore.

THE RINGING TOUCH

Each time the doorbell rings at home . . . Before I leave my
chair . . . I usually can guess the type . . . Of caller waiting there
. . . The uninvited visitor . . . Will give a timid ring . . . While
children small and salesmen bold . . . Will lean upon the thing
. . . The mailman has an even touch . . . And so does parcel
post . . . But special stamps and telegrams . . . Can never make
that boast . . . Some rings will say, "Please let me in" . . . And
some will call, "Hello" . . . While others shout, "Hey, open up!
. . . I'm in a rush to go" . . . But soft and short or loud and
long . . . The one I like the best . . . Is that congenial friendly
ring . . . Of some expected guest.

CADDIE

The caddie lugs the golfer's bag . . . And follows him around
. . . And when the guy gets set to shoot . . . He must not make a
sound . . . He has to keep an expert eye . . . Upon the sailing
ball . . . And find the pellet when it bounds . . . Into the grasses
tall . . . He has to be alert to name . . . The proper club to choose
. . . But be prepared to take the blame . . . When some old
duffers lose . . . At times it pays him well to praise . . . Or else to
sympathize . . . Though he must never once display . . . The gall
to criticize . . . The caddie may not like his job . . . But if he
watches well . . . It may improve his stance and stroke . . . And
help him to excel.

A FRIEND LIKE YOU

I think it is so wonderful . . . To have you for a friend . . . That
I have no desire now . . . To reach the rainbow's end . . . For I
have gathered all the gold . . . That life could offer me . . . By
reason of the fact that I . . . May share your company . . . You
make the day more glorious . . . And when the stars appear . . .
There is no shadow anywhere . . . As long as you are near . . .
Your friendship is the only faith . . . And confidence I need . . .
To carry on courageously . . . And do some worthy deed . . . My
heart is filled with happiness . . . And all my dreams come true
. . . Because I am so fortunate . . . To have a friend like you.

WHITE COLLAR

The average office worker is . . . A fellow or a girl . . . Who
may not seem to be but is . . . A sort of priceless pearl . . . Who
rides the bus and seldom fails . . . To punch the clock on time
. . . And does a fair amount of work . . . To help the profits
climb . . . Yet he or she is hardest hit . . . In our economy . . .
Because the boss will seldom give . . . A raise in salary . . . When
business takes a sudden dive . . . There is a cut in pay . . . And
even though the times improve . . . The rate is there to stay . . .
The average office worker has . . . No union or the like . . . To
arbitrate for cash increase . . . Or vote to call a strike.

TEACH ME TO PRAY

I seldom look at any book . . . But I read one today . . . A book
for little children that . . . Is called, *Teach Me To Pray* . . . It is a
handsome volume and . . . The pictures all are nice . . . And
what the pretty pages say . . . Is more than worth the price . . . I
read each story carefully . . . And each suggested prayer . . . And
every golden line is one . . . That all of us should share . . . Not
only little boys and girls . . . But every parent too . . . That we
may give our love to God . . . And learn what prayer can do . . .
There is no more important task . . . In life from day to day . . .
Than being worthy parents and . . . To teach our child to pray.

OUR NEWSPAPERBOYS

Today we pay our tribute to . . . The boys who walk or ride . . .
To bring the daily paper to . . . Our friendly fireside . . . Who
forward pass it to the porch . . . Or toss it on the lawn . . . Some
time along the afternoon . . . Or in the early dawn . . . They are
the young, ambitious men . . . Who want to earn their way . . .
And have no use for foolishness . . . Or any idle play . . . Of
course they go for healthy sports . . . And try to get their share
. . . But first they see that school and work . . . Receive their
proper care . . . They are tomorrow's leaders of . . . A world that
cannot die . . . As long as youth is shooting straight . . . And
keeps its courage high.

IT PAYS TO ADVERTISE

What would we do without the ads . . . That grace the printed
page . . . To publicize the merchandise . . . For every class and
age? . . . The messages and pictures that . . . Adorn the daily
press . . . The magazines and billboards and . . . The mail to each
address? . . . How would the people be informed . . . Of services
they need . . . And where the best will cost the least . . . For
those who look and read? . . . The art of advertising is . . . A real
necessity . . . To business, government, and home . . . In each
community . . . And in the commerce of the world . . . The
merchant who is wise . . . Is he who has discovered that . . . It
pays to advertise.

AWAY FROM HOME

Some families must be apart . . . Throughout the night and
day . . . While husbands earn their daily bread . . . In places far
away . . . And that requires sacrifice . . . And lonely hours too
. . . Until their ships are sailing home . . . And happy dreams
come true . . . Their only songs and rainbows are . . . The letters
they receive . . . With promises depending on . . . The progress
they achieve . . . The weeks and months are endless and . . . The
stars are seldom bright . . . For loving lips that cannot meet . . .
To kiss and say good night . . . But all the long and lonely while
. . . That they must be apart . . . They share the faith of perfect
love . . . That never leaves the heart.

OUR SEAL OF JOY

What is this little Easter Seal . . . That seals the envelope? . . .
It is the seal of happiness . . . Encouragement and hope . . . For
boys and girls who cannot walk . . . Or run around and play
. . . But who must occupy a chair . . . Or lie in bed all day . . .
Each Easter Seal that decorates . . . Whatever mail we send . . .
Assures our crippled children that . . . They have a faithful friend
. . . Because the penny that it costs . . . Will help them to get
well . . . Or comfort them and teach them ways . . . In which
they can excel . . . So let us spend for Easter Seals . . . As much
as we can pay . . . And seal our friendship with the youths . . .
Who need our help today.

THE PRAYERS WE SAY

There is a prayer of thankfulness . . . For blessings of the day
. . . And one that asks almighty God . . . To take the clouds away
. . . There is a prayer for comfort in . . . The loneliness of
dawn . . . And supplication for the will . . . And strength to carry
on . . . And there are those petitions for . . . The things we want
to do . . . And how to fill our place in life . . . And make our
dreams come true . . . Yes, there are prayers of every kind . . . Our
humble hearts may tell . . . To ask for wealth and prominence
. . . Or just to keep us well . . . But God prefers the heartfelt
prayer . . . We take the time to say . . . To love and praise and
thank Him for . . . Our blessings of the day.

HOME OFFICE

A firm's home office is the place . . . Where policies begin . . .
And that to which its branches all . . . Must send their business in
. . . Where corporate papers are on file . . . And officers preside
. . . And advertising emanates . . . With hesitance or pride . . .
It is the hand that sweeps the land . . . To point the chosen way
. . . And carry out promotions with . . . Their corresponding pay
. . . And yet in many instances . . . Its very life depends . . .
Upon the way its branches meet . . . The local business trends
. . . And so the big home office should . . . Be always glad to share
. . . The credit and the profits with . . . Its agents everywhere.

NO LONG ROAD BACK

If I must leave you now I hope . . . It will not be for long . . .
But in your faith and fervent love . . . My courage will be strong
. . . I shall be thinking of you when . . . The wind is wild and
free . . . And when the waves in giant boots . . . Are trampling
on the sea . . . I shall be praying in the hills . . . And through the
fearful night . . . When flames are licking at the sky . . . To blaze
a fiendish light . . . And when the days are bare and bleak . . .
With snow and mud and rain . . . I shall remember that you said
. . . It cannot be in vain . . . And I shall hope that every step . . .
Will mean a fresher track . . . And there will be no tears and there
. . . Will be no long road back.

A FRIEND TO YOU

If you will be a friend to me . . . When skies are gray or blue
. . . I promise you that I will be . . . A faithful friend to you . . .
I promise you that I will heed . . . Your every beck and call . . .
And I will gladly serve your need . . . However great or small . . .
I will be with you day and night . . . In time of peace or stress
. . . And whether you are wrong or right . . . In failure or success
. . . Because a friendship cannot last . . . Unless it has a place
. . . For all the future and the past . . . That we may have to
face . . . And so if you will promise me . . . To be forever true
. . . You may be sure that I will be . . . A faithful friend to you.

OUR SEAL OF SYMPATHY

On every card and every gift . . . Prepared for Christmas Day
. . . Let us remember those who need . . . Some help along the
way . . . Let us declare the kindness and . . . The charity we feel
. . . By purchasing and pasting on . . . Another Christmas Seal
. . . To comfort those whose lungs are weak . . . And give them
special care . . . With every dime and dollar that . . . Our pocketbooks can spare . . . The Christmas Seal is more than just . . . A
stamp of color bright . . . And more than just the noble badge . . .
Of doing what is right . . . It is the seal of sympathy . . . The
symbol of our love . . . With all the faith and promise of . . . A
prayer to God above.

185

OUR GOOD EXAMPLE

Each deed we do, each word we say . . . Affects some other soul
. . . And we may help it to attain . . . Or keep it from its goal
. . . For if our influence is bad . . . We shall impair the weak
. . . And undermine their courage for . . . The virtues they would
seek . . . But if we guard our actions and . . . We speak with
grace and care . . . Our influence on others will . . . Be equal to
a prayer . . . Our greatest service and the best . . . Example we
can give . . . Are gentle conversations and . . . The noble way we
live . . . And surely God will bless us in . . . The hour of our need
. . . If we will try to be like Him . . . In every word and deed.

DRIVER JIMMIE

Our Jimmie wants to drive the car . . . From morning until
night . . . And we confess his vision and . . . His timing are all
right . . . And we admit how handily . . . He passed his driving
test . . . Indeed the score he made that day . . . Was just about
the best . . . But we are slightly conscious of . . . The gasoline he
burns . . . And his idea of when and how . . . We should be
taking turns . . . He used to walk or ride the bus . . . Each time
he had a date . . . Where now he has to have the car . . . And
keep it out quite late . . . And now it seems our budget will . . .
Be getting mighty slim . . . Because the only answer is . . . Tc
buy a car for him.

MOTHER'S PRAYER

I thank You, God, for blessing me . . . With motherhood on
earth . . . And I adore and praise You for . . . The miracle of
birth . . . I pray I may be worthy of . . . Your wondrous gift to
me . . . And I may do my part in life . . . For all humanity . . .
That I may raise my children right . . . And teach them what to
do . . . To grow in strength and character . . . And always honor
You . . . For they belong to You and they . . . Are only in my
care . . . To comfort and protect them and . . . To help them
with a prayer . . . And that is why I make this plea . . . For wisdom and for grace . . . That I may do Your holy will . . . And fill
my humble place.

ESPECIALLY GOOD

Christmas Day will soon be here . . . And our dear children know it . . . Because their good behavior and . . . Their perfect manners show it . . . It seems they cannot do enough . . . To prove their deep affection . . . Including clothes and teeth that pass . . . The most minute inspection . . . Including hands and faces clean . . . And quite a disposition . . . To work for us without reward . . . Or special recognition . . . It happens every winter when . . . That certain day is nearing . . . And someone very jolly is . . . About to be appearing . . . If only they would be like that . . . Throughout each week and season . . . Without the hope of Santa Claus . . . Or other wishful reason!

IN YOUR SORROW

Your sorrow is a tragedy . . . That nothing can erase . . . And there is no one on this earth . . . To take your dear one's place . . . And I can only offer you . . . My sympathetic prayer . . . That God will keep the one you loved . . . In His eternal care . . . But I assure you truly that . . . My heart goes out to you . . . And there is nothing for your sake . . . I would not gladly do . . . I hope that you will call on me . . . Tomorrow or today . . . That I may serve your slightest need . . . In every friendly way . . . Because I want to ease your pain . . . And brighten every dawn . . . And by each little word and deed . . . To help you carry on.

NO WINTER OF LOVE

The days and weeks and months go by . . . The seasons come and go . . . And winter seems to linger more . . . The older that we grow . . . The cobwebs sort of gather and . . . The dust is everywhere . . . And colder is the shoulder of . . . The wind that fills the air . . . But, darling, when I think of you . . . And all the joy we hold . . . There is no wintertime of love . . . Nor any growing old . . . For every moment is like spring . . . And we are young of heart . . . As long as life is ours to share . . . And we are not apart . . . Your hand is warm, your eyes are soft . . . The stars are always bright . . . And life is sweeter every time . . . I kiss your lips good night.

PREACHER'S PRAYER

Inspire me, O God, to preach . . . A sermon good and true . . . That all who hear my voice may heed . . . And give themselves to You . . . Let me be humble and sincere . . . In every word I say . . . To comfort and encourage them . . . And teach them how to pray . . . I want to spread Your gospel to . . . The hearth of every home . . . And help You save the sinners and . . . The profligates who roam . . . To foster love and charity . . . And light the lamp of hope . . . That none may falter in the faith . . . And none may have to grope . . . Endow me with the wisdom, God . . . To preach a sermon good . . . That Your commandments may be known . . . And fully understood.

CIRCULATION MANAGER

The circulation manager . . . Has quite a task at hand . . . Including how to hurry each . . . Edition to the stand . . . And how to keep his drivers and . . . The newsboys on their toes . . . So there will be no papers left . . . When it is time to close . . . But that is only part of it . . . For he must find a way . . . To publicize and bring in more . . . Subscriptions every day . . . He must co-ordinate his work . . . With all the staff at large . . . Collect accounts and figure out . . . How much he ought to charge . . . He well deserves his salary . . . And share of happiness . . . Because he circulates the veins . . . That keep alive the press.

KRISTINA BELIEVES

Kristina now is smart enough . . . To notice many flaws . . . But still her little heart believes . . . In jolly Santa Claus . . . With pencil, pen, or blackboard chalk . . . She struggles hard to say . . . What presents she is hoping to . . . Receive on Christmas Day . . . Of course she tells us what she wants . . . Because she knows so well . . . That Santa may not recognize . . . The words she tries to spell . . . But every night she dreams about . . . A pretty Christmas tree . . . With bright and gorgeous gifts for her . . . And all the family . . . And as I gaze into her eyes . . . I wish that I could hold . . . The faith and trusting spirit of . . . Our darling five-year-old.

THANK YOU FOR MERCY

Dear Lord, when I have done a wrong . . . And I repent my sin
. . . I thank You that I may regret . . . And once again begin . . .
That I may kneel before You with . . . Contrition in my heart
. . . And with the fervent hope and prayer . . . That we may never
part . . . You are so ready to forgive . . . The weakness of my will
. . . And with Your everlasting grace . . . My lonely soul instil
. . . As long as I am sorry and . . . I strive to make amends . . . To
You, my Lord, and unto all . . . My enemies and friends . . . And
as I say my sorrow and . . . My promise I renew . . . I praise and
honor You and give . . . My gratitude to You.

TIME FOR CAUTION

That holiday is here again . . . When people like to drive . . .
And when the only lucky ones . . . Are those who stay alive . . .
The highways will be crowded and . . . The tempers will be short
. . . And business will be booming for . . . The graveyard and the
court . . . And there will be the swimming saps . . . And empty-
headed jerks . . . Whose carelessness will kill or maim . . . With
common fireworks . . . But there is still a chance that we . . .
Can keep the total down . . . So let us all be careful on . . . The
highway and in town . . . Let us be doubly cautious when . . . We
walk around or drive . . . And do our best in every way . . . To
keep the world alive.

ONCE AND FOREVER

The only time I fell in love . . . Was when I looked at you . . .
And in that moment it appeared . . . That all my dreams came
true . . . For you were everything to me . . . That I had ever
wanted . . . And in your presence I became . . . Encouraged and
undaunted . . . I was inspired to attain . . . The summit of success . . . And every golden glory that . . . Would give you happiness . . . The only time I fell in love . . . I fell in love forever . . .
And every prayer I said was one . . . That you would leave me
never . . . Because you are so wonderful . . . And now the same as
then . . . I know that I could never sigh . . . Or be in love again.

SHOW-OFF

A show-off is a fellow who . . . Believes he is a treat . . . Or else a girl who likes to think . . . That she is mighty sweet . . . In either case we recognize . . . The flimsy mask they wear . . . And know the glory they display . . . Is never really there . . . Because they are too obvious . . . In what they do or say . . . And by their efforts to pretend . . . They give themselves away . . . A show-off either talks too much . . . Or plays too big a part . . . And shows that he or she has no . . . Sincerity of heart . . . And when the show-offs get some sense . . . And really try to rate . . . They usually discover they . . . Are just a little late.

OUR CONGRESS

The members of our Congress are . . . The men and women great . . . Who go to Washington each year . . . From each and every state . . . The many representatives . . . Including old and new . . . The pompous senators who are . . . Comparatively few . . . They sponsor resolutions and . . . The bills they introduce . . . And after many arguments . . . They try to reach a truce . . . Of course there are the cloakrooms and . . . The lobbies by the score . . . Infrequent filibusters and . . . The deals behind a door . . . But Congress is the color of . . . Our democratic way . . . A system that has never failed . . . And that is here to stay.

TALK TO STRANGERS

I like to talk to strangers who . . . Are gentle and polite . . . Because it always helps to pass . . . The time of day or night . . . It broadens my philosophy . . . Of life on every hand . . . And teaches me to analyze . . . And try to understand . . . But many times the one who has . . . An unfamiliar name . . . Is somebody who merely wants . . . To argue or to blame . . . Who does not ever sympathize . . . Or give the slightest smile . . . But who believes that nothing now . . . Is really worth our while . . . And so I study carefully . . . The stranger on the street . . . Before I take another chance . . . On triumph or defeat.

OUR HEALTH

We seldom think about our health . . . Or give it proper care
. . . Until some illness comes along . . . To make our minds aware
. . . And then we get to thinking and . . . We worry and we
fret . . . And buy up all the medicine . . . And pills that we can
get . . . We lie in bed and we bemoan . . . Our horrifying fate
. . . And wonder whether life will last . . . Or if it is too late . . .
When all along we could have been . . . Concerned a little more
. . . And kept ourselves in shape to work . . . And win our every
war . . . Our health is more important than . . . The many things
we do . . . Indeed we have to have its help . . . To see each project through.

THE GODLY WAY

The Godly way of life on earth . . . Is being good and true . . .
Sincere and fair and generous . . . In everything we do . . . It is
the path of friendship and . . . Of kind and loving care . . . Not
just for kin and neighbor but . . . For people everywhere . . . The
road of daily sacrifice . . . Unselfishness and pain . . . Where we
may help some other soul . . . To its eternal gain . . . The Godly
way is paved with thorns . . . Of time and energy . . . And with
the trials that beset . . . The whole community . . . But if we
keep in sight the goal . . . That we are working toward . . . We
may be sure that God will give . . . His wonderful reward.

ONLY YOU

There never was or will be . . . Another one like you . . . Another one to thrill me . . . And make my dreams come true . . .
You are so captivating . . . You take my breath away . . . And I
am always waiting . . . For every word you say . . . You are my
inspiration . . . For every song I sing . . . And every celebration
. . . I keep remembering . . . My minutes and my hours . . . Belong to you, my sweet . . . And all of them are flowers . . . I lay
before your feet . . . I see the stars above you . . . As bright as
they can be . . . And in my heart I love you . . . And hold you
close to me.

I THANK MY FRIENDS

I thank the many friends I have . . . For all they do for me . . .
With their encouragement and with . . . Their faithful company
. . . They sympathize when I am sad . . . They lift me when I
fall . . . And they are always at my side . . . To heed my beck and
call . . . Indeed they are the truest friends . . . That anyone could
find . . . And that is why their faces are . . . Forever in my mind
. . . And that is why their special names . . . Are ever in my heart
. . . And why I treasure them and hope . . . That we shall never
part . . . I thank my friends eternally . . . Who are so good and
true . . . And hope that I may serve them with . . . The deeds I
try to do.

THE MONTH OF GOD

December is the month of God . . . In quite a special way . . .
Because it holds the beauty and . . . The joy of Christmas Day
. . . It tells again the story of . . . The Child the shepherds saw
. . . Where Mary and where Joseph knelt . . . Beside a bed of
straw . . . In poverty and humbleness . . . With little warmth for
them . . . Beyond the shining glory of . . . The Star of Bethlehem
. . . December is the time of year . . . To live in peace and love
. . . And give our gratitude for all . . . Our blessings from above
. . . Indeed it is the month of God . . . When all the world
should be . . . United in the cheerful bonds . . . Of boundless
charity.

OUT OF LINE

When I am waiting in a line . . . I see a bit of red . . . As someone brazenly attempts . . . To wiggle in ahead . . . Invariably
this he or she . . . Will see a certain friend . . . And get in front of
him instead . . . Of starting at the end . . . In stores and cafeterias
. . . And at the movies too . . . These parasites are right on hand
. . . To show their colors true . . . They think that they are
mighty smart . . . To beat the others out . . . But they should hear
the choice remarks . . . When they are talked about . . . For they
are strictly moochers whom . . . Their neighbors all reject . . .
Because they are so selfish and . . . They have no self-respect.

NURSE'S PRAYER

I pray that I will ever be . . . A good and faithful nurse . . . And
help each patient to get well . . . Or keep from growing worse . . .
To aid the doctor and obey . . . The orders I receive . . . And
always be available . . . And willing to relieve . . . And when my
country calls me in . . . The hour of a war . . . I pray that I will be
prepared . . . To serve on sea or shore . . . To heal the sick and
wounded and . . . Attend the lame and blind . . . And comfort
those whose nerves are frayed . . . Or who are ill of mind . . . I
ask for strength and courage and . . . That I may never fail . . .
To honor God, my uniform . . . And Florence Nightingale.

BUSINESS BALANCE

Along about this time of year . . . It is the same old story . . .
Of balancing the business books . . . By taking inventory . . . By
checking all the merchandise . . . And marking every debit . . .
And digging through the paid-up bills . . . To find another credit
. . . There are accounts receivable . . . In statements still out-
standing . . . And those deductions for the cost . . . Of building
and expanding . . . And then there is the sinking fund . . .
Against depreciation . . . And there are stocks and dividends . . .
And bonus computation . . . And after that and just about . . .
The time that one relaxes . . . There is the horrifying thought
. . . Of governmental taxes.

KRISTINA DEAR

Kristina loves the flowers and . . . The grasses and the trees . . .
And in her little heart she holds . . . A thousand memories . . .
The pictures of the pleasant past . . . That time has tucked away
. . . To bless the happy childhood that . . . Is still her own today
. . . She loves her two big brothers and . . . Her mother and her
dad . . . Her home and all the neighborhood . . . Where life is
good and glad . . . And as we watch her growing up . . . In
sweetness, charm, and grace . . . We cherish every golden smile
. . . That lights her lovely face . . . And in the miracle of life . . .
That she is really here . . . We say a prayer of thanks to God . . .
For our Kristina dear.

OUR CALENDAR

Each night and day in every way . . . I love you more and more
. . . Because you are the only one . . . I constantly adore . . . You
are the current calendar . . . I hang upon the wall . . . Where
every date with you is one . . . I treasure and recall . . . And now
another calendar . . . Is just about to end . . . And there are
special sentiments . . . That I would like to send . . . So I have
marked the months and weeks . . . And all the days to be . . . As
those my heart is hoping will . . . Belong to you and me . . . I
want your coming calendar . . . To have my own design . . . So
you may share whatever dream . . . And happiness are mine.

ALL UNTO GOD

Whatever else this life may seem . . . To hold for you and me
. . . There is but one, eternal God . . . And one eternity . . . And
only as we worship Him . . . And bow before His throne . . . May
we enjoy the blessings and . . . The benefits we own . . . The roof
and walls that shelter us . . . Against the storms that rage . . . And
all that spells security . . . According to our age . . . Because whatever we achieve . . . And put upon our shelf . . . Is finally and
happily . . . A gift from God Himself . . . So let us love our Lord
and God . . . And let us try to be . . . His good and faithful
followers . . . For all eternity.

PEACH

A peach is such a luscious thing . . . When it is ripe to eat . . .
And in so many different ways . . . It is a special treat . . . You
have it sliced on cereal . . . Or in a dish of cream . . . Inside a
jellied salad or . . . Upon a cake supreme . . . It fills the bushel
baskets from . . . The orchards here and there . . . Or comes in
cans to stock the shelves . . . Of grocers everywhere . . . The
peach provides delicious juice . . . And it contains a stone . . .
That youngsters carve or use to start . . . An orchard of their own
. . . And in the conversation of . . . Our youthful social whirl . . .
It is the definition of . . . A very pretty girl.

CIVIC LEADER

The civic leader is the one . . . Who really tries to be . . . Of
service to the folks in his . . . Or her community . . . Who studies
all the problems and . . . The ways and means at hand . . . To
fill the cup of every need . . . And meet the least demand . . .
Who gives unselfishly of time . . . And energy and brain . . . For
all the common welfare and . . . For everybody's gain . . . Not
just today, tomorrow, or . . . Throughout the current year . . .
But every dawn and every night . . . That he or she is here . . . To
be of help to others and . . . Inspire them to be . . . The future
civic leaders in . . . The same community.

OUR HEARTS MUST WAIT

I know your heart is lonely and . . . You know that mine is too
. . . But what is there this side of earth . . . That you or I can
do? . . . I cannot walk across the sea . . . Or overpass the land
. . . To see your loving smile again . . . And hold your gentle
hand . . . I cannot turn the clock around . . . To bring the hour
near . . . And I have not the magic wand . . . To make the
weather clear . . . And so we have to save our dreams . . . While
we are still apart . . . And live on silent messages . . . That warm
the waiting heart . . . But there will be a morning when . . . The
shore will anchor ships . . . And when your charms will fill my
arms . . . And I shall kiss your lips.

GOD, MAKE ME GOOD

Dear God, I hope today will be . . . The best I ever spent . . .
For every friend and neighbor and . . . To serve my government
. . . I pray that You will be with me . . . In all I do or say . . .
And never let me hesitate . . . Or fall along the way . . . Inspire
me to serve You, God . . . With all my heart and soul . . . And
make each sacrifice I need . . . To reach my richest goal . . . To
earn my pass to Paradise . . . And happiness with You . . . Where
all the angels sing their songs . . . And holy dreams come true . . .
Enable me to put away . . . The sinful side of me . . . And grant
that I may be with You . . . For all eternity.

PENCIL

The pencil is an instrument . . . That human beings use . . . To carry on their daily tasks . . . Or merely to amuse . . . It serves the scholar young or old . . . The doctor and the clerk . . . The banker, engineer, and judge . . . And all who ever work . . . The salesman and stenographer . . . Reporter, racketeer . . . Accountant, farmer, laundryman . . . And preachers far and near . . . The pencil drafts the speeches and . . . The treaties that are made . . . And writes the notes anonymous . . . Of those who are afraid . . . Of course at times it makes mistakes . . . In office, home, or shop . . . But that is why it carries an . . . Eraser at the top.

CLOTHIER

He makes or sells the garments and . . . The goods that people wear . . . For gentlemen to be more neat . . . And ladies to be fair . . . He has to know the quality . . . Of all the merchandise . . . And take the proper measurements . . . And sometimes take them twice . . . He must convince the customer . . . That when it comes to cost . . . The bargain that is overlooked . . . May be forever lost . . . Sometimes the buyer has complaints . . . And things must be repaired . . . And sometimes there are shortages . . . And tempers must be spared . . . But every clothier tries to show . . . That friendly, winning smile . . . And no one is more competent . . . To keep the world in style.

PHONE BOOK

The telephone directory . . . Is such a useful thing . . . Not just to call a number and . . . To listen to it ring . . . Not just to dial and to hear . . . What other people say . . . Or tune in on a record that . . . Will tell the time of day . . . But also when you want to write . . . Without the need to guess . . . At someone's place of business or . . . A residence address . . . And when you want to buy or sell . . . Without much energy . . . Or when you have to summon help . . . In some emergency . . . The phone book is an index to . . . The more convenient things . . . The very best of service and . . . The friendliest of rings.

I THANK THEM ALL

So many friends have touched my life . . . In one way or another . . . I feel that everybody is . . . My sister or my brother . . . They all have been so good to me . . . That each has been a blessing . . . And boundless is the gratitude . . . That I would be expressing . . . I thank them for the kindness of . . . Their smallest commendation . . . And every criticism that . . . Has been an inspiration . . . I thank them for their letters that . . . Have brought me so much pleasure . . . And for their dear companionship . . . That I will always treasure . . . I cannot pay them back in full . . . However much I serve them . . . But with the best that I can do . . . I hope I may deserve them.

MY WIFE AND I

My wife is very fond of me . . . And I am fond of her . . . But there are things that she enjoys . . . And those that I prefer . . . And she would like to have her way . . . When I am wanting mine . . . And that is why our moods and plans . . . Are never quite in line . . . She wants to sit and talk with me . . . When I would rather write . . . And when I sleep I wish that she . . . Would please put out the light . . . She window-shops when I am in . . . A hurry to get home . . . And when she hugs an easy chair . . . I get the urge to roam . . . It seems we never quite agree . . . On when to work or play . . . And yet somehow we get along . . . And stay in love each day.

BUSINESS CARD

The business card is something that . . . Provides a handy way . . . To reach a person on the phone . . . Throughout the working day . . . Or else to find the firm's address . . . When sending letters out . . . Or visiting the premises . . . With things to talk about . . . It is a memo of a name . . . That might escape the mind . . . Or of a certain restaurant . . . Where happy friends have dined . . . The business card saves time and words . . . And pen and paper too . . . And costs so little in the light . . . Of all that it can do . . . However plain or fancy, it . . . Will often ring the bell . . . For it is such a cordial way . . . To advertise and sell.

DONNIE'S HOBBIES

Our Donnie saves up stamps and coins . . . And streetcar tokens
too . . . As well as famous autographs . . . Of persons old and new
. . . He likes to keep collections and . . . He always wants to
be . . . Informed on everything that has . . . A place in history
. . . And so each time I travel or . . . I walk along the street . . . I
try to get the signatures . . . Of famous folks I meet . . . And
every foreign coin or one . . . That looks a little old . . . Is one
that I admire and . . . That I decide to hold . . . Because each
hobby helps to keep . . . Our Donnie occupied . . . And does so
much to magnify . . . Our pleasure and our pride.

PERSONAL AD

Dear L, please get in touch with me . . . And say that you forgive . . . And say that you will be my friend . . . And help my
heart to live . . . I am so deeply sorry and . . . I really want to do
. . . As much as I am able, dear . . . To make it up to you . . . I
love you and adore you and . . . I want you to be mine . . . And
only in your image will . . . The sun forever shine . . . I treasure
all your whispers and . . . The letters that you sent . . . Because I
know each sentence was . . . A message that you meant . . . Please
phone me, dear, or write a note . . . And in your own way say . . .
That you are still in love with me . . . Your own—forever—J.

OUR HONOR

There is no greater glory than . . . The honor that we bear . . .
Among our friends and relatives . . . And people everywhere . . .
The honor of our loyal heart . . . In joy and tragedy . . . Our
honesty and fairness and . . . Dependability . . . For what is there
to gain from wealth . . . And from financial fame . . . To match
the golden tribute of . . . A good and worthy name? . . . Mere
money melts and flattery fades . . . Our armor gathers rust . . .
And towers tremble in the dark . . . And crumble into dust . . .
But virtue lives forever and . . . The noble deeds we do . . . Are
lamps that light the deepest cave . . . And gleam the whole night
through.

ACTIVE KRISTINA

Kristina climbs up on a chair . . . And then on top the table
. . . And tries to be an acrobat . . . As much as she is able . . . She
runs around from room to room . . . And somersaults and dances
. . . And all the while she hopes and looks . . . For our approving
glances . . . Of course she likes to exercise . . . But I might also
mention . . . That little girls are slightly vain . . . And they enjoy
attention . . . They want to have the pleasure and . . . The perfect satisfaction . . . Of being very pretty and . . . The center of
attraction . . . And probably Kristina is . . . No different from the
others . . . But I adore her on my lap . . . And when she jumps on
Mother's.

POMPOUS PERSON

He wears the latest fashion from . . . The bottom to the top
. . . His nails are pretty and he smells . . . Just like a barbershop
. . . He hails a taxi or he waits . . . To ride his chauffeured car
. . . While blowing rings of vapor from . . . His fifty-cent cigar . . .
His head is far above the clouds . . . His feet are off the ground
. . . And there is nobody who dares . . . To order him around . . .
He does not thrive on vitamins . . . Of brain or energy . . . But he
survives on compliments . . . And feasts on flattery . . . And
usually he goes his way . . . And he is unaware . . . That every
seat he occupies . . . Is still an empty chair.

GOD WILLING

The joys and sorrows of this life . . . Are neither strange nor
odd . . . Because they are the symbols that . . . Reflect the will of
God . . . We have a freedom of our own . . . To choose the way
we walk . . . And only we ourselves may move . . . The lips and
tongue that talk . . . But God designed the sun and moon . . .
And gave the stars their light . . . And He ordained the brightest
day . . . Beyond the darkest night . . . He has a certain master
plan . . . For all humanity . . . That moves along the channels of
. . . Success and tragedy . . . And so whatever smiles or tears . . .
Pursue the path we plod . . . We must perceive that life itself . . .
Is by the grace of God.

RESTFUL WORK

It always seems enjoyable . . . To rest and to relax . . . And put
aside the duties that . . . So often strain and tax . . . And yet
when I am idle or . . . The work is very light . . . I always feel
fatigued and worn . . . As I go home at night . . . And every time
throughout the day . . . That there is any lag . . . The seconds are
like minutes and . . . The hours sort of drag . . . But when my
hands are busy and . . . I struggle and I try . . . The hardest task
is easy and . . . The moments really fly . . . And somehow when
the day is done . . . I feel my very best . . . And not the least bit
tired or . . . In need of any rest.

POSTAGE STAMP

The postage stamp is used to send . . . A letter on its way . . .
So it will reach the addressee . . . Without the least delay . . . We
lick it and we stick it on . . . The envelope we seal . . . To guard
the messages that we . . . Would rather not reveal . . . Or else
our fingers fasten it . . . On packages and such . . . So Uncle Sam
may see at once . . . That we have paid that much . . . Sometimes
we miss the right amount . . . Because we merely guess . . . And
our dispatch should carry more . . . Or it could go for less . . . At
any rate the price we pay . . . Is just a minor cost . . . Considering
the service and . . . How little mail is lost.

ROSES IN SEPTEMBER

I know that roses bloom in June . . . In April and July . . . In
January and in March . . . According to the sky . . . And there
are roses every month . . . Each season of the year . . . To offer
fond remembrance of . . . A special smile or tear . . . But now it
is September and . . . The roses at your feet . . . Are those that
blossom in my heart . . . Because you are so sweet . . . They are
the roses red and white . . . That I present to you . . . Around my
wish that all your dreams . . . Will soon be coming true . . . My
roses in September are . . . The flowers I have grown . . . With
all my love and every hope . . . That you will be my own.

PIANO TUNER

He takes away the top and back . . . And then he tries the keys
. . . To see if our piano plays . . . The proper melodies . . . He
seems to have a thousand tools . . . And yet they seem as one
. . . Because of the uncanny way . . . He gets his duty done . . .
He pounces on a single note . . . Until our eardrums ring . . .
And suddenly the music swells . . . As only angels sing . . . He is
at once a craftsman who . . . Pursues his humble trade . . . And
some immortal genius who . . . Has never really played . . . But
when at last he goes away . . . And leaves his friendly smile . . .
We feel that our piano will . . . Endure a long, long while.

POT HOLDER

It is a piece of padded cloth . . . To hold a heated pot . . .
But sometimes it is something more . . . And really means a lot
. . . Not just because the fabric is . . . A texture soft and fine . . .
Or just because of color or . . . Of beautiful design . . . Nor is the
cost important in . . . The sense of value true . . . According to
appearance or . . . What it is fit to do . . . But sometimes it is
woven in . . . The hours that are spent . . . By friendly hands that
long to say . . . Their loving sentiment . . . And then each stitch
of thread or yarn . . . Is like another knot . . . That joins the
warmth of hand and heart . . . With every heated pot.

POST-MORTEM

Last Saturday's collegiate game . . . Is fought again today . . .
By all who get together and . . . Review it play by play . . . Of
course it is not quite the same . . . As football records show . . .
Because there are some errors that . . . Officials did not know
. . . And then there were some breaks to which . . . Opponents
had no right . . . In view of how the hometown boys . . . Put up a
valiant fight . . . A thousand ifs are talked about . . . And if they
had not been . . . The other team would not have had . . . The
lousy luck to win . . . But when the hotheads simmer down . . .
The alibis grow pale . . . Because the game is over and . . . The
scoreboard tells the tale.

BOY SCOUT DONNIE

Our Donnie is a Boy Scout now . . . And that is what he likes
. . . Especially the camping trips . . . And when he goes on hikes
. . . And we are truly happy and . . . We think that it is fine . . .
But now and then we sort of wish . . . That we could draw the
line . . . For when those expeditions start . . . He gives us quite a
fit . . . With all the stuff he has to get . . . To fill his Boy Scout
kit . . . The beans, spaghetti, and the eggs . . . The bacon and
the bread . . . The tent and all the blankets for . . . His pioneer-
ing bed . . . Well, by the time we satisfy . . . His every want and
need . . . We feel that we have really done . . . Our daily Boy
Scout deed.

REMEMBER, SWEET?

Do you remember when we met . . . One evening at a dance
. . . And how I was enchanted by . . . Your first delightful glance?
. . . Do you remember what I said . . . And what your lips replied . . . And how I hungered in my heart . . . To linger at your
side? . . . It was a magic moment, sweet . . . That made my
dreams come true . . . And all the sky was like a shawl . . . Of
silver and of blue . . . We left the crowd and strolled away . . .
Beyond the slightest sound . . . And life was like a paradise . . .
With beauty all around . . . I know that you remember, sweet
. . . And in my grateful heart . . . The love that you have given
me . . . Will never grow apart.

GOD'S HELP

However much I try to do . . . In moments bright or dim . . . I
know that all my courage and . . . My strength depend on Him
. . . I know my God is watching me . . . And helping me each
day . . . And He is always interested . . . In every prayer I say
. . . He gives me grace and fortitude . . . But He expects of me
. . . My share of faithful gratitude . . . And loving sympathy . . .
He wants me to obey His word . . . As ably as I can . . . And be of
willing service to . . . My every fellowman . . . I know my courage
and my strength . . . Depend on God each day . . . And He is
always kind enough . . . To help me on my way.

COPY BOY

The copy boy is one who learns . . . The journalistic game . . .
By starting at the bottom of . . . The ladder to his fame . . . He
carries rewrite stories to . . . The desk and to the slot . . . And
stands and waits for copy when . . . The news is extra hot . . . He
also gets the cigarettes . . . The coffee and the rolls . . . That help
remind the local staff . . . That they have human souls . . . For
him there is no glory and . . . Indeed no handsome pay . . . But
if he perseveres he will . . . Behold a better day . . . The day the
city editor . . . Decides to try him out . . . With who, what,
where, and when and why . . . The news is all about.

SO GOES THE WORLD

In every store and office and . . . In every factory . . . There
seems to be a great amount . . . Of greed and jealousy . . . In
government and business and . . . Athletics and in class . . .
There is a scheme behind the dream . . . To conquer and to pass
. . . To beat the other fellow and . . . To grab the winning place
. . . Regardless of the ethics or . . . Of decency and grace . . .
Instead of being neighborly . . . And generous and fair . . . And
giving each competitor . . . His just and equal share . . . And
thus the country carries on . . . Its selfish history . . . With all the
false encouragement . . . Of greed and jealousy.

SINCERELY YOURS

There are so many words of love . . . I want to say to you . . .
And special deeds to please your heart . . . That I would like to
do . . . There are so many wishes and . . . So many dreams to
share . . . And all the other ways to tell . . . How much I truly
care . . . And I could buy you presents, dear . . . And promise
you the moon . . . And I could fashion you a song . . . Around a
perfect tune . . . But all I ever think about . . . Is just to let you
know . . . That I adore you every day . . . And it is really so . . .
That you mean more than every breath . . . And all the atmosphere . . . And I could never be more sure . . . And never more
sincere.

GOODNESS IS EASY

It is so easy to be good . . . If only we will try . . . And everything is brighter when . . . The sun is in the sky . . . While evil draws the darkness and . . . The shadows that are long . . . And there is never happiness . . . In doing what is wrong . . . It may provide some pleasure and . . . Some comfort here and there . . . But it is bound to bring regret . . . And possibly despair . . . In goodness there is peace of mind . . . In sinfulness is fear . . . And there is no success unless . . . We have a conscience clear . . . For God decreed the goal of life . . . And how to play the game . . . And if we violate the rules . . . We have to take the blame.

C.P.A.

The certified accountant is . . . The one who verifies . . . The profits or the losses of . . . Your business enterprise . . . He checks the books and records for . . . A salary or fee . . . And generally is noted for . . . His skill and accuracy . . . He may have studied privately . . . Or in a college class . . . But there are special state exams . . . That he has had to pass . . . You hire him to figure out . . . The tax you have to pay . . . And back your published statements with . . . His fame as C.P.A. . . . Unless he works for Uncle Sam . . . And is the one who looks . . . For evidence that somebody . . . Has falsified the books.

KRISTINA LOVES US

Kristina says when she grows up . . . She will not want to roam . . . Because she loves her mommy and . . . Her daddy and her home . . . She says that she may marry and . . . Have children by the score . . . But only if she lives with us . . . Or has a house next door . . . Of course her age is only five . . . And she may change her mind . . . But what if she should carry out . . . The plan she has defined? . . . I'm not so sure that Mommy dear . . . And I would welcome it . . . Because the chances are that we . . . Would have to baby-sit . . . And who can tell what other tasks . . . And clever little schemes . . . Would come from our Kristina and . . . The hero of her dreams.

HE DIED FOR US

Upon a hill called Calvary . . . They nailed Him to a cross . . .
And there were those who never knew . . . Their overwhelming
loss . . . And there are those who live today . . . In ignorance and
shame . . . Who do not honor or respect . . . The glory of His
name . . . But He was God who died for us . . . With thorns
around His head . . . And He was Jesus, Son of God . . . Who
suffered and Who bled . . . He showed the way to Heaven and
. . . He opened wide the door . . . To love and peace and holiness
. . . And joy forevermore . . . So let us kneel before His cross . . .
And worship at His side . . . And let us sorrow for the sins . . .
For which our Saviour died.

PRESS CLUB

The press club is that sacred spot . . . Where journalists may
meet . . . To talk about the weather or . . . Deplore their daily
beat . . . To sympathize or argue or . . . Express the private views
. . . For which there is no proper place . . . When they present
the news . . . Where publishers, photographers . . . And cub reporters go . . . For dinner and refreshments or . . . To see a talent
show . . . Or just to fill an easy chair . . . And happily relax . . .
In snores and dreams that plainly seem . . . To scorn the world of
facts . . . The press club is the habitat . . . Of those who strive to
write . . . And who maintain or quench the flame . . . Of literary
light.

THE OFFICE

The office is a place to work . . . And not to powder noses . . .
And where one does as he is told . . . And not as he proposes
. . . Where clocks are not for eyes to watch . . . But rather as a
warning . . . To hurry up production and . . . To be on time each
morning . . . The office telephone is there . . . To answer business
queries . . . And not to use for making dates . . . Or gossiping
with dearies . . . While paper, pencil, pen, and ink . . . Are meant
for calculations . . . And not for drawing doodle bugs . . . Or
writing to relations . . . The office is a place to work . . . With
little intermission . . . But where results and loyalty . . . Receive
their recognition.

APRON

The apron is an article . . . That girls and women wear . . .
When there is housework to be done . . . Or dinner to prepare
. . . It keeps their dresses neat and clean . . . And it is pretty too
. . . Especially the frilly kind . . . The fancy and the new . . .
On ladies young it is a sign . . . They do not care to roam . . . But
they would rather dust and sweep . . . And fill their place at home
. . . It is the shining symbol of . . . Their wish to do their part
. . . And always serve their loved ones with . . . A true and hum-
ble heart . . . And when a certain apron is . . . A gift from some-
one dear . . . It means so much and helps so much . . . To add
a world of cheer.

MY SOUL IS SOFT

I wish that I could be a saint . . . In everything I do . . . A
perfect creature—good, sincere . . . And generous and true . . . A
human being with the strength . . . To conquer every strife . . .
And bear the crosses that become . . . The Godly way of life . . .
But many times my heart is frail . . . My soul is soft and weak
. . . And I ignore the nobler things . . . I know I ought to seek
. . . I yield to some temptation and . . . Commit another sin . . .
And then I lose the spirit and . . . The confidence to win . . .
Except I keep my faith in God . . . Because I know that He
. . . Is always willing to forgive . . . And help and comfort me.

DEAREST DADDY

I love you, dearest Daddy, for . . . Your many gifts to me . . .
And for the father and the pal . . . That you have tried to be
. . . For all the nickels and the dimes . . . The movies and the
toys . . . The circuses and candy and . . . A thousand other joys
. . . For parties and for picnics and . . . The meals that Mommy
makes . . . The turkey, ham, and chicken and . . . The luscious
pies and cakes . . . But mostly for the way you work . . . Each
moment of the day . . . To feed and clothe and comfort me . . .
Along my youthful way . . . And for the noble character . . . You
struggle to instil . . . That I may keep my faith in God . . . And
all your hopes fulfill.

DEAREST MOTHER

There is no flower fair enough . . . Or box of candy sweet . . .
To give the gratitude that I . . . Would offer at your feet . . .
There is no song so heavenly . . . Or word of praise sincere
. . . Sufficient to express my love . . . For you, my mother dear
. . . You are the angel of my life . . . The guardian of my youth
. . . And every inspiration for . . . Fidelity and truth . . . I turn
to you in trouble and . . . You smile and comfort me . . . Indeed
your heart is always filled . . . With love and sympathy . . . God
bless you, dearest Mother, and . . . May all your dreams come true
. . . I love you and I thank you and . . . I think the world of you.

POCKET OF LOVE

Each time I see your picture, dear . . . I seem to hear it say . . .
That you remember me as much . . . As every yesterday . . . And
that is more than frequently . . . Because I find your face . . . On
every wall and mirror and . . . In nearly every place . . . But most
of all I keep you in . . . The pocket of my heart . . . Where I can
dream that you are mine . . . And we will never part . . . I kiss
you in the sunshine and . . . I hold you in the rain . . . And everything is wonderful . . . And nothing is in vain . . . And though
the walls may vanish and . . . The mirrors disappear . . . Inside
the pocket of my heart . . . Your face will linger, dear.

CREDIT FIRM

The credit organization strives . . . To keep a constant file . . .
On what your income is and how . . . You try to live in style . . .
How prompt you are in paying bills . . . Or possibly how slow
. . . And whether you deserve to have . . . A rating high or low
. . . Of course it cannot always get . . . The fullest facts on you
. . . And now and then the trade reports . . . Are not precisely
true . . . And now and then at first approach . . . It has to take a
chance . . . According to the wisdom of . . . Its judgment at a
glance . . . Indeed its task is difficult . . . And it may get the
blame . . . If it gives too much credit to . . . Your pocketbook or
name.

ONLY VISITORS

The world is so important to . . . The youngsters of today . . .
That sometimes it must seem to them . . . That they are here to
stay . . . They strive for pleasure and success . . . With all their
hearts and souls . . . And nothing matters much to them . . .
Beyond their earthly goals . . . But we who watch the sun go
down . . . And long to have our rest . . . Are not so much concerned about . . . The ordinary quest . . . We understand that
everything . . . Belongs at last to God . . . And we are only
visitors . . . Who cultivate the sod . . . We know that we are only
here . . . To help the world go on . . . And try to be deserving of
. . . The everlasting dawn.

STEER CLEAR

Vacation days are here again . . . The lakes and mountains call
. . . And one way or another there . . . Is happiness for all . . .
But also there is tragedy . . . That lurks along the road . . . For
those who make no effort to . . . Obey the traffic code . . . Who
try to hog the highway and . . . Who never dim a light . . . Or
throttle down when hills or curves . . . Are coming into sight . . .
There will be many accidents . . . And many hurt or killed . . .
And laughter on a childish lip . . . Will be forever stilled . . . Un-
less we watch the winding road . . . And exercise more care . . .
And in a sober manner take . . . Our time in getting there.

KRISTINA HIDES

Kristina likes to hide from me . . . Without a sound or stir . . .
And she is always happy when . . . I go to look for her . . . And
so I roam from room to room . . . And peek in every place . . . To
find my little five-year-old . . . And kiss her pretty face . . . Of
course I have to make some noise . . . And I must call her name
. . . Because she knows as well as I . . . That it is just a game . . .
I keep right on pretending and . . . I help Kristina play . . . Until
she starts to giggle and . . . She gives herself away . . . And then I
find her instantly . . . And take her in my arms . . . And tell her
there is no one else . . . Who has so many charms.

POET'S PRAYER

O God, if I may sing the songs . . . That fill my soul today . . .
And if my music may be soft . . . Inspiring and gay . . . And if the
pictures that I paint . . . In rhythm and in rhyme . . . May please,
encourage, and console . . . The people of our time . . . Then
give Your blessing to the muse . . . That haunts and follows me
. . . And guide my pen across the page . . . Of life and memory
. . . Give me the grace to lead them through . . . Your wondrous
universe . . . To teach Your everlasting love . . . And all their
fears disperse . . . Help me to serve Your creatures, God . . . To
make their dreams come true . . . And in my small and humble
way . . . To praise and honor You.

LOYAL FRIEND

However I may meet the dawn . . . Or how the day may
end . . . I do not fear my fortune if . . . I have a faithful friend
. . . A friend to share my thoughts with me . . . And tell me all
his own . . . To keep each other company . . . And never feel
alone . . . I do not mind the loudest storm . . . Or any vale of
tears . . . As long as there is friendship true . . . To treasure
through the years . . . A smile of welcome at the door . . . A hand
to hold in mine . . . And friendly footsteps on the floor . . . When
it is time to dine . . . There is no borrowed sorrow and . . . There
is no grief to lend . . . As long as I have somebody . . . Who is a
faithful friend.

STARS IN MY CUP

When I have tea or coffee and . . . The stars are in the sky . . .
I dream of all the hours, love . . . That we are passing by . . . The
moments made for beauty and . . . The happiness of heart . . .
That would be all our own to share . . . If we were not apart . . .
And when I chance to drop my gaze . . . Instead of looking up
. . . I seem to see the silver stars . . . Reflected in my cup . . .
Each one of them is like a gem . . . Magnificent and new . . .
And every little sparkle is . . . A memory of you . . . And when I
lift the vessel, love . . . And drink in silent sips . . . I only taste the
lusciousness . . . Of your delightful lips.

CREDIT MANAGER

The credit manager is one . . . Who has to know his task . . .
And when to give or to refuse . . . The credit people ask . . . And
when to turn the faucet off . . . Or graciously extend . . . The
time in which the payment due . . . Must reach its final end . . .
It may be just a small account . . . At some convenient store . . .
Or it may be a business deal . . . Where doubtful debits soar
. . . But always he must keep informed . . . And he must be alert
. . . To see that everything goes well . . . And nobody gets hurt
. . . And only as he does his job . . . And struggles to be fair . . .
Will everybody prosper and . . . Receive his equal share.

JOY IN FRIENDSHIP

In friendship there is happiness . . . That draws the night away
. . . And ushers in the sunshine of . . . A new and brighter day
. . . It takes away the teardrops and . . . The rain along the street
. . . And substitutes a welcome warm . . . Wherever souls may
meet . . . In friendship there is comfort and . . . No cause to be
afraid . . . And there are flowers soft and fair . . . And stars that
never fade . . . And there are hopes that fill the heart . . . And
dreams that never die . . . As surely as the world is round . . .
And God is in the sky . . . And there are frames and picture books
. . . That hold the happy past . . . Of faithful love and promises
. . . As long as life may last.

TIME FOR LUNCH

When we get good and hungry in . . . The middle of the day
. . . We hurry out to patronize . . . Our favorite café . . . It may
be quite a fancy place . . . Or just a common stand . . . Where
coffee and a barbecue . . . Are taken right in hand . . . Or else a
cafeteria . . . Where we must wait our turn . . . To choose our
food according to . . . The money that we earn . . . Perhaps we
count our pennies and . . . Perhaps we do not care . . . About
the cost of any dish . . . Upon the bill of fare . . . But there is no
suggestion and . . . There is no wish or hunch . . . That pleases
anybody more . . . Than taking time for lunch.

GLORIOUS FOURTH

Today is Independence Day . . . And all throughout the land
. . . The stars and stripes are flying high . . . And folks are feeling
grand . . . It is the time to celebrate . . . Our glory in the sun . . .
From all the fights for human rights . . . That we have waged and
won . . . We are entitled to be proud . . . Of every victory . . .
And all our efforts in behalf . . . Of peace and liberty . . . By
land and sea, and in the air . . . Against whatever blow . . . Our
good and great United States . . . Have never ceased to grow
. . . So let us now salute the flag . . . And cheer the roaring guns
. . . And pray that God will always bless . . . Our fathers and our
sons.

SO GENTLE AND SINCERE

Each minute of my life on earth . . . Has sixty seconds, dear
. . . In which to thank you for your love . . . So gentle and sincere
. . . To put my arms around you and . . . To hold you close to me
. . . And whisper softly to your heart . . . My joy and ecstasy . . .
The happiness that you bestow . . . With every word and smile
. . . And every inspiration deep . . . To make my life worth while
. . . And every second on this earth . . . I do express to you
. . . My gratitude for all the dreams . . . That you have made
come true . . . And yet I know that what I say . . . Is not suffi-
cient, dear . . . To thank you for your boundless love . . . So
gentle and sincere.

SMUG AND SELFISH

Some people who direct their sights . . . To goals they never
reach . . . Are those who will not sacrifice . . . Or practice what
they preach . . . They dream of some tomorrow while . . . Today
is young and new . . . And they are not concerned about . . .
What other people do . . . They will not paint the future on . . .
The canvas of today . . . Because they have their own ideas . . .
Of progress and of play . . . And while they seem to be so smart
. . . In all they undertake . . . They never do a worthy deed . . .
For someone else's sake . . . They figure up their prominence
. . . With their financial sums . . . And they demand their loaf of
bread . . . Including all the crumbs.

D. A.

The prosecutor for the state . . . Or U. S. Government . . . is
usually deserving of . . . The money that is spent . . . He tries to
do his best to see . . . That justice will prevail . . . And only guilty
citizens . . . Are fined or sent to jail . . . He has to keep the laws
enforced . . . Whatever they may be . . . And whether folks are
rich or poor . . . In their community . . . His public brief case
must be filled . . . With all the legal tricks . . . And in addition he
must play . . . His part in politics . . . Indeed it is a trying job . . .
At no enormous pay . . . And everybody ought to back . . . The
brave and good D. A.

HELP ME TO SMILE

Give me a cheerful spirit, God . . . Inspire me to smile . . .
That I may help a weary world . . . Along each passing mile . . . I
want to be an optimist . . . And gaze beyond the rain . . . Instead
of always looking for . . . Some reason to complain . . . I want to
greet my fellowmen . . . With faith and courage true . . . And
with the confidence they need . . . In everything they do . . . Enable me to hide my fears . . . If any I possess . . . That I may lift
each lonely heart . . . With hope and happiness . . . Give me the
wisdom and the strength . . . To conquer every strife . . . And
pave the path for others, God . . . To live a cheerful life.

THIS IS MY LOVE

The hills may fade, the stars may fall . . . And we may be apart
. . . But my impassioned love for you . . . Will never leave my
heart . . . My love for you is stronger than . . . The wildest wind
or rain . . . And it will live when life itself . . . Appears to be in
vain . . . Above the roar of chaos and . . . Against the raging sea
. . . And after all the sands of time . . . Have joined eternity . . .
My love is more enduring than . . . The ever-faithful friend . . .
And far beyond the fondest hopes . . . That touch the rainbow's
end . . . And though the universe may burn . . . And melt away
the sky . . . My love for you will be the same . . . And it will
never die.

JIMMIE'S SHIRTS

Our Jimmie has a passion for . . . The latest style in dress . . .
And getting clothes appears to be . . . His key to happiness . . .
He likes a suit of fancy cut . . . A shiny pair of shoes . . . A lot of
sox and quite a bunch . . . Of ties from which to choose . . .
But more than any other thing . . . The shirt is on his mind . . .
Especially the colorful . . . And very sporty kind . . . He goes
around from store to store . . . To gather up the best . . . And
even spends his hard-earned cash . . . To cover up his chest . . .
And that apparently is why . . . His bureau drawers abound . . .
And closet hangers never are . . . Enough to go around.

MY BEST FRIEND

Some friends of mine are old as I . . . And some of them are
new . . . But none of them in any way . . . Could quite compare
with you . . . Because you are so loyal and . . . Considerate and
kind . . . That you are constantly the first . . . And foremost in
my mind . . . You are the one whose special name . . . My telephone would call . . . For something very urgent or . . . For anything at all . . . The same as if you needed me . . . You know you
could depend . . . On all the aid and comfort in . . . My power to
extend . . . You are the friend I treasure and . . . Who means
the most to me . . . For we have formed a partnership . . . Of love
and sympathy.

HE WALKS BESIDE ME

Although I cannot touch His hand . . . Or look upon Him here
. . . I worship God, and in my soul . . . I feel that He is near . . .
He calls me in the morning when . . . The sun is in the sky . . .
He walks beside me through the day . . . While clouds are rolling
by . . . He whispers in the sunset and . . . The silver of a star
. . . And comforts me in all my thoughts . . . No matter what they
are . . . In trial and in sorrow and . . . In every joy and dream
. . . He is my hope eternal and . . . My confidence supreme . . .
And every day I pray that I . . . May give the best in me . . . To
honor and in every way . . . To serve Him faithfully.

PRICE OF PARKING

Whenever I drive into town . . . In daylight or the dark . . . I carefully select the spot . . . Where I decide to park . . . I much prefer the public street . . . (If I can find a space) . . . To any plain or beautiful . . . Commercial parking place . . . Because in most garages and . . . Upon the average lot . . . The treatment that my car receives . . . Is not exactly hot . . . Attendants drive it recklessly . . . Their brains are very few . . . And they are not concerned about . . . The damage that they do . . . It seems to me their bosses would . . . Insist on greater care . . . But either they are unconcerned . . . Or sadly unaware.

THEY OVERWORK

Some people work from dawn to dawn . . . With never any rest . . . To gather glory or the gold . . . To buy the very best . . . And all the while they suffer and . . . They tear the body down . . . Until the head is weary and . . . Too weak to wear a crown . . . It is a sad mistake they make . . . Because they shorten life . . . And do so little to relieve . . . The struggle and the strife . . . Whereas they ought to labor less . . . And take the time to play . . . And happily appreciate . . . The beauty of the day . . . With leisure and with proper rest . . . They could accomplish more . . . And ultimately gain the goal . . . That they are striving for.

TEACHER'S PRAYER

I want to teach my students how . . . To live this life on earth . . . To face its struggle and its strife . . . And to improve their worth . . . Not just the lesson in a book . . . Or how the rivers flow . . . But how to choose the proper path . . . Wherever they may go . . . To understand eternal truth . . . And know the right from wrong . . . And gather all the beauty of . . . A flower and a song . . . For if I help the world to grow . . . In wisdom and in grace . . . Then I shall feel that I have won . . . And I have filled my place . . . And so I ask Your guidance, God . . . That I may do my part . . . For character and confidence . . . And happiness of heart.

TOO MUCH PROFIT

A fair amount of profit should . . . Be made in every deal . . .
But sometimes people get so much . . . That in effect they steal
. . . They try to claim the higher sum . . . Is fully justified . . .
By economic circumstance . . . Or business sense applied . . .
But in their hearts they know that they . . . Have taken in too
much . . . And all because the buyer was . . . A mighty easy touch
. . . It may be their alertness or . . . A good and timely tip . . .
But there are times when profiting . . . Is just another gyp . . .
And though they may go on like that . . . The day is bound to
dawn . . . When suckers will be few and they . . . Will find their
business gone.

TO BRING YOU BACK

When day is done and when the sun . . . Is swallowed by the
sea . . . I pray the stars will guide your ship . . . And bring you
back to me . . . I pray the wind will blow your sail . . . Beyond
the smallest storm . . . And every wave will pillow you . . . To
keep you safe and warm . . . That every lantern will be bright
. . . To lead and light the way . . . And you will anchor safely
in . . . The shelter of our bay . . . The harbor of our happiness
. . . Where every voyage ends . . . And as we share our thoughts
and dreams . . . We are forever friends . . . I pray the moon will
bring its beams . . . To sweep the widest sea . . . And help my
heart to find your ship . . . And bring you back to me.

SNUGGY SLEEPERS

Kristina puts pajamas on . . . When it is time for bed . . . And
they are quite a special kind . . . As we have always said . . . For
they are soft and woolly and . . . They keep her snuggy-warm . . .
Whenever there is snow or sleet . . . Or any windy storm . . . We
call them snuggy sleepers and . . . She loves to have them on . . .
Especially to cuddle up . . . When it is early dawn . . . But when
she eats her breakfast egg . . . And lifts her glass or cup . . . She
always manages somehow . . . To get them spotted up . . . And
when she starts to dress herself . . . She does not seem to care
. . . Because she pulls her snuggies off . . . And throws them anywhere.

DIPLOMAT

The diplomat is one who speaks . . . And strives to win his point . . . Without his larynx or his lung . . . Becoming out of joint . . . His tone is soft and gentle and . . . He has a subtle way . . . Of making black appear as white . . . And changing night to day . . . His words are not dishonest and . . . His pledge is not untrue . . . And yet he is not bound by all . . . He promises to do . . . He struggles for advantages . . . In diplomatic chess . . . To check opponents and insure . . . Political success . . . He is the formal figure in . . . The game of hit and run . . . Who shapes a sacred treaty or . . . Invites the opening gun.

HIS DAILY BLESSING

I see the moon and all the stars . . . And I behold the sun . . . And I consider all my past . . . And what I should have done . . . I know that God created life . . . And in His wondrous way . . . He has bestowed His blessings and . . . His grace from day to day . . . I may have tried to do my best . . . And maybe I have not . . . And there are many happenings . . . That I have long forgot . . . Yet if I start anew today . . . And give my all to Him . . . His love will never leave me and . . . His light will never dim . . . But He will see me safely through . . . The darkest night ahead . . . And with His daily blessing He . . . Will keep me comforted.

FRIENDLESS WORLD

The world would be a sorry place . . . And soon would reach its end . . . If no one knew the happiness . . . Of having found a friend . . . For we would all be strangers in . . . A selfish atmosphere . . . With nobody contributing . . . Good fellowship or cheer . . . There would be no community . . . Of happy songs and smiles . . . But we would walk our separate ways . . . Along the weary miles . . . We would not be concerned about . . . Our neighbor or the poor . . . And every illness great or small . . . Would be our own to cure . . . The world would be a lonely place . . . And reach an early end . . . If everyone ignored the rest . . . And no one had a friend.

DOOR TO DOOR

I sympathize with salesmen who . . . Must go from door to door . . . To gain the meager livelihood . . . That they are striving for . . . They surely earn their daily bread . . . In terms of weary feet . . . And I would like to help them out . . . Whenever they entreat . . . But there are some who ring my bell . . . And try to fill my ear . . . With offers that are dubious . . . Or plainly insincere . . . There are so many rackets in . . . This neighborhood appeal . . . That it is hard to recognize . . . The phony from the real . . . And so although I sympathize . . . I seldom buy a thing . . . From those who pierce my privacy . . . With their soliciting.

VACATION PLANS

I look at all the folders of . . . Vacation trips to take . . . From wooded streams and mountains to . . . The seashore and the lake . . . I visualize the comforts of . . . A ship or luxury train . . . The joy of motor travel and . . . The swiftness of a plane . . . A place to lie beneath the sun . . . And live a life of ease . . . With no responsibility . . . Nor any boss to please . . . A week or two or even three . . . Where life is fun and play . . . And there is never any need . . . To know the time of day . . . There are so many beauty spots . . . Where I would like to roam . . . But when I count my cash on hand . . . I think of staying home.

RAINBOW OF BIKES

I wandered by a school today . . . And I took in the view . . . Of bicycles of red and green . . . And yellow, brown, and blue . . . There seemed to be a thousand bikes . . . Of every make and style . . . That cluttered up the campus for . . . A portion of a mile . . . I noticed all the colors bright . . . But also I beheld . . . The eager boys and girls and all . . . The promises they held . . . I saw the youngsters who would grow . . . And rule the land some day . . . And how much confidence they need . . . To help them on their way . . . And all the colors of their bikes . . . Were like a rainbow bright . . . With Mother, Dad, and Teacher too . . . To keep them going right.

FRIENDLY ENEMY

Not always is an enemy . . . The one to fear or dread . . . For he may be the very one . . . To help us get ahead . . . His criticism may be just . . . And when we read the slate . . . We may discover we are wrong . . . And we deserve his hate . . . Perhaps we caused the enmity . . . Through what was said or done . . . Although in our opinion it . . . Was meant to be in fun . . . An enemy may really be . . . An angel in disguise . . . To whom in all sincerity . . . We should apologize . . . So let us not be vengeful now . . . But let us strive to see . . . The better side of one who seems . . . To be an enemy.

G-MAN

The G-Man is an average man . . . The same as you and I . . . Who has to earn his daily bread . . . And wear a shirt and tie . . . The G is not for Genius or . . . For Glorious or Great . . . But it is meant for Government . . . And shielding every state . . . The G-Man has to study hard . . . And work with all his might . . . And often he must sacrifice . . . The sleep he needs at night . . . He has to be alert and calm . . . And loyal to the core . . . And do the best and most he can . . . In time of peace or war . . . He is our guardian against . . . The gangster and the spy . . . And makes us glad and grateful that . . . We have the FBI.

ALWAYS MY ALL

If now the moon should disappear . . . And every star should fall . . . And if I walked in wilderness . . . And could not hear your call . . . And if the rain came running down . . . Or snowflakes turned to sleet . . . I still would trudge the country road . . . And roam the city street . . . Because I want to share your life . . . Wherever you may be . . . And give you every golden gift . . . That God has given me . . . Because I love you and because . . . The world is never right . . . Unless I say good morning and . . . I kiss your lips good night . . . And if the earth should vanish and . . . If every star should fall . . . I still would be your very own . . . And you would be my all.

IF YOU ARE GOOD

If you are thoughtful of the world . . . If you are good and
kind . . . Then God is in your heart today . . . And God is in
your mind . . . If you endeavor to fulfill . . . Your duty to your
town . . . Then God is in your soul and He . . . Will never let
you down . . . For He rewards the faithful and . . . The generous
and true . . . And all who are sincere and fair . . . In what they
strive to do . . . So keep the path and live your life . . . According
to His way . . . And there will be no idle dawn . . . Or useless
yesterday . . . There is no reason to regret . . . Or any fate to fear
. . . If you obey the word of God . . . As long as you are here.

ROBIN HOOD

Perhaps it is a legend and . . . Perhaps the tale is true . . . But
Robin Hood could bend a bow . . . As few could ever do . . .
And he was one who robbed the rich . . . And gave it to the poor
. . . That life might be more equal and . . . More easy to endure
. . . His method was illegal and . . . He cut a bloody path . . .
However much he may have thought . . . He had a righteous
wrath . . . But would it not be wonderful . . . If each of us could
be . . . A kind and gallant Robin Hood . . . For our community?
. . . I mean, if we would share our goods . . . Sufficiently to give
. . . At least the bare necessities . . . Our neighbors need to live?

AT TWELVE TONIGHT

Tonight at twelve o'clock we end . . . Another year on earth
. . . And only God and we can tell . . . What it was really worth
. . . The books are closed and there will be . . . A balance sheet
tonight . . . To debit and to credit us . . . With every wrong and
right . . . Perhaps we made mistakes and we . . . Have reason to
regret . . . And there may be a lot of things . . . We wish we
could forget . . . Or we have had a perfect year . . . And we may
be content . . . With all of our accomplishments . . . And how
the time was spent . . . But there is always one more year . . .
To choose the right from wrong . . . If God will keep the earth
intact . . . And let us live that long.

LITTLE MAILMAN

Each day I get a batch of mail . . . With all its dreams and hopes . . . And after I have sorted it . . . I save the envelopes . . . Because they are the ones I give . . . Kristina every day . . . To keep her gay and help her feel . . . Important in her play . . . She looks them over carefully . . . And then she makes believe . . . That she herself delivers all . . . The mail that I receive . . . She goes outside and rings the bell . . . And when I pull the door . . . She showers me with circulars . . . And envelopes galore . . . She has a great big bundle and . . . I have to play my part . . . By telling her she surely is . . . The mailman of my heart.

I HAVE TO PRAY

I labor for my daily bread . . . My shelter and my clothes . . . But I must pray if I would gain . . . The gifts that God bestows . . . The strength to bear my burden and . . . The grace to persevere . . . To be of public service and . . . To live a life sincere . . . I have to pray for wisdom and . . . The love and sympathy . . . That are the guiding principles . . . Of perfect charity . . . I know that even bread and clothes . . . And shelter in the night . . . Are gifts that God bestows on me . . . To see me through my plight . . . But if I want His special help . . . To sanctify each day . . . I know that I must fold my hands . . . And bow my head and pray.

I HEAR THE WIND

O God, each time I hear the wind . . . I know that You are here . . . Because You are my every breath . . . And all the atmosphere . . . The same as You ordain the sun . . . The mountain, and the sea . . . The smiles and tears of passing years . . . And every memory . . . You are the song immortal and . . . The smallest flower fair . . . You shape the moon and all the stars . . . And You are everywhere . . . My heart and soul belong to You . . . And everything I own . . . Because You are my Master and . . . You are my God alone . . . And whether I have kept the faith . . . Or whether I have sinned . . . You offer me Your friendship in . . . The whisper of the wind.

EMPLOYMENT MANAGER

He interviews the applicants . . . To study and decide . . .
Which ones appear most competent . . . And truly qualified . . .
He listens to their answers and . . . He looks them up and down
. . . And tries to analyze their thoughts . . . In every smile and
frown . . . He may be very capable . . . Or he may just pretend
. . . And choose a girl for beauty or . . . A man who is a friend
. . . Or he may want to show the great . . . Importance that he
feels . . . And waste their time with needless talk . . . Or make
them cool their heels . . . But if he knows his business and . . .
He struggles to excel . . . He helps the jobless and the boss . . .
And does his duty well.

WEALTH OR HEALTH?

They say the wealthy business man . . . Has ulcers quite severe
. . . And nothing short of greater wealth . . . Can bring him any
cheer . . . And yet when he has reached the height . . . Of glory
and success . . . He still is looking everywhere . . . For health and
happiness . . . Well, he can have his progress and . . . The pleasure of his fame . . . And all the painful ulcers of . . . His money-
making game . . . But I would rather take my time . . . And always feel all right . . . And have a share of daily fun . . . To keep
my troubles light . . . For how am I to profit by . . . The luxury
of wealth . . . If I must suffer in my mind . . . And sacrifice my
health?

I LOVE YOU, LORD

I love You, Lord, for all the gifts . . . That You have given me
. . . The breath of life, eternal faith . . . And every memory . . .
The strength to walk, the tongue to talk . . . The will to rise and
grow . . . And every truth of age and youth . . . That I have come
to know . . . I love You for my health of heart . . . And for my
daily bread . . . And for the comfort of the dreams . . . That fill
my sleepy head . . . For greater courage in defeat . . . And hope
beyond despair . . . And for the eagerness in life . . . To do my
equal share . . . I love You, Lord, and thank You for . . . Each
moment I am here . . . And pray that I will always be . . . Devoted and sincere.

GRAIN BROKER

He deals in corn and soybeans . . . In wheat and oats and rye
. . . And other grain commodities . . . That people sell and buy
. . . He moves the products of the field . . . For merchants and
for millers . . . For grocery stores and auto firms . . . Investors
and distillers . . . He has to watch the market price . . . Of each
and every grain . . . To get for all his customers . . . Their best
financial gain . . . His livelihood depends upon . . . The sum of
his commission . . . And his success is equal to . . . His public
recognition . . . A buyer and a seller and . . . A business go-
between . . . He does his part to stabilize . . . Our economic
scene.

ALL THROUGH LIFE

My friends embrace so many names . . . I cannot count them
all . . . In fact there are a few of them . . . I cannot now recall
. . . But all of them have brought me joy . . . In one way or
another . . . Completely and as surely as . . . A sister or a brother
. . . They have encouraged me to smile . . . And conquer every
pain . . . And find the hidden sunshine when . . . The heavens
turn to rain . . . And I have always found a way . . . To overlook
the weather . . . As long as they have said hello . . . And we have
been together . . . I have so many friendships and . . . They do
so much for me . . . That I am sure my life will last . . . At least
a century.

AS LONG AS I LIVE

I miss you, my darling, with all of my heart . . . And more than
my lips can say . . . I long for your smile in the beautiful while
. . . Of our marvelous yesterday . . . I dream of the dusk and the
silver stars . . . That fashioned a crown for you . . . And the
magic night when the moon was bright . . . And the world was
young and new . . . I cry and I sigh for your loving lips . . . And
I pray on my bended knee . . . But dim is the dawn, and your
laughter is gone . . . And nothing can comfort me . . . Wherever
I go and whatever I find . . . It never is quite the same . . . For
I am alone and forever unknown . . . And no one remembers
your name . . . Yet as long as I live and as long I breathe . . .
And as long as the sand may run . . . Whatever I do, I shall treasure you . . . My wonderful, wonderful one.

POLICEMAN'S PRAYER

I am a plain policeman, God . . . And so I turn to You . . . To
give me grace and guidance for . . . The job I have to do . . . I
need a bit of patience and . . . The wisdom to untie . . . The
loud and snarling traffic when . . . Parades are passing by . . .
The courtesy of keeping calm . . . When drivers disobey . . . The
simple rules intended to . . . Keep accidents away . . . And now
and then I have to shoot . . . The criminals who flee . . . And
take the chance that tragic news . . . Will touch my family . . .
But I adore and praise You, God . . . And in my every prayer
. . . I know that You will hold me in . . . Your kind and loving
care.

MATTER OF EATING

I like to gather groceries . . . And stock the highest shelf . . .
To please my wife and youngsters and . . . To satisfy myself . . .
And now and then I really buy . . . A lot of things to eat . . . In-
cluding milk and vegetables . . . And cereals and meat . . . And
then the pantry shelves are filled . . . Until they overflow . . .
And there is plenty to appease . . . And help the children grow
. . . But it is never long before . . . The cabinets are bare . . .
And all the plain and fancy foods . . . Have vanished into air
. . . And as I write my grocery list . . . And try to stretch my
pay . . . I marvel at the speedy rate . . . We stow the stuff away.

MY MENTAL CLOCK

The old alarm clock seldom fails . . . To rouse my sleepy head
. . . Precisely at the moment when . . . I should get out of bed
. . . It interrupts my deepest dream . . . And gives my ears a fit
. . . Relentlessly and stubbornly . . . Until I silence it . . . But
I have still a better and . . . A more efficient way . . . To free
myself from slumber and . . . Begin another day . . . And that is
just to tell my mind . . . Before I go to sleep . . . That I have
made a promise that . . . I simply have to keep . . . And all night
long my mental clock . . . Keeps ticking in my head . . . And
quicker than the loudest bell . . . It gets me out of bed.

HOTEL MAID

She is the most unnoticed soul . . . In all our traveling days
. . . And yet she keeps us comfortable . . . And clean in many
ways . . . She makes the beds with linen fresh . . . She renovates
the floor . . . And puts the towels and the soap . . . Beyond the
bathroom door . . . She empties ash trays and she dusts . . . Each
table and each chair . . . And straightens up the dresser with . . .
The very best of care . . . If we need stationery or . . . A blotter
or a match . . . We merely phone our order and . . . She brings
it with dispatch . . . And any time we do not like . . . Our slumber to be curbed . . . We post the card that says that we . . .
Don't want to be disturbed.

STARS IN YOUR EYES

Not all the stars of magic pulse . . . Are in the nightly skies
. . . For there are those that charm me when . . . I gaze into your
eyes . . . I see a star that seems to smile . . . And one that sheds
a tear . . . And one of deep sincerity . . . That shines from year
to year . . . A star of faith, a star of hope . . . A star of courage
true . . . And all the stars that comfort me . . . And kiss my
dreams of you . . . And, oh, there are so many more . . . That
cast their spell on me . . . As if to promise happiness . . . For all
eternity . . . I think when I behold the stars . . . That fill the
nightly skies . . . They merely are reflections of . . . The starlight
in your eyes.

THE LETTERS I SAVE

When I have answered letters I . . . Destroy them one by one
. . . Because when my replies are mailed . . . My duty has been
done . . . And letters merely clutter up . . . What little space I
own . . . With messages that mean no more . . . Than how the
winds have blown . . . But now and then some envelope . . . Is
filled with friendly lines . . . That mean a great deal more to me
. . . Than oral words or signs . . . A narrative of warmth and
cheer . . . And just a bit of praise . . . To keep my old umbrella
up . . . On disappointing days . . . And that is one I treasure and
. . . I never would destroy . . . Because its every sentence is . . .
A source of endless joy.

VACATION TIME

Vacation time will soon be here . . . And that is bad for me
. . . For I am just another Joe . . . Who has a family . . . And so
I have to read the maps . . . And load the car and drive . . . And
somehow figure out a way . . . To keep myself alive . . . I seek
the perfect fishing spot . . . And struggle with a tent . . . Or go
to some hotel and pay . . . The mortgage with my rent . . . I have
to patch the punctures and . . . To fight the gnats and flies . . .
And purchase all the souvenirs . . . That catch the youngsters'
eyes . . . Vacation time is quite the time . . . For me to go berserk
. . . And just about the only time . . . I miss my daily work.

ICEMAN

He used to come in sloppy clothes . . . To knock upon your
door . . . And leave his wet and muddy tracks . . . Across your
kitchen floor . . . But now he wears a uniform . . . And he is very
nice . . . And in his special drip-proof bag . . . He brings your
cake of ice . . . Or maybe you prefer it chipped . . . For oyster,
shrimp, or tea . . . In any case he is on hand . . . To serve you
faithfully . . . He cools the milk and vegetables . . . In stores,
hotels, and such . . . And keeps the patient's fever chart . . . From
going up too much . . . His product helps the railroad and . . .
The chemist in his work . . . The farmer and the florist and . . .
Of course the soda jerk.

THANK GOD AND YOU

Each night, I thank Almighty God . . . That you belong to me
. . . Because I am so happy in . . . Your loving company . . .
Your faith inspires me to reach . . . A greater goal each day . . .
Your solace is the rainbow bright . . . That draws my tears away
. . . Your kindly spirit comforts me . . . When I am sad and
blue . . . And everything that I achieve . . . Is just because of
you . . . I know that I must fill my place . . . Whatever I prefer
. . . But in the happiness you give . . . My life is easier . . . And
so I thank Almighty God . . . And praise your gentle heart . . .
And constantly I pray that we . . . Will never be apart.

OUR GARDENER

We have a certain gardener . . . Who tends to all our needs . . .
Of nourishing the flowers fair . . . And getting rid of weeds . . .
He trims the bushes, turns the beds . . . And plants the grass
around . . . And sponsors all the miracles . . . That come up from
the ground . . . He does not make a fortune but . . . He seems to
be content . . . With flowers and philosophy . . . And God and
government . . . His smile is always genuine . . . His every word
is kind . . . And sunshine is the only thing . . . He ever leaves
behind . . . And that is why I envy him . . . Who tends to all our
flowers . . . And wish I were a gardener . . . As wonderful as ours.

APPLYING FOR A JOB

When you apply in person for . . . A steady occupation . . .
You should pursue your purpose with . . . At least some prepara-
tion . . . You should be ready to present . . . The things you want
to mention . . . But your apparel should not be . . . The kind to
draw attention . . . You should not be too humble nor . . . Display too much aggression . . . But you should tell the truth and
try . . . To make a good impression . . . The rest depends upon
your past . . . And how you have been rated . . . Which quietly
and thoroughly . . . Will be investigated . . . And if the interview
results . . . In permanent employment . . . The chances are your
work and pay . . . Will bring you much enjoyment.

AUTO RACING

There is no grind more grueling . . . Than driving in a race . . .
Or one that takes more courage as . . . You try to set the pace
. . . You guide your car around the track . . . And as you near
each curve . . . You jiggle it and steer it so . . . The auto will not
swerve . . . The dust and smoke are in your eyes . . . The signal
flag is faint . . . But there is neither time nor cause . . . To
register complaint . . . You have to stop for fuel and . . . To wipe
away the dirt . . . And in your heart there is a prayer . . . That no
one will be hurt . . . And if you are the lucky one . . . Who roars
to victory . . . Your final lap has put you in . . . The lap of luxury.

OUR BRIEF TODAY

The pleasures of the world are few . . . And they can never last
. . . And there will be a day when we . . . Will melt into the past
. . . A day when every song and sigh . . . And all our smiles and
tears . . . Will only serve to gather up . . . The dust of yesteryears
. . . And that is why it matters not . . . How much we gain on
earth . . . Except as we may do a deed . . . Of everlasting worth
. . . Except as we may try to help . . . Our neighbor and our kin
. . . And overcome temptation and . . . Avoid the way of sin . . .
This life is temporary as . . . The earth itself must be . . . But
God is Master of the soul . . . For all eternity.

I NEED YOU, GOD

Dear God, I do not want to know . . . What things there are in
store . . . But I implore Your help to live . . . And to accomplish
more . . . Your hand alone can lead me through . . . The darkness
of the night . . . And bless me with encouragement . . . To keep
on doing right . . . I try to be prepared each day . . . To take my
life in stride . . . But I need grace to guide my steps . . . And
never leave Your side . . . Almighty God, in every thought . . . I
most sincerely pray . . . For just enough assistance now . . . That
I may never stray . . . Be with me every morning when . . . The
sky is gray or blue . . . And let me find the stars at night . . . That
light the way to You.

OUR HOME MOVIES

Our movies of the family . . . Are like a memory book . . .
Where we may turn the pages back . . . And take another look
. . . We see our Jimmie on his bike . . . Young Donnie rolling
eggs . . . And dear Kristina stumbling as . . . She tries her baby
legs . . . The home where happy dreams were born . . . The
pretty birthday cake . . . The parties and the picnics and . . . The
trips we used to take . . . Each frame reflects our memories . . .
In colors bright and gay . . . Our progress and our friendship and
. . . The children at their play . . . We cherish and we keep with
care . . . Our motion picture book . . . With those endearing
views of how . . . Our youngsters used to look.

ALL FRIENDS

My friends are all the folks I know . . . Wherever they may be
. . . And they are all the letters that . . . The mailman brings to
me . . . They are the people on the bus . . . And in the picture
show . . . Along the busy thoroughfare . . . And everywhere I go
. . . Yes, even those whose names appear . . . Upon the printed
page . . . Of paper, magazine, or book . . . Whatever be its age
. . . They are the proud and humble and . . . The wealthy and
the poor . . . The happy humans and the souls . . . With sorrows
to endure . . . My friends are right beside me and . . . Beyond the
seven seas . . . If only in the knowledge that . . . I have no
enemies.

FOR THOSE WHO DIED

In silence and in gratitude . . . We bow our heads and pray . . .
For those who fought for liberty . . . One distant yesterday . . .
Who marched to war with courage high . . . To heed our country's call . . . Who sacrificed unflinchingly . . . And gave their very
all . . . May God remember every cross . . . And every ocean
grave . . . And bless our dear departed for . . . The loyalty they
gave . . . And let us too remember now . . . And strive to keep
the peace . . . That hands may toil and fields may grow . . . And
guns forever cease . . . Let us be humbly grateful for . . . The
passing of the night . . . But also let us guard the day . . . And be
prepared to fight.

I PRAY AGAIN

Dear God, when I was just a child . . . I used to talk to You
. . . And ask Your guidance every time . . . I had a problem new
. . . And somehow in my heart I felt . . . You always heard my
prayer . . . And that was why I seldom cried . . . Or worried anywhere . . . But as the early years went by . . . And I became
mature . . . I sort of slipped away from You . . . And I was not so
sure . . . I wandered in a wilderness . . . Where selfishness pre-
vailed . . . Until I realized I was lost . . . And I had really failed
. . . But now the way is lighted and . . . I know the course is true
. . . And now once more I pray I may . . . Be always close to You.

INTERN

He is the young apprentice who . . . Has gotten his M.D. . . .
But who must still attain the goal . . . Of true ability . . . He doffs
his cap and gown, and dons . . . An apron and a mask . . . To
watch and help his elders as . . . They go about their task . . . In
sickroom and in surgery . . . He learns to diagnose . . . And when
to operate and when . . . The risk appears too close . . . His
books are always handy and . . . He studies night and day . . . To
heal the wounds of all the world . . . And keep disease away . . .
And only as he perseveres . . . With skill and dignity . . . Does he
deserve his license and . . . His medical degree.

BEING PROMOTED

Promotion is a special thing . . . That comes occasionally . . .
To one who works with extra skill . . . And constant loyalty . . .
It may include an office new . . . With quite a handsome raise . . .
Or just a lofty title and . . . Some words of passing praise . . . It
may be very well deserved . . . Or it may be routine . . . Because
someone expired or . . . Retired from the scene . . . But each
promotion does some good . . . If only to create . . . A greater
effort to produce . . . And to co-operate . . . And whether lucra-
tive or not . . . It is a compliment . . . And it is bound to warm
the heart . . . Of the recipient.

YOUR SEVENTH BIRTHDAY

Kristina, you are seven now . . . And sweet as you can be . . .
The princess and the darling of . . . Our happy family . . . You
are a lovely little girl . . . With eyes of grayish blue . . . And all
the charm that you could want . . . To win the world to you . . .
And yet you never think about . . . Yourself in any way . . . Except to be Kristina and . . . To go to school and play . . . You
love your two big brothers and . . . Your mother and your dad
. . . And with your every word and smile . . . You make us proud
and glad . . . Congratulations, honey, and . . . May all your future hold . . . The best of health, the finest friends . . . And
moments made of gold.

AUTUMN REVERIE

The autumn woods are calling now . . . With leaves of red and brown . . . And it is time to get away . . . From everything in town . . . To wander over pleasant paths . . . With all the world at ease . . . And meditate and contemplate . . . A thousand memories . . . The laughter and the merriment . . . Of many moons ago . . . And all the little heartaches and . . . The tears we used to know . . . The dream of perfect happiness . . . The everlasting search . . . The doctor and the lawyer and . . . The graveyard and the church . . . It is the time to roam the woods . . . And think about the past . . . And contemplate tomorrow and . . . How long this life may last.

I THANK YOU

Dear God, I thank You for my health . . . My children and my wife . . . And all the other blessings You . . . Have added to my life . . . I thank You for my many friends . . . Their kind and timely aid . . . My daily occupation and . . . The progress I have made . . . My home and all the comforts I . . . Enjoy from day to day . . . And for the church where I may go . . . To worship You and pray . . . My heart is ever grateful for . . . The sun and wind and rain . . . And for the moon and stars that shine . . . Upon my windowpane . . . Dear God, I thank You for each dawn . . . Of dreams and smiles and tears . . . And for the wistful memories . . . Of youthful yesteryears.

AWARDS

There is a custom everywhere . . . Of giving out awards . . . According to the judgment of . . . Committees or of boards . . . The medals and the loving cups . . . The scholarships and pins . . . The plaques and pretty ribbons and . . . The cash that someone wins . . . There is no end to prizes that . . . Are given every day . . . To recognize accomplishment . . . In special work or play . . . And that is good for everyone . . . Because it helps create . . . The urge to competition in . . . The struggle to be great . . . And only in that effort and . . . The will to do the best . . . Can all the world be equal to . . . And pass the toughest test.

DOUBLE HOLIDAY

All holidays are happy ones . . . But they are extra nice . . .
When they occur on Sunday and . . . We celebrate them twice
. . . They make the week end longer and . . . We have more
leisure then . . . Before we have to rise and rush . . . To get to
work again . . . The double holiday affords . . . A chance to rest
and play . . . As though we all were millionaires . . . And we
could have our say . . . We figure we have lots of time . . . For
what we want to do . . . To please our inclinations and . . . To
make our dreams come true . . . But when that Tuesday morning
comes . . . Our manner may be gruff . . . Because the job ahead
of us . . . Is always twice as rough.

PATH TO PERFECTION

We do not like to make mistakes . . . However great or small
. . . And constantly we hope to keep . . . From making them at
all . . . But hope alone is not enough . . . To reach that perfect
height . . . And wishful thinking will not turn . . . A wrong into
a right . . . It takes our earnest effort and . . . Our perseverance
too . . . To be exacting and correct . . . In everything we do . . .
We have to strive relentlessly . . . And always be on guard . . . If
we would write the highest score . . . On every tally card . . . And
when a few mistakes occur . . . Despite our diligence . . . We
should be willing and prepared . . . To take the consequence.

I PRAY FOR ALL

I pray for those who are my friends . . . And who are kind to
me . . . That God will bless them with His love . . . For all eternity . . . I pray for every neighbor and . . . The stranger on the
street . . . Whatever be his standing or . . . Wherever we may
meet . . . And most of all I plead the cause . . . Of those whom I
offend . . . And those who may despise me and . . . Ignore me to
the end . . . For in my heart there is no hate . . . Or eagerness to
win . . . But only warmth and gentleness . . . And sorrow over
sin . . . I do not thirst for bitterness . . . Or crave the smallest
strife . . . But just to be a friend to all . . . Whom God has given
life.

BANK ACCOUNT

A bank account is where we save . . . Or take our money out
. . . And where the records seldom leave . . . The shadow of a
doubt . . . Where earnings grow from day to day . . . And every
penny counts . . . Or drafts are drawn and now and then . . . A
certain check will bounce . . . It promises security . . . And shows
our credit good . . . Especially among the folks . . . Who fill our
neighborhood . . . A bank account is something that . . . Is always
well to own . . . Regardless of the poverty . . . Or riches we have
known . . . Because it is a record of . . . Our cash from day to day
. . . And whether we are keeping it . . . Or tossing it away.

FIRST SHAVE

There comes a day when every boy . . . Beyond a certain grade
. . . Believes that it is time for him . . . To use a razor blade . . .
He gazes in the mirror and . . . The evidence is there . . . That
all the fuzz around his face . . . Has turned to human hair . . .
And so he gets some shaving cream . . . And with a razor keen
. . . He operates upon himself . . . To keep his features clean . . .
Of course he draws a little blood . . . That leaves a scar or two
. . . But after all the process is . . . Unusual and new . . . And
after all he does the best . . . That any youngster can . . . To
prove that he is growing up . . . And wants to be a man.

HELP THE HEART

Sometimes it seems the whole wide world . . . Is full of heart
disease . . . And yet so few are interested . . . In finding remedies
. . . I do not mean the doctors who . . . Are caring for the ill . . .
And not the research specialists . . . Who struggle up the hill . . .
But common people everywhere . . . Including you and I . . .
Who know about our neighbors and . . . Our relatives that die
. . . We should be so much more concerned . . . About each heart
attack . . . Our hospitals and surgeons and . . . The money that
they lack . . . We are the lucky folks on earth . . . Who ought to
do our part . . . By opening our pocketbooks . . . For every ailing
heart.

232

GOD LOVE THEM ALL

They sleep in peace who bravely faced . . . The blazing guns of
war . . . That we might live and set aside . . . Our hates forevermore . . . They are at rest beneath the sun . . . The rain, the
wind, and snow . . . Who did not ask for honors or . . . The
medals we bestow . . . Their only purpose was to serve . . . The
land they loved so well . . . And multiply the magic tones . . . Of
freedom's lofty bell . . . We praise them for their valor and . . .
The sacrifice they made . . . And to the end of time their deeds
. . . Will hold the highest grade . . . God love their souls whose
lives became . . . The patriotic price . . . And help us to be
worthy of . . . Their noble sacrifice.

WILL TO WORK

I used to hate to go to work . . . And punch the clock each day
. . . And wonder how my boss would feel . . . And what he had
to say . . . I did not like to ride the bus . . . And hurry to the room
. . . Where everything around me seemed . . . To hold a certain
gloom . . . Until I took an interest in . . . The task I had to do
. . . And found that it was really fun . . . To see the project
through . . . To be a very vital part . . . Of something being done
. . . And try to set a record new . . . Before the final gun . . . And
then I understood how much . . . My job could mean to me . . .
And just how good and generous . . . My boss could really be.

THANK YOU, DARLING

I know I seldom shower you . . . With gratitude and praise . . .
For all your kind, unselfish deeds . . . And for your loving ways
. . . I know the credit you receive . . . Is never half enough . . .
And often I am thoughtless and . . . Perhaps a little gruff . . . But,
darling, when I search my heart . . . The truth is always there
. . . That life is sweet because you are . . . The answer to my
prayer . . . I cannot do without your help . . . And all your good
advice . . . And I can only gain my goal . . . Because you sacrifice
. . . I know I seldom say my thanks . . . For everything you do
. . . But, darling, all the credit and . . . The praise belongs to you.

233

I RESOLVE

Almighty Father, I resolve . . . With all my heart sincere . . .
To live a better life today . . . And all throughout this year . . .
To overcome my prejudice . . . And every selfish stand . . . And
try in every way I can . . . To lend a helping hand . . . For kins-
man, neighbor, friend, and foe . . . Wherever we may meet . . .
And for the passing stranger and . . . The beggar on the street
. . . I want to serve You faithfully . . . And be of greater worth
. . . Not only to my family . . . But everyone on earth . . . Al-
mighty Father, hear my prayer . . . And give Your grace to me . . .
That I may keep my promise with . . . Profound humility.

WISHFUL WANDERING

Sometimes I wish that I could roam . . . To places far away
. . . To sail across the seven seas . . . Or fly there in a day . . . Not
just to go around the globe . . . And see the other side . . . But
also to relax a bit . . . And sort of change my stride . . . To get
away from common things . . . That make a dull routine . . .
And try to find a different and . . . A more refreshing scene . . . I
dream of strange, exotic lands . . . With danger all around . . .
And legendary treasures that . . . Are hidden in the ground . . .
But then I think about my job . . . And it is plain to me . . . I
could not reach those places on . . . My time and salary.

SUNDAY TO SUNDAY

I love you every Sunday, dear . . . And every Monday too . . .
On Tuesday I adore you and . . . My heart belongs to you . . . I
cherish you on Wednesday and . . . When Thursday takes its place
. . . While Friday, dear, and Saturday . . . I live for your embrace
. . . And yet not all the seven days . . . Of every week we share
. . . Are long enough for me to tell . . . How much I really
care . . . Or any month or season or . . . Whatever moon may be
. . . Nor are the years that multiply . . . Into eternity . . . Because
my love is boundless as . . . A sea of stars sublime . . . And it is
just as endless, dear . . . As are the hands of time.

FIRST TOOTH OUT

Kristina's tooth came out last night . . . And she was mighty glad . . . Because it was the first one out . . . Of all the teeth she had . . . For many days it had been loose . . . And wobbly as could be . . . And then her mother plucked it and . . . She handed it to me . . . I gave it to Kristina when . . . She climbed into her bed . . . To put beneath the pillow soft . . . On which she laid her head . . . And when the sun appeared and when . . . She opened up her eyes . . . She raised her pillow and she found . . . A wonderful surprise . . . The baby tooth had vanished and . . . A fairy or a friend . . . Had left a piece of money for . . . Our little girl to spend.

POPSICLE MAN

Each day we hear his jingle bells . . . As he comes up the street . . . With ice-cream bars and popsicles . . . To beat the summer heat . . . Our children hurry out and jump . . . Upon his running board . . . To get the little treat we feel . . . That we can well afford . . . Because the purchase price is just . . . A nickel or a dime . . . And it assures the youngsters of . . . A most delightful time . . . They wait for him each morning with . . . A healthy appetite . . . And watch him drive away until . . . His truck is out of sight . . . We hope he makes a fortune from . . . The goodies that he sells . . . Because it means so much to us . . . To hear his jingle bells.

ALWAYS A FRIEND

There is a friend for each of us . . . Who dwell upon this earth . . . Whatever our possessions or . . . How little we are worth . . . There may be thousands who pursue . . . Our glory in the sun . . . Or in the poverty of life . . . We may have only one . . . But always there is one at least . . . Who tries to understand . . . And who is loyal and who wants . . . To lend a helping hand . . . We may not really recognize . . . The friend who comes to call . . . And sometimes we may tell ourselves . . . There is no friend at all . . . But even if we never hear . . . A knock upon our door . . . We know we have a friend in God . . . And will forevermore.

PICTURE-BOOK PAST

Memories are picture books . . . Of many smiles and tears . . .
That lead the way along the lanes . . . To all the yesteryears . . .
The laughter on a summer lawn . . . When life was young and
gay . . . The sweetness of a song in spring . . . With little else to
say . . . The wistfulness of autumn and . . . The melancholy rain
. . . The winter loneliness that snowed . . . Upon the window-
pane . . . Memories to treasure now . . . And memories to keep
. . . If only as the heart may dream . . . When angels are asleep
. . . All the world has memories . . . And all the world may look
. . . Beyond the fears of yesteryears . . . In every picture book.

JANITOR

The man who is a janitor . . . Is one who goes about . . . The
job of cleaning up a place . . . And taking garbage out . . . He
makes repairs, he checks the lights . . . And keeps the water warm
. . . And tries to guard the premises . . . Against whatever storm
. . . He may not always be on hand . . . To do his timely deed
. . . But usually he is prepared . . . To serve the slightest need . . .
Sometimes the tenants seem to feel . . . That he is overpaid
. . . Although if they pursued his task . . . They could not make
the grade . . . And though he makes more money than . . . The
average family . . . He tries to look as humble as . . . They think
he ought to be.

FEEDING OUR JIMMIE

Our Jimmie haunts the kitchen in . . . The house where we
abide . . . And yet at every chance he gets . . . He wants to eat
outside . . . He loves his mother's chicken and . . . Her ham and
apple pie . . . And every time she bakes a cake . . . We hear his
hungry sigh . . . But often he is restless and . . . He wants to go
his way . . . To join his high-school buddies at . . . A neighborhood café . . . Especially when we exclaim . . . How wearisome
we feel . . . And send him to the kitchen to . . . Prepare his evening meal . . . Perhaps his hunger reaches past . . . The food
upon the shelf . . . Or he may be too indolent . . . To wait upon
himself

I WANT TO SERVE YOU

O Lord, if there is anything . . . That You would have me do
. . . Please let me know how I can be . . . Of service unto You
. . . Enlighten me in all respects . . . According to Your will . . .
And let my every sacred vow . . . Be one that I fulfill . . . I do
not seek the comfort and . . . The luxury of life . . . But only how
to do my best . . . In facing every strife . . . How I can help my
neighbor and . . . The stranger on the street . . . And how to lead
each lonely soul . . . To happiness complete . . . Believe me,
Lord, and hear me now . . . In this my prayer sincere . . . That I
may have the courage and . . . The strength to persevere.

SORRY FOR SELF

Some people always wonder why . . . Their dreams do not come
true . . . And feel so sorry for themselves . . . They know not what
to do . . . They blame their lack of luck on fate . . . And sit
around and fret . . . Because they do not share the breaks . . .
That other people get . . . In their opinion they deserve . . .
Much more than other souls . . . And they should be the first to
gain . . . Their all-important goals . . . They would not publicly
admit . . . Or privately confide . . . That they have not progressed
because . . . They have not really tried . . . But all they seem to
want to do . . . Is murmur and complain . . . While other people
do their best . . . And make the greater gain.

WHO WORK AT NIGHT

Some people have to work at night . . . And they must struggle
on . . . Until the world is getting up . . . To greet another dawn
. . . And that is seldom pleasant or . . . An easy thing to do . . .
No matter what the wages or . . . The goal they have in view
. . . For while their neighbors slumber, they . . . Have hours they
must keep . . . And when the others are awake . . . They have to
be asleep . . . And usually they do not have . . . The vigor and
the vim . . . Of those who labor in the light . . . And share the
social swim . . . But they deserve a lot of thanks . . . And all the
praise in sight . . . Because they keep the world alive . . Throughout the weary night.

FOR EVERY A

When our two boys get marks in school . . . We promise we will pay . . . A certain sum for every card . . . On which they have an A . . . But it is strictly understood . . . That they must surely pass . . . In all their subjects and they must . . . Behave in every class . . . Of course it is no simple task . . . To make a perfect score . . . Especially in some pursuits . . . That are inclined to bore . . . But when there is a prize at stake . . . It makes the youngsters try . . . And usually the cards reflect . . . Their grades are mighty high . . . And we are just as pleased to pay . . . The money they receive . . . As we are proud of what our boys . . . Are able to achieve.

THEY PRAY IN VAIN

Some people wonder why they pray . . . To have their dreams come true . . . Because the way they look at it . . . It seems they never do . . . Each time they ask for sunshine bright . . . The rain is at their door . . . And when they want to win a game . . . They make a losing score . . . They blame their tragedies on God . . . And say He did not hear . . . The fervent pleas and promises . . . They whispered in his ear . . . They never try to understand . . . How richly they are blest . . . Or realize in their smiles and tears . . . That God knows what is best . . . They never seem to recognize . . . Their own intrinsic worth . . . Or quite agree in theory . . . His will be done on earth.

SWEET AND WONDERFUL

I love you more than you suspect . . . And you will ever know . . . Because I am too bashful for . . . The love I want to show . . . Because you are so gentle and . . . So wonderful and sweet . . . And all I ever want to do . . . Is worship at your feet . . . I love you for the things you say . . . The sweetness of your smile . . . And just the joy of knowing you . . . For every little while . . . I love you, darling, from your toes . . . To all your finger-tips . . . And more than any other wish . . . I long to kiss your lips . . . I long to hold you in my arms . . . And whisper in your ear . . . That you are sweet and wonderful . . . And I am most sincere.

PUBLISHER

Some people think the publisher . . . Is one whose block of
stock . . . Enables him to play all day . . . And never mind the
clock . . . Well, he may be a wealthy man . . . And he may have
his say . . . But he is one who usually . . . Puts in a working day
. . . Although he has subordinates . . . He has his job to do . . .
And he is never satisfied . . . Until he sees it through . . . The
daily flow of printers' ink . . . Is running through his veins . . .
The same as in the writers and . . . Reporters whom he trains
. . . He may not have the time to give . . . Each one his special
care . . . But by his proven policies . . . He surely does his share.

ONE LITTLE LETTER

One little letter in the mail . . . From in or out of town . . .
May move the world in which I live . . . And turn it upside down
. . . It may be for the better or . . . It may be for the worse . . . In
terms of friendly greeting or . . . In phrases cold and terse . . .
Perhaps it brings some money from . . . An unexpected source
. . . Or threatens me with tragedy . . . By legal means or force
. . . But whether it is news from home . . . Or just another ad
. . . I wonder and I worry if . . . The words are good or bad . . .
And that is why I hesitate . . . To slit the envelope . . . And
struggle with the fears that seem . . . To challenge every hope.

JOINER

The joiner is a person who . . . Is eager as can be . . . To take a
part in every club . . . And each fraternity . . . He wants to join
the civic groups . . . Wherever they may meet . . . And proudly
wears their emblems as . . . He walks along the street . . . At
church and social gatherings . . . His name is on the list . . . And
he would like to be in all . . . The orders that exist . . . He
usually is prompt to pay . . . Whatever sums are due . . . And tries
to interest others in . . . Becoming members too . . . And while
some folks may criticize . . . The sort of life he spends . . . He
surely helps his fellowman . . . And makes a lot of friends.

THE DAY WILL COME

I know it seems impossible . . . But there will be a day . . .
When all your memories of him . . . Will melt and fade away . . .
When you will go about your tasks . . . With other goals to win
. . . And no concern for anything . . . That was or might have
been . . . Of course it will be gradual . . . And you will hardly see
. . . How he becomes the shadow of . . . A passing fantasy . . .
But there will come a time in life . . . When he will mean no more
. . . Than just another circular . . . That decorates your door . . .
I know you think you love him and . . . Your heart is torn in two
. . . But there will be a day when he . . . Means nothing more to
you.

· NO REAL BOSS

Some people say they do not like . . . To work for any boss . . .
Because they would much rather take . . . The profit or the loss
. . . They want a business of their own . . . In which they may
pursue . . . The policies and kind of work . . . That they prefer to
do . . . Of course it is all right for some . . . And they attain
success . . . Without too great a sacrifice . . . Or too much strain
or stress . . . But no one really is the boss . . . In any business way
. . . Because it is the customer . . . Who has the final say . . .
And so the noun we know as "boss" . . . Is not the proper term
. . . For one who shines a pair of shoes . . . Or runs the biggest
firm.

FOOTBALL DONNIE

In helmet and in uniform . . . Our Donnie takes the field . . .
With football pep and eagerness . . . That never are concealed
. . . He hits the line and runs the ends . . . He kicks and passes
too . . . And when opponents have the ball . . . He knows just
what to do . . . But best of all our Donnie likes . . . To be the
referee . . . To blow the whistle, drop the flag . . . And call the
penalty . . . And then again he likes to coach . . . And teach the
tricky plays . . . That he has skillfully designed . . . And schemed
for many days . . . In junior high he seems to be . . . An expert at
the game . . . And we are sure that he is bound . . . To win
collegiate fame.

OFFICE MEMOS

I do not like the memos that . . . The boss forever sends . . .
About the working world and all . . . The economic trends . . .
About the need for promptness and . . . The sin of being late
. . . And how we ought to be alert . . . And try to concentrate
. . . He criticizes what we do . . . And stresses what we don't . . .
And then assumes we do not care . . . And we just simply won't
. . . I never like the memos that . . . Are filled with his advice . . .
To labor hard and gladly make . . . Whatever sacrifice . . . But I
adore the memos that . . . Present a word of praise . . . And prom-
ise us that we will get . . . A bonus or a raise.

I VISIT GOD

Today is Sunday and today . . . I turn my thoughts to God . . .
To ask His blessing and His grace . . . Along the path I plod . . . I
want to serve Him faithfully . . . In every humble way . . . With
every thought and every deed . . . And every word I say . . . Because it is that special day . . . To honor Him and rest . . . And
in our praise to Him we are . . . His most beloved guest . . . And
so I want to visit Him . . . And offer Him my prayers . . . And ask
for courage to endure . . . My troubles and my cares . . . I want
to thank Him for the gifts . . . That He has given me . . . And
strive to win a happy place . . . In His eternity.

JUNKMAN

The junkman used to come around . . . With operatic voice
. . . To gather worn-out articles . . . According to our choice . . .
He called for rags, old iron, and . . . Whatever we would give . . .
Or sell for next to nothing to . . . Enable him to live . . . He used
to roam the alleys with . . . A wagon and a horse . . . Or with a
creaky pushcart he . . . Pursued his humble course . . . But now
his chant is seldom heard . . . And he is seldom seen . . . And
probably on Sunday now . . . He drives a limousine . . . Because
he pays so little for . . . The junk we have today . . . And frequently he charges us . . . To haul the stuff away.

ON FRIDAY

I like to work on Friday and . . . I always do my best . . . Because it finishes the week . . . And gives me time to rest . . . Because I know that Saturday . . . And Sunday will be here . . . To make my moments pleasant and . . . To fill my heart with cheer . . . And so I strive and concentrate . . . To give the best in me . . . To gather greater progress and . . . Promote efficiency . . . I do not mind the hours or . . . The efforts great or small . . . When Friday marks the calendar . . . That hangs upon the wall . . Because the week end is at hand . . . And I may loaf and play . . . Until blue Monday comes again . . . With heavy clouds of gray.

AVERAGE FOLKS

Our family is not aloof . . . Sedate or dignified . . . But we are just the average folks . . . Who labor side by side . . . Our children are our partners and . . . They share in all the fun . . . Of happy schemes, delightful dreams . . . And all that we get done . . . We have no conversations that . . . The youngsters may not hear . . . Because they are a part of us . . . And they are sweet and dear . . . We live together day and night . . . And every moment share . . . Each little problem and success . . . And every hope and prayer . . . Let other people pride themselves . . . On pomp and dignity . . . We only want the love that makes . . . A happy family.

THERE IS A FRIEND

There is a friend for every need . . . Whatever it may be . . . To help in time of stress or just . . . To keep us company . . . To write a letter or to call . . . And pass the time of day . . . And with the magic of a smile . . . To take our tears away . . . There is a friend for every song . . . That echoes from the past . . . With melody that moves the heart . . . And memories that last . . . A friend who never leaves our side . . . No matter where we go . . . And one who walks along the street . . . And merely says hello . . . Whatever our ambition or . . . The course we may pursue . . . There is a passing friend and one . . . Who is forever true.

OLD MEANY

The boss is always telling us . . . How much he has to spend
. . . And that we must economize . . . To meet the business trend
. . . Economy is all we hear . . . From morning until night . . .
Including paper, pen, and ink . . . And turning off the light . . .
Machine repairs and towels and . . . The rubber bands and clips
. . . And most of all the tragedy . . . Of late or absence slips . . .
Of course we have our office faults . . . And anyone can see . . .
That we have yet to gain the goal . . . Of full efficiency . . . But
now and then we wish the boss . . . Would just economize . . .
On his desire to be strict . . . And always criticize.

TIME FOR A PRAYER

We have so many minutes and . . . So many hours too . . . In
which we may accomplish all . . . The things we want to do . . .
That certainly there ought to be . . . Sufficient time to spare . . .
To think about almighty God . . . And say a little prayer . . . We
rest at home and go to shows . . . Or entertain a friend . . . And
many are the greeting cards . . . And packages we send . . . We
eat when we are hungry and . . . We sleep when we need rest
. . . And in the circle of our wealth . . . We buy the very best . . .
And so the least that we can do . . . Is go to church today . . .
And give our gratitude to God . . . By taking time to pray.

THE UNINVITED

We do not like the kind of folks . . . Who never let us know
. . . When they decide to ring our bell . . . To sort of say hello
. . . Who come without a warning or . . . The least apology . . .
And barge right in to force us to . . . Accept their company . . .
Or those who join our table in . . . A tearoom or café . . . Without an invitation or . . . A courteous display . . . We know how
nice it is to get . . . Surprises now and then . . . But there are
times when we should say . . . When folks may call again . . . For
everybody has the right . . . To ask and to expect . . . A sense of
good behavior and . . . Appropriate respect.

PROMOTION DIRECTOR

He struggles night and day to make . . . The circulation grow
. . . And many are the problems and . . . The answers he must
know . . . He must be sure that big events . . . Are definitely
booked . . . And no promotional idea . . . Is ever overlooked . . .
He tries to search the public mind . . . And learn what it would
say . . . About the different features that . . . Appear from day to
day . . . Each reader must be happy and . . . Each advertiser too
. . . And in that undertaking he . . . Has quite a job to do . . .
He boosts his paper everywhere . . . As much as he is smart . . .
And hopes that his promotion work . . . Will win the public's
heart.

BADGE

A badge identifies a man . . . For what he strives to do . . . The
G-Man, the policeman, and . . . The politician too . . . The fireman and watchman and . . . Convention delegate . . . The bailiff
and the officer . . . Who guards the border state . . . Some badges
are the silver kind . . . And some are made of gold . . . And all of
them inspire men . . . To be a little bold . . . They carry some
importance and . . . They spell authority . . . And make their
owners recognized . . . In their community . . . But more than
any metal badge . . . That may acquire rust . . . Is that unseen
insignia . . . Of loyalty and trust.

OUR UPS AND DOWNS

Sometimes the mail is heavy and . . . Again the mail is light
. . . The same as joy may live today . . . And loneliness tonight
. . . There is no pattern to our stride . . . Or to the river's flow
. . . Except that each is changeable . . . As are the winds that
blow . . . For life is just a melting pot . . . Of many smiles and
tears . . . And of the mingled memories . . . That tabulate the
years . . . Our songs of sweetest sentiment . . . Our injuries and
scars . . . The driving rain, the gentle snow . . . And dreams that
touch the stars . . . We have to have our ups and downs . . . With
failure and success . . . And do our best to cultivate . . . And harvest happiness.

KIND OF WORKER

There is a kind of worker who . . . Is loyal as can be . . . And does the best and most he can . . . To help the company . . . And then there is the other kind . . . Who shirks and loafs all day . . . And grabs each opportunity . . . To fool around and play . . . He is the one who never will . . . Admit his own mistake . . . And in a pinch will never give . . . The other guy a break . . . He does not have the least regard . . . For ethics or respect . . . And getting by with murder is . . . The least you can expect . . . But by the law of averages . . . It seems that he—or she . . . Is finally discovered by . . . The watchful company.

OUR SHARE OF LIFE

There is no life from start to end . . . That never knows a tear . . . Nor any soul that does not doubt . . . Or suffer any fear . . . There is no heart that does not ache . . . For something great or small . . . Or any mind that does not dream . . . Of anything at all . . . For inasmuch as each of us . . . Is brought upon this earth . . . There must be glory and defeat . . . And misery and mirth . . . There must be strength and weakness and . . . Some pride and some regret . . . As time must show a profit or . . . The total of a debt . . . So let us smile and weep and sigh . . . According to our share . . . And not be overconfident . . . Or given to despair.

A FATHER'S JOB

A husband and a father is . . . The one who ought to be . . . A generous provider for . . . His growing family . . . The one whose job supplies the roof . . . The clothes and daily bread . . . The doctor, school, and all the things . . . That keep them comforted . . . But his important place in life . . . Is not confined to these . . . For he must face so many more . . . Responsibilities . . . He should be constantly prepared . . . To share the smiles and tears . . . And all the hopes the family . . . Is blending with the years . . . He ought to take an active part . . . In everything they do . . . To carry out their happy plans . . . And make their dreams come true.

THE STARS ARE OURS

I think the stars were made for us . . . Because they seem to be
. . . A part of all our dreaming and . . . Of every memory . . .
Whenever they are in the sky ، . . We plan the days ahead . . .
And when we kiss and say good night . . . They follow us to bed
. . . Each one reminds me of the day . . . When life was young
and new . . . And it became my happiness . . . To fall in love
with you . . . Each one is like a jewel in . . . The golden crown
you wear . . . When I behold the paradise . . . That we agreed to
share . . . I think the stars were made for us . . . Because they
are a part . . . Of everything I want to bring . . . To your beloved
heart.

TO DO MY TASK

My Lord and God, I pray to You . . . That I may keep in stride
. . . With every moment of my life . . . Completely occupied . . .
Let not my hands be idle when . . . There is a task to do . . . But
fill me with the courage and . . . The strength to see it through
. . . Allow no vain or foolish words . . . To leave my lips today
. . . Or any sinful longing now . . . To draw my heart away . . . I
want to do the best I can . . . And struggle endlessly . . . For every
friend and stranger and . . . For all humanity . . . My Lord and
God, be with me when . . . The road is steep and long . . . Inspire me to persevere . . . And keep my courage strong.

SCHOOL LUNCH

Today I went to school for lunch . . . And there I had a treat
. . . For it was good as any meal . . . That I would want to eat
. . . Kristina dear invited me . . . To join her at the table . . . And
gobble some of everything . . . As much as I was able . . . I found
the food was wonderful . . . And wholesome as could be . . . And
even more I was impressed . . . By its economy . . . The cost was
such a little sum . . . That anyone could pay it . . . And many are
the parents who . . . Are often heard to say it . . . And though
there may be subsidies . . . To keep the prices low . . . My heart is
grateful for the food . . . That helps our children grow.

PRINTER

The printer takes our written words . . . And with a little ink . . . He tells the world in black and white . . . What we would have it think . . . He may be in the pressroom of . . . A paper small or great . . . With molds for mats designed by type . . . Or photographic plate . . . Or he may serve a magazine . . . Or business of his own . . . With wedding notes and calling cards . . . And where to write or phone . . . But one way or the other, his . . . Importance is supreme . . . Because his craft is needed in . . . Promoting every scheme . . . His letters spell the words we mean . . . Or hide the ones we think . . . Whenever we communicate . . . In terms of printer's ink.

OUR TRUE SUCCESS

What good are all our worldly gains . . . In places near and far . . . Unless our friends admire us . . . For what we really are? . . . Unless they love us for ourselves . . . And what we try to be . . . And feel that it is worth their while . . . To share our company? . . . For money cannot buy the kind . . . Of friendship that will last . . . And fame is merely something more . . . To glorify the past . . . But true devotion never dies . . . And never disappears . . . And love alone can comfort us . . . And overcome our fears . . . Our happiness and our success . . . Are only warm and real . . . According to whatever way . . . Our friends sincerely feel.

SONG AFTER SONG

There is a song for every day . . . And season of the year . . . Including one that seems to make . . . Our every meaning clear . . . Whatever be the weather or . . . The hour of the night . . . The weariness of afternoon . . . Or bliss of morning bright . . . The melancholy autumn and . . . The winter with its snow . . . The loveliness of springtime and . . . The summer's golden glow . . . There is a song for every heart . . . According to its tune . . . From Christmas in December to . . . Vacation days in June . . . A song that brings a memory . . . And one that brings a sigh . . . And all the songs of loneliness . . . When lips have said good-by.

PARASITE

And then there is the person who . . . Will mooch or sponge his way . . . From food and drink and money to . . . The minutes of your day . . . Who looks around for handouts and . . . The favors you bestow . . . And grabs as much as possible . . . Wherever he may go . . . He wants to drive your auto and . . . To use your telephone . . . And brazenly monopolize . . . Whatever else you own . . . Of course he never offers to . . . Return the smallest share . . . And if you ask for anything . . . His hands are always bare . . . He is a friend to your success . . . A stranger to your plight . . . And in a single, truthful word . . . He is a parasite.

WHEN TO VACATION

Today the boss reminded us . . . Of summer on the way . . . With annual vacations at . . . The standard rate of pay . . . He asked us all to let him know . . . The time we liked the best . . . To travel and to swim and fish . . . Or stay at home and rest . . . Of course I promptly called my wife . . . And listened to her voice . . . While she in no uncertain terms . . . Declared our only choice . . . And after I had marked it down . . . I sent it to the boss . . . And prayed that it would not turn out . . . To be a total loss . . . My wife decreed September with . . . Its fading summer moon . . . But if my luck runs true to form . . . The boss will make it June.

TEACH ME TO SERVE

Teach me, O Lord, to love the world . . . And always strive to be . . . Of greater worth and benefit . . . To my community . . . To be unselfish in my heart . . . And with my every deed . . . To serve each neighbor faithfully . . . However small the need . . . For if I live unto myself . . . I cannot truly say . . . My gratitude for all the gifts . . . You give me every day . . . I cannot mean the simplest prayer . . . Unless I try to do . . . The generous and friendly things . . . That please and honor You . . . So teach me, Lord, and give me grace . . . To do my humble part . . . For universal welfare and . . . For happiness of heart.

THE STARS ARE FADED

Do you remember what you said . . . One evening long ago . . .
When stars were in the sky and when . . . We sauntered in the
snow? . . . Do you remember, darling, that . . . You gave your
love to me . . . And that you told me it would last . . . For all
eternity? . . . You said it would not matter if . . . The world
should disappear . . . Your heart would still be faithful and . . .
Your love would be sincere . . . But now the stars are faded and
. . . The snow is not the same . . . And empty is the echo when
. . . I call your gentle name . . . The shadows lengthen in the
night . . . The dawn is cold and gray . . . And I must wonder to
myself . . . Why did you go away?

AMONG MY FRIENDS

I like to meet with friends and talk . . . About the things they
do . . . And whether anything they know . . . Is interesting and
new . . . I like to hear their problems and . . . Compare them
with my own . . . Because when they are quite the same . . . I
do not feel alone . . . I could not tell my friends in full . . . How
much they mean to me . . . But they are always in my heart . . .
And in my memory . . . They make the sunshine brighter and . . .
They keep the rain away . . . With all their smiles and all the
words . . . Of cheerfulness they say . . . They lift me up when I
am down . . . And offer me their aid . . . In every way I ever
need . . . To make a better grade.

FAMILY TABLE

The family table is the place . . . To eat and drink each day . . .
And sit around and gossip when . . . The plates are cleared away
. . . Where children do their homework by . . . The lamp's invit-
ing light . . . And Mother sews and struggles hard . . . To keep
the budget tight . . . Where tea is served and games are played . . .
And birthday cakes are set . . . And baby splashes water from
. . . The handy bathinette . . . The family table may be old . . .
Or it may be quite new . . . And large enough for many folks . . .
Or just a very few . . . It may be highly polished or . . . A plain
and common thing . . . But countless are its uses and . . . The
comforts it can bring.

THE ROSE YOU GAVE ME

I took the rose you gave me and . . . I put it in a vase . . . Along
with all the memories . . . I never could erase . . . And it was red
and beautiful . . . And fragrant as could be . . . And happily I
told myself . . . That you remembered me . . . But one by one the
petals fell . . . As shadows touched the dawn . . . And in the pur-
ple of the sky . . . I knew that you were gone . . . And now the
day is lonely and . . . I wonder in my heart . . . Why you and I
were meant to meet . . . And why we had to part . . . And now I
save the petals of . . . The rose you gave to me . . . And each is
soft and gentle as . . . A loving memory.

THESE ARE MY FRIENDS

My friends are countless as the stars . . . That fill the clearest sky
. . . And every time we say hello . . . I hate to say good-by . . .
They are the neighbors on my street . . . The folks who work with
me . . . And all who serve the slightest need . . . In our community . . . The grocer and the druggist and . . . The pal who prunes
my hair . . . The movie usher and the one . . . Who takes my
trolley fare . . . The mailman, milkman, laundryman . . . Policeman, and the rest . . . Who always make me feel as though . . . I
am their honored guest . . . They are the friends who comfort me
. . . And help my heart to smile . . . And do so much to make this
life . . . A little more worth while.

I WILL NOT REST

I will not lay my pen aside . . . Until my work is done . . . Until my God has summoned me . . . Beyond the setting sun . . .
But I will write of love and stars . . . And moonbeams on the sea
. . . Of youth and age on every page . . . Of time and memory
. . . And I will write of fertile fields . . . That grow beneath the
sky . . . Of smiles and tears, of hopes and fears . . . And dreams
that never die . . . And always I will honor God . . . And sing His
highest praise . . . For giving me this life to live . . . And blessing
all my days . . . May I be worthy of His trust . . . And give the
world my best . . . For other souls to worship Him . . . And be
forever blest.